Bush Food

ABORIGINAL FOOD AND HERBAL MEDICINE

Bush

ABORIGINAL FOOD AN

Food

HERBAL MEDICINE

JENNIFER ISAACS

NEW
HOLLAND

Published in Australia by
New Holland Publishers (Australia) Pty Ltd
Sydney • Auckland • London • Cape Town

14 Aquatic Drive Frenchs Forest NSW 2086 Australia
218 Lake Road Northcote Auckland New Zealand
86 Edgware Road London W2 2EA United Kingdom
80 McKenzie Street Cape Town 8001 South Africa

First published by Rigby 1987
Reprinted by Weldon Publishing 1988, 1989, 1991, 1992
Reprinted by Lansdowne Publishing Pty Ltd 1994
Limp edition 1996, 1997
Reprinted by New Holland Publishers (Australia) Pty Ltd 2002

Project Coordinator: Cecille Haycock
Managing Editor: Sheena Coupe
Editor: Carson Creagh
Maps and illustrations: Stan Lamond
Design and art direction: John Bull, Bull's Graphics
Production: Kate Smyth, Mick Bagnato

A CiP record for this title is available from the National Library of Australia

ISBN 1 86436 816 0

Typeset in Australia by Deblaere Typesetting Pty Ltd, Sydney
Colour separations by J. Film Process Co. Ltd
Printed in China

10 9 8 7 6 5 4 3 2 1

CAPTIONS FOR PHOTOGRAPHS PAGES 1-5
Page 1: Thelma Minor Djambijimba enjoys sweet nectar from the
desert grevillea *(Grevillea juncifolia).* PHOTO: LEO MEIER/WELDON TRANNIES

Pages 2-3: Arnhem Land billabongs provide a range of plant and
animal foods, which are gathered by women while searching
for weaving materials. PHOTO: REG MORRISON/WELDON TRANNIES

Pages 4-5: Harvesting waterlilies at Yathalamara billabong,
near Ramingining, central Arnhem Land. PHOTO: LEO MEIER/WELDON TRANNIES

Maude Nungarai, and her relatives enjoy daily trips to gather food and medicine in the foothills west of Papunya.

PHOTO : LEO MEIER/WELDON TRANNIES

CONTENTS

Freshly cooked bivalve mussels.
PHOTO : JENNIFER ISAACS

Dhuwandjika Marika gathering *rakay*.
PHOTO : JENNIFER ISAACS

Seedpods of desert acacias offer fresh green beans.
PHOTO : LEO MEIER/WELDON TRANNIES

Honey ant, a Dreaming ancestor and food source.
PHOTO : LEO MEIER/WELDON TRANNIES

Plate fungi, a herbal medicine.
PHOTO : JENNIFER ISAACS

Banduk Marika, Yirrkala

Dhuwandjika Marika, Yirrkala

Mararu, Yirrkala

Elsie Ganbada, Yathalamara

Thancoupie, Weipa

Joyce Hall, Weipa

Maude Nungarai, Mt Liebig

Nellie Patterson, Amata

PHOTOS: JENNIFER ISAACS

PHOTO: REG MORRISON/WELDON TRANNIES

INTRODUCTION

Before European settlement two hundred years ago, Aboriginal Australians ate rich, exciting and balanced diets of seasonal fruits, nuts, roots, vegetables, meats and fish — all indigenous varieties and species and each totally adapted to this unique environment, the continent of Gondwanaland.

Today, while traditional Aboriginal communities in northern and central Australia are still great botanists and naturalists, white Australian newcomers remain tunnel visioned. The 'bush' or 'scrub' must be cleared for crops of alien grain or orchards of exotic fruit inevitably besieged with pests while the rich bounty of the native trees and shrubs nearby is ignored. Most Australians have never even *tasted* bush foods. Yet the variety and quality of culinary experience they offer is enormous and Aborigines, the gourmets, are generous in sharing their knowledge learnt over 50 000 years of trial and error and from adhering to religious rules governing seasonal harvesting and ways of preparation. Some foods are just 'pickings'; others are staples. All will be a fascinating new world for most Australians.

The journey of discovery I embarked on in this book will reward me all my life — the forests, open savannah and coastal dunes will never be the same; plants, fruits, seeds and tubers now look so inviting that I find myself salivating as though beholding 'a golden peach upon the bough'.

Some words of caution are necessary lest true blue Aussies in outback vehicles decide to play 'survival', denuding trees and bushes of every berry, digging swollen roots or eating fallen nuts. Many Australian species contain toxins, or at least irritants. Aborigines leached, fermented or cooked a great many foods before eating them. Some had to be eaten in moderation to avoid gastric problems. Most importantly, Aborigines are the caretakers of their tribal lands and the plants and animals created by the ancestral beings. Each food, therefore, has ceremonial or religious importance. Tracts of land are owned by different people and permission must be gained before gathering food, hunting animals or catching fish.

Aboriginal food experts from the communities of northern Australia and the central desert have shared their immense knowledge of the properties of native fruits and plants generously in the hope that all Australians and visitors to this country will learn to respect their land ownership and their heritage — an Australian heritage of unique value to world zoology, botany, cuisine and medicine.

ONE

NATURALISTS, HUNTERS
AND GATHERERS

Aboriginal people have an encyclopaedic knowledge of Australian plants and animals and of seasonal changes in the Australian environment. A batwing coral tree flowers, its orange blossoms fall and women know it is time to go and dig crabs from their hides under the mangrove mud. Their fat, too, will be orange, and the flesh good and filling. Another flower blooms to warn that poisonous stingers are in the northern waters, while the milky white flowers known as 'oyster flowers' tell people to move camp to the oyster beds, for the oysters are fat and white.[1] Every child learns the importance of such natural signs. The winds, the blooming of plants and the seeding of grasses, rather than a fixed calendar of dates and months, herald the changes of seasons.

Aboriginal awareness of the environment includes an understanding of the life cycles of animals, insects and sea creatures – not only those harvested for food, but others that may be totem animals linked to religious beliefs. The Australian continent covers an enormous range of botanical environments: from tropical coast to rainforest, from open scrub to wet sclerophyll forest, from woodland to desert, and from temperate riverine environments to snowy alpine mountains. Aboriginal people once lived in

Above: Marrirriwuy Marika digs a freshwater well beneath the sand at Yelangbara.

The forests of central Arnhem Land provide fruits, nuts and roots which the women on outstations gather daily while collecting pandanus leaves for weaving.

PHOTO: LEO MEIER/WELDON TRANNIES   13

all these areas and continue to live in most, utilising the natural foods and medicines unique to Australia. Their knowledge has not always been recognised, to the peril of those early European-Australian explorers who died of thirst and starvation close to permanent rock springs or under trees bearing thousands of edible seeds.

Most nineteenth-century colonists looked with horror at the eating habits of Aborigines, and had little insight into the depth of knowledge and experience of their hosts. Tentatively they sometimes tried foods they observed 'the blacks' eating, but just as often they looked for herbs and botanical equivalents of plants of the old country and experimented with 'damson jam' or intoxicating drink made from local bushes that looked like hops. These efforts met with mixed results. Quandongs were admired as fruit and their hard inner nuts used as counters in Chinese chequers, but old journals describe many other bush foods as 'not tolerable', 'a passable substitute for ...' or 'flavourless but sustaining'.

MacDonnell Ranges. Desert areas consist of spinifex and sandhill lowlands punctuated by rocky ridges. Water and a variety of foods are generally found at the base of these ridges.

PHOTO: LEO MEIER/WELDON TRANNIES

Opposite page
Rainforest at Dorrigo, New South Wales. Rainforests were once significant food sources for Aborigines, offering an array of fruits, nuts and small creatures. The growing tips or core of many species of palms were also delicacies.

PHOTO: LEO MEIER/WELDON TRANNIES

A blue-winged kookaburra rests on a pandanus tree. The coming and going of birds, flowers and seeds heralds the changing seasons, the ripening of fruits or the time to harvest food.

PHOTO: LEO MEIER/WELDON TRANNIES

Accustomed as they were to the soft texture of potatoes rather than the stringy consistency of yams, and sweet pulpy fruits rather than bitter, acrid or acidic fruit, the newcomers found little in the new country to encourage them to cultivate local foods. Similarly, an aversion to untried meats and the unusual appearance of Australian animals thankfully spared the wholesale slaughter of traditional Aboriginal meats such as echidna, flying foxes, possums, wallabies and birds.

It would not be too bold a generalisation to say that every part of any plant that can be used for food is probably used by Aborigines. Naturally, some areas of the Australian continent are much richer in food resources than others. The environment of Arnhem Land and Cape York is so rich that it is never necessary for people to gather grasses and grind their seeds, as is done in the arid centre. Aborigines have always given of this knowledge generously. Indeed this open revelation of details of water storage, seeds, foods, fruits and how to catch animals has often been the catalyst that convinced sceptical outback people of the veracity of Aboriginal claims to tribal lands.

Sex roles are well defined in traditional Aboriginal communities. Women generally gather food; men hunt it. While men hunt large land and sea mammals and catch fish, women collect vegetables, shellfish, small animals and eggs.[2] Women, of course, as bearers and rearers of children, must carry out all their food-gathering activities with children present. However, they gather food extremely successfully and can provide up to 80 per cent of the food in the community.[3]

Food is gathered quietly and efficiently. Groups of women spend long days with their children in the bush, with perhaps occasional bouts of excitement as the older children chase wallabies or small marsupials or track a goanna to its hole and dig it out. Women usually gather food in specific areas that they know of before setting off in the morning, so the food resource becomes predictable and reliable. Every day, women think about and discuss the whereabouts of plant foods within striking distance of camp, whereas men are preoccupied with preparing for the hunt.

I would suggest, therefore, that the greatest repository of centuries of botanical knowledge and experience lies with Aboriginal women, rather than men. Certainly men theoretically know the names and locations of all food sources, and they often report to the women the foods they have sighted, but on all bush tucker trips undertaken for this book the women were indisputably the experts. Men came along for the ride or, more commonly, the food, unless they were seeking large fish or kangaroos, when they completely took over. The importance of bringing home game is a considerable attribute of manhood. Spearing a kangaroo, for example, is one of the first tests of manhood for central Australian desert people. Hunting game frequently requires reserves of great endurance and strength as it means trekking animals day after day, often without success. When hunters are successful the meat is highly prized and praised.

Arkapenya and Lou Yunkaporta search for mud crabs on swampy land close to Aurukun, western Cape York.

PHOTO: JENNIFER ISAACS

Liverpool River, Maningrida.
PHOTO: JENNIFER ISAACS

Wooden water container from New South Wales. These vessels were carved from the gnarled protuberances of eucalyptus trees. Collection: Australian Museum.

PHOTO: JENNIFER ISAACS

Although utensils, weapons and containers varied from community to community across Australia before European contact, there was a basic range of equipment common to all tribes. This included spears, spear throwers, throwing sticks, sometimes in the shape of boomerangs, digging sticks, animal traps, nets along the coast and rivers and a variety of hand-held or handled axes and stone tools. Wooden containers, bark troughs, hand-woven fibre bags and digging sticks were important food-gathering utensils used by women. In Cape York the tool kit was extended with outrigger canoes, harpoons and harpoon floats (also used in eastern Arnhem Land, particularly for dugong hunting), bamboo knives, bark containers and bailer shell water holders and cooking vessels.

Along the southern river networks, particularly the Murray and Darling rivers, stone fish traps and fibre fish weirs, similar to those used in Arnhem Land, were ingenious techniques for catching fish, and the remains of several stone fish traps can still be seen in northern New South Wales. Canoes were once used everywhere along coastal and river systems, although fish hooks were relatively rare. Fish poisons were well known throughout the country and similar plants were used in the desert to stun emus drinking at waterholes.

Today the situation has changed quite dramatically, though many communities still use a range of traditional weapons and utensils. The main

Freshwater rock hole in the ranges near Papunya.
PHOTO: JENNIFER ISAACS

changes have been in fishing and hunting game: the rifle has replaced the spear, and the European fishing net and twine have largely superseded the hand-spun variety. What has not altered, though, is Aboriginal hunters' knowledge of the seasonal changes in the Australian environment, or their understanding of the habits of their prey. These factors are just as important in the hunt for food today as any individual weapon or utensil that might have been used for thousands of years. In this sense, Aborigines are gifted, knowledgeable and experienced survivors.

Authors and researchers have provided long lists, sometimes totalling hundreds, of Australian plants used by Aborigines as food, largely based on the evidence of white observers – explorers, travellers, settlers, government officials and, in recent times, anthropologists and ethnobotanists.[4] Often, though many plants were known as sources of food, only nine or ten were staples, and sometimes only a few were available in any given month. The more sedentary life of today's Aborigines has reduced their need to find 'bush tucker' to satisfy hunger. Stores now provide white flour, tinned and packaged foods and frozen meats. Hunting and gathering have always been hard work and most families living exclusively off the land would have had to spend half of each day getting food. If the store is open, why bother? As Gertie Motton said to me at Weipa, 'You don't find no bush tucker with full belly!' Traditional bush foods are high in natural protein

The Arnhem Land outstation diet includes a high proportion of bush food. Children enjoy the rich harvest of numerous wild fruits.

PHOTO: LEO MEIER/WELDON TRANNIES

Collecting pandanus leaves to weave baskets, dilly bags and mats. Pandanus nuts are tasty but difficult to extract.

PHOTO: JENNIFER ISAACS

The Malangi family playing in the bush after rain at Yathalamara.

PHOTO: JENNIFER ISAACS

Rrapu Bukulatjpi from Yirrkala
holds the colourful pods and
black-cased *balk balk* or bush
peanuts *(Sterculia quadrifida)*
PHOTO: JENNIFER ISAACS

and vitamins and the health of Aboriginal people has suffered drastically because of the foods that have been substituted. Over the past decade or so, Aboriginal people have been moving from communities to satellite out-stations and homelands centres where they are nutritionally better off as they eat a higher percentage of bush foods.

The Northern Territory Department of Health has established programs for gathering bush food and samples have been analysed for their nutrient content at the University of Sydney in the hope that further programs can be developed to provide Aborigines with greater access to 'bush tucker'. This bush food analysis has revealed Australian wild foods to be often richer in vitamins, trace elements and protein than equivalent cultivated plants. Grass and acacia seeds, for example, are much higher in protein and fat levels than commonly cultivated cereal plants such as wheat and rice. Many wild fruits also have surprisingly high protein levels, and good fat and carbohydrate contents, compared with apples, pears and stone fruits. Vitamin C has been found in appreciable amounts in wild desert oranges and in some yams, while the spectacular amounts discovered in the wild Arnhem Land plum *(Terminalia ferdinandiana)* have already aroused interest around the world.[5]

Having once ignored Aboriginal botanists, environmental scientists are now attempting to replace a little of what has been lost by researching the scientific cultivation of these highly nutritious bush foods. It is still possible to ask Aboriginal people about their own foods and will be for many decades to come. We can therefore gain not only direct experience and the excitement of sharing the knowledge of gathering foods of the Australian environment and eating them far from the nearest store, but also an understanding of the importance of food in the intellectual and mythological life of the people.

Aborigines believe that each food was created by the ancestral spirits. Some, are in fact, like the honey ants of Papunya, ancestral spirits metamorphosed. The Mulga Seed Dreaming is extremely important to the people of Haast's Bluff. While this is a nutritious food, it also has such ceremonial importance that the legal proceedings of the land claim of the Haast's Bluff people were held in camera and only Aboriginal women directly concerned were allowed to present evidence.

All food has meaning. The animal and plant kingdoms are one with people and are linked totemically as relatives. The laws that govern Aboriginal society are strict and include many rites and observances related to food. Some animals and plants are totemic relatives of every group of Aborigines. These may not be killed or eaten, though they may be considered quite legitimate food by another tribe not far away. Some foods are not eaten at certain times of the year. Others are elaborately prepared to remove toxins. Some are forbidden to children or pregnant women. Others are especially gathered for lactating women and babies. There is indeed a time and a season for every living thing.

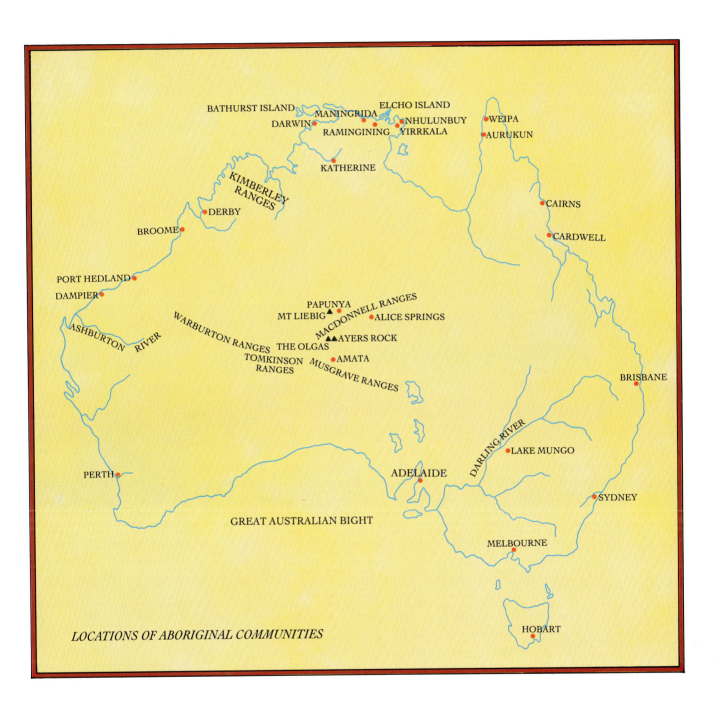

LOCATIONS OF ABORIGINAL COMMUNITIES

PHOTO: WELDON TRANNIES

TWO

SEASONS AND THE AUSTRALIAN ENVIRONMENT

THE ARID ZONE

In the centre of Australia is a vast arid area stretching from the centre westward toward the coast of Western Australia, south to the treeless Nullarbor Plain, east into New South Wales and northeast into Queensland. Survival in this area, where rain is unreliable, depends on a detailed knowledge of waterholes and the behaviour of plant and animal species. Today the need to find water is not as urgent as it once was. Aboriginal people often hunt from a camp they have reached by four-wheel drive vehicle and they generally take water with them in large containers, though most frequently they camp near an available water supply. However, until quite recent times, the location of water dominated all other concerns of Aboriginal people in arid regions and the search for food could not be separated from the need for water. Food gathering, in fact, took place at and around waterholes or soaks.

The chains of waterholes or soaks in the desert often follow the Dreaming tracks, which occur in a sequence of locations memorised as part of the sacred ceremonial song cycles. From a very young age children are required to memorise these songs and, therefore, the chain of waterholes by their proper names. The water sources vary enormously

Above: The open expanse of arid salt flats.

South Alligator River, Northern Territory.
PHOTO: WELDON TRANNIES

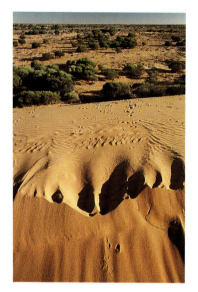

Simpson Desert sand dunes.
PHOTO: WELDON TRANNIES

from huge pools beside deep gorges containing many thousands of litres of water, like those found in the ranges at Papunya, to small soaks at the foot of rocky outcrops where the run-off is caught in concave rocks below. In other areas the supply can be as small as a few cupfuls of water left in basin-like rocks or cavities formed in the branches of eucalyptus trees.

As rainfall is fickle in the arid zone, the Aboriginal pattern of movement is to proceed from one water source to the next, concentrating on the smaller sources first and eating the food in those areas before settling at an alternative soak. People are adept at forecasting the weather because the direction in which rain has been falling can often be visible in the desert for up to eighty kilometres. The people also have a large amount of botanical knowledge and a mental map of the location of staple foods at any particular time of the year. Depending on the amount of rain, they know whether water supplies are likely to be available.

In their seasonal movements, small groups move large distances across the land. Although the hunting activities of the men offer spectacular meat harvests of kangaroo and emu, the women provide the main food supply at most times of the year. They gather fruit of various *Solanum* species, harvest quantities of shrub and grass seeds, which are pounded and baked, and track and capture small reptiles and mammals. The witchetty grub is a prized food source, as well as various kinds of gum and flowers rich in nectar. Lizards and reptiles were once the most common source of protein, but in recent years these have been largely replaced by rabbits and feral cats, particularly in the area from Uluru south into South Australia where the country is potholed with rabbit warrens.

The desert area is divided into two lowland regions by a central zone of ranges. The lowlands consist largely of spinifex and sandhill country through which travel is difficult. The ranges extend east-west for between 450 and 600 kilometres in a series of ridges, including the MacDonnell Ranges. To the south are the Musgrave, Everard and Mann ranges. The main water courses rise in the ranges and flow through deep gorges on to the flats beyond: these are usually the only permanent sources of water. The lowlands are characterised by sand plains, dunes and stony or gibber plains and in this country water can be obtained for most of the year only from soaks and springs, and from claypans after rain.

The flora and fauna in each area are very different. Large mammals are rarely found in the spinifex areas, though small mammals such as kangaroo rats, desert rats and hopping mice are common. There are many kinds of lizards in the desert areas, while kangaroos and wallabies appear on the grassy plains near ranges and euros and rock wallabies live in the hills. Emus span both environments.

Spinifex grass is the dominant ground cover of the sand plains, which are characterised by grey-green mulga and acacia stands. Sand ridges are fixed in place with spinifex, cane grass and sparse shrubs. Only the desert oak appears as a characteristic tree. After rain the beautiful desert

Ellery Gorge, Northern Territory.
PHOTO: REG MORRISON/WELDON TRANNIES

After rain the red desert is carpeted with wildflowers, everlasting daisies and red hop bush, an introduced plant which has spread rapidly.

Finke River, Northern Territory. Huge river gums grow along the dry watercourses of the arid centre. The bark is used as a medicine.

grevilleas and hakeas bloom and flowers cover the ground. The sand glows red and the desert no longer seems inhospitable. Important plant foods include yams such as *Ipomoea costata*, the fruits of many solanums, the seeds of acacias and grasses, and bush onions (*Cyperus bulbosus*). These foods as well as figs and other desert fruits, are most commonly found on rocky outcrops. Cypress pines, wild figs and wild oranges cling to granite hills. Huge and elegant river red gums grow along the dry watercourses, while the ghost gum favours hillsides.

The fruiting and flowering of all these species are well understood by desert Aborigines and food gathering was once organised according to season. Today the truck that brings supplies from store to outstation provides a significant proportion of food though, depending on the availability of vehicles, bush food is still eagerly sought when hunting trips are possible. Most of the communities are now settled and there is little game within twenty kilometres or so of their outstations. As a result, vehicles are necessary for successful hunting trips.

Anthropologist Richard Gould, who lived for some time with a group of western desert Aboriginal people twenty years ago, then surviving almost exclusively on bush food, described the area as probably the harshest in Australia. He found that in any given year only eight vegetable staples were gathered and eaten. The main species eaten in a normal year

Pale tufts of spinifex catch the light near the Olgas, a major religious site to desert Aborigines.

PHOTO: WELDON TRANNIES

were berries, seeds, fruit of the native tomato and other solanums, wild fig and quandong. In a drought year, which occurs approximately every five to seven years in the desert area, only three of these species were available. The diet was supplemented by whatever animals and birds could be trapped or hunted, as well as seed damper, the dietary mainstay. According to Gould:

> Survival rests on knowing precisely where to find water along with other resources in a given area. Knowledge of this kind is precisely what the Aborigines possess in abundance, and the mechanisms for transmitting this knowledge from one generation to the next form an important part of traditional Aboriginal culture. More than their technology or their great physical endurance, it is this complex system of knowledge— what anthropologists sometimes call 'cognitive map' of both the terrain and the resources of their environment — that stands as the key to the adaptive success of the Aborigines in this harsh region.[1]

It was clear to Gould that people moved specifically from water soaks to waterholes knowing in advance both the location of the food plants and whether they would be ripe given the amount of rain that had fallen.

THE TROPICAL COAST

Most of Arnhem Land is open canopy forest with a large proportion of *Eucalyptus* species, particularly the stringybark (*Eucalyptus tetrodonta*). Here and there are more fertile areas of soil that hold moisture, and pockets of jungle or rainforest that spring up around large banyan trees, which are frequently important in Aboriginal mythology. Wattles and bloodwoods (*Eucalyptus polycarpa*) are frequently interspersed in the woodlands and paperbark swamps. Paperbark swamps have a cover of waterlilies and are often edged by large areas of sedge, which is harvested for its succulent corm. Mangrove areas are rich sources of food: crabs, shellfish, edible shoots and worms are harvested there. The richest food environment is, of course, the sea, where fish abound. Casuarinas line the sandy beaches, which are broken by occasional rocky outcrops covered with oysters and edible shellfish.

The open woodlands and rainforests offer the greatest quantity of tubers, fruits and nuts, the tidal floodplains being poorest as a source of food. The black soil of the swamps is almost permanently damp and here the long-necked turtle hibernates in the dry season, emerging at the beginning of the wet season as the swamps fill with water. Some coastal areas have very high tides and the large river systems, including the Blyth, Liverpool and Alligator rivers, have extremely fast moving currents. Fishing and using the rivers are dependent on knowledge and skill in watercraft. The relatively inaccessible beaches along the northwest tip of the Gulf of Carpentaria are lined with sand dunes, the breeding grounds of sea turtles. The eggs of these turtles are gathered in season and the turtles themselves are occasionally cooked for feasts or ceremonies.

At the edge of the swamp, Elsie Ganbada strips off large sheets of bark from a giant paperbark tree to cover a ground oven. This versatile bush fibre is also used to wrap the food into bundles, to fold into food and water carriers and as soft bedding.

PHOTO: LEO MEIER/WELDON TRANNIES

A small group of edible pigface plants cling to the cliffs of the Great Australian Bight on the edge of the barren Nullarbor Plain. Many foods of coastal environments throughout Australia were harvested seasonally by Aborigines.

PHOTO: REG MORRISON/WELDON TRANNIES

Maree Puruntatameri watches her children play on the tidal flats on Bathurst Island.

PHOTO: JENNIFER ISAACS

Children quickly become experts at prising delicious crabs out of their hides in the sand.

PHOTO: JENNIFER ISAACS

Mangrove colonies are one of the main sources of shellfish. Liverpool River, central Arnhem Land.

PHOTO: JENNIFER ISAACS

The environment of northern Queensland is similar, with a higher percentage of rainforest. Cape York is a vast tract of country that stretches for 950 kilometres from the Gulf of Papua to the southern part of the Gulf of Carpentaria in Queensland. In general, open canopy savanna woodlands prevail, though there are many pockets of rainforest, swamp and coastal thicket where most of the wild Aboriginal food plants grow. The area encompasses mangroves and saltpans.

Game such as wallabies and scrub fowl are generally hunted in the grasslands as well as the open canopy forests. These forests also provide most of the fruits, stems and roots. Rainforests, however, offer nuts, figs, wild gingers, wild bananas and wild palms, of which the starchy pith in the stem is eaten.

The mangrove colonies and freshwater swamps are the main source of staple plant foods, particularly the mangrove root (*Bruguiera gymnorrhiza*), which has a surprisingly high nutritional value, and the tubers of the colloquially termed 'arrowroot' (*Tacca leontopetaloides*). A wild species of taro is also harvested as well as the delicious corms of the water rush (*Eleocharis dulcis*).

Up to ten species of yam are eaten, including many bitter varieties that must be peeled, mashed and leached in water before being cooked and eaten. On the western coast of Cape York many species of shellfish,

South Alligator River, Northern
Territory.

especially mangrove shellfish, are gathered and eaten. Throughout the coastal area, saltwater and freshwater fish contribute more animal food than do terrestrial animals and birds, though eggs are gathered and kangaroos, wallabies, goannas, cassowaries, ducks, turkeys and fowls are hunted. The west coast of Cape York and northeastern Arnhem Land are the traditional hunting grounds of the dugong.[2]

Traditionally, the seasons of the Top End—Arnhem Land, Cape York and northwestern Australia—are divided into two: the Wet and the Dry. The Wet is the time of monsoons, when the rivers swell and the flood-plains are under water. The Dry is the season when no rain falls, under-growth dries and withers and bushfires clear out the scrub. The Aboriginal perspective of nature is much more descriptive. There are six seasons in the north, each with distinctive weather patterns and vegetation changes and each marked by the availability of plant and animal foods.

In the 1930s ethnographer Donald Thomson wrote an influential early description of the Aboriginal seasons and foods of Cape York.[3] Recently Stephen Davis, a teacher on Milingimbi Island off the Arnhem Land coast, compiled a sensitive modern study of the Aboriginal perspective on the seasons of central Arnhem Land.[4] The two studies agree to a remarkable extent and show that in Arnhem Land, Aboriginal people have totally retained their integral relationship with the environment.

In central Arnhem Land the year begins with *Dhuludur,* from October to November at the end of the dry season when sprinkling rains cause the burnt out grass plains to shoot. 'The male thunder shrinks the waterholes and the female thunder brings the rain called Dhuludur'. The huge tides cover the floodplains with water for the first time since the end of the Wet in April. At low tide large trumpet shells and bailer shells are exposed on the sandbars. An occasional small bushfire burns and the winds are mixed up with the southwest wind, each blowing at different times on the same day. The white-breasted wood swallow arrives to signal the coming of rain. Then the kangaroos and wallabies give birth and their young feed on the first yellow shoots that crack the earth and turn green.

This is an important time for the new growth symbolises regeneration. Water is still scarce and the swollen paperbark trunks are tapped for their hidden reserves. A few fruits begin to ripen and the last of the long yams are dug before the rains. Round yams are ready to be dug. As the waterholes slowly fill, whistling ducks arrive and, like the brolgas and jabirus, begin to nest. The rain begins to fall every day, brolgas dance together, the mud of dried billabongs cracks and the hibernation of the long-necked turtles is over.

The Wikmonkan of western Cape York and the people of central Arnhem Land recognise five main seasons, categorised in similar ways by signs, winds, fruits and rain. *Turrpak,* the equivalent of *Dhuludur,* is characterised by lightning, the scarcity of vegetable foods and a hot, still oppression. Burnt grass has destroyed traces of yam but nonda plums are ripe on the trees, to be later stored with the yams, bulbs and tubers.

Swollen Cape York rivers meander through mangroves.

Waters of the Gulf of Carpentaria teem with fish, which are hunted daily in all coastal Aboriginal communities.

PHOTO: REG MORRISON/WELDON TRANNIES

From late December to early March the Wikmonkan season is *Karp,* the height of the Wet. In central Arnhem Land, this season is *Barramirri.* The country floods rapidly as the river systems overflow into swamps and movement between communities becomes impossible. This is the time when plant life flourishes and all things grow. A few small fruits are available, including black fruit *(Vitex glabrata)* and lady apple *(Syzygium suborbiculare)* as well as the fruits of certain species of fig. The matchbox bean *(Entada phaseoloides)* is used as an occasional standby, together with dried nonda plums or round yams stored from earlier seasons. For communities camped along waterways fish, shellfish and crabs become the staple diet. As the Wet eases, the eggs of many waterfowl, marine turtles and crocodiles provide protein.

Rainbow lorikeets flock across northeastern Arnhem Land and groups of red-tailed black cockatoos come to eat seeds and nuts. In the mangroves worms are fat, though swarms of mosquitoes make hunting hard. Water floods over the plain and barramundi trapped in the grasses are easily speared. As the rains abate, the bush passionfruit *(Passiflora foetida)* flowers, a sign that *Mayaltha,* the season of flowering plants, is commencing. There is very little bush food, but in *Mayaltha*—around February and March—many flowering plants scent the bush and bring nectar-loving birds to the herbs and grasses. Bushlarks build their nests on the ground and sing day and night to each other. Peaceful doves gather around the puddles left by the rain. The grasses grow to maximum height and as they seed the parrots descend to feed, marking *Midawarr,* the season of seeding grass and fruiting plants.

The northeast wind begins the season, to swing later from the east. Then the seas are calmer and the air clear. Storms interrupt the peace but, when the weather is calm, the seas are flat and glass-like, good for turtle hunting. The flowers of *Mayaltha* have dropped and their fruits are ripe. Many tubers and bulbs, including round yams and long yams, are ready for digging, and there are fruits and berries to collect. Cycad nuts are ripening in *Midawarr,* and women gather large amounts to detoxify and cook into ceremonial 'bread'. Waterlilies cover the billabongs and grasses begin to bend with the weight of their seeds. This season is the 'good eating' time when the bush offers its richest harvest of plant and vegetable foods. In Cape York it is the *Ontjin,* the great vegetable harvest, from March to July. The vegetables of Cape York differ: white and black mangroves are important and, in particular, the arrowroot *(Tacca leontopetaloides)* is harvested and processed into cakes of starch.

At the height of the Dry, in May, June and July, food sources diminish. This is the Arnhem Land *Dharratharramirri* and the Cape York *Kaiyum.* As the winds blow the grasses flat and they begin to dry out, the first fires are lit and *Dharratharramirri* begins. Nights are cool, mornings misty and the winds change again. Now the southeast wind moves to south-southeast. The saltpans dry out and begin to crack. Yams are still dug in the

Spectacular lotus blooms abound in the billabongs of the Kakadu National Park.
These billabongs are inviting sanctuaries to Aboriginal families and
offer abundant food.
PHOTO: WELDON TRANNIES

File snake. These are found in northern Australian waterholes and are hunted for food.

PHOTO: LEO MEIER/WELDON TRANNIES

bush and the billabongs offer waterlily bulbs, flowers and stems. The only fruit available now is the green plum (*Terminalia ferdinandiana*). Insects and birds begin to leave. Snakes, however, increase and file snakes, water pythons, king brown snakes and olive pythons provide food.

Honey can be found in the open forest, while the colonies of fruit bats, or flying foxes, roosting in the tall banyan trees are sought for food during this season. Many varieties of shellfish and crustacea are gathered. During *Dharratharramirri*, when bush foods are few, the sea offers many fish and becomes the focus for hunting on the Arnhem Land coast. Turtles, too, are still hunted. When the red pandanus fruit drop to the ground and the cheese fruit (*Morinda citrifolia*) ripen, *Dharratharramirri* is finishing. It is replaced by *Rrarrandharr,* from August to October.

In *Rrarrandharr*—called *Kaiyim* in Cape York—sea turtles are fat and their eggs are hunted high on long sandy beaches. This is an important meat-hunting season, for the bandicoots, kangaroos, wallabies, brolgas, geese and emus are fat. Nuts of *Brachychiton paradoxum* are gathered and eaten. There is an abundance of honey, sought eagerly as soon as stringy-bark trees flower. Young saltwater crocodiles, born in the wet season, now sleep on their mothers' backs. Land snails (*Xanthomelon pachystylum*) are collected from beneath the root debris at the foot of forest trees. Mangrove worms, shellfish and reef fish also become important as the fruit bats leave the mango trees around the settlements. Another cycle begins with the thunder of *Dhuludur*.

Although northern Aboriginal families now purchase a great many foods from the store, they also eat several species of yams, water chestnuts and waterlilies and many wild fruits gathered in the bush. In addition, eggs and honey provide welcome nourishment and variety in the diet when available. They still catch or hunt fish and shellfish, freshwater turtles, birds, wallabies, snakes and lizards. In 1948, as part of an American-Australian scientific expedition to Arnhem Land, Margaret McArthur studied the eating patterns of northern Aborigines. Her research is interesting today in that most of the foods she listed are still gathered and eaten throughout Arnhem Land.

THE TEMPERATE SOUTHEAST

Most of our information about the food of southeastern Aboriginal communities before European contact comes from reports of nineteenth-century explorers such as Edward John Eyre, Thomas Mitchell and Charles Sturt. At most times, a large quantity and variety of food were available. The rivers offered freshwater yabbies, crayfish and shellfish, and in the dry forests beside the rivers, there were many varieties of marsupials and lizards, snakes and echidnas, emus and turkeys to be hunted and trapped. Waterfowl and other birds were caught and their eggs were gathered, as were insect larvae and wild honey. Various species of yams played an important part in the diet here, as they did in other areas of

Freshwater yabbie, Lamington National Park, Queensland. These delicacies were once widely hunted and eaten by Aborigines throughout Australia.

PHOTO: LEO MEIER/WELDON TRANNIES

Australia; most were cooked, though some were eaten raw. Many fruits of the forest were collected: quandong, wild orange, fig and lemon, plums, pigface and wild raspberries. Grasses and many species of cress provided nectar and the hearts of palms were eaten raw.

As in other parts of Australia, women concentrated on collecting shellfish, fishing, hunting small land animals and collecting and processing vegetable food, while the men caught large fish and hunted land animals such as kangaroos and emus. Their fishing techniques were ingenious and highly sophisticated. Weirs were built and along coastal and river regions large stone arrangements formed tidal fish traps. A wide range of nets, up to three hundred metres long and complete with floats and stone weights, were constructed from lawyer vine and other strong fibres.

Kangaroos, emus and smaller birds were also caught with nets. Water-birds were trapped in nets strung across rivers; the women drove the ducks downstream by flapping the water and making a lot of noise, while the men threw boomerangs into the sky to imitate the flight of bird predators or mimicked the call of hawks to lure the ducks into the nets. Boomerangs were also used to kill birds.

Along the coast large numbers of people assembled at different sites to take advantage of seasonal resources. Aboriginal people in New South Wales retain an oral history of great gatherings and feasts, and archaeological evidence corroborates this tradition. At Durras North, on the south coast of New South Wales, great quantities of muttonbird bones testify to the feasts that were held when these birds came to the area during their seasonal migrations. There were large gatherings during summer at Wombah on the north coast to feast on fat oysters. Early settlers refer to gatherings of between two and three hundred feasting on particular foods.

In winter these large groups split up into smaller segments, sometimes young men preparing for or going through initiation, sometimes family units of husband, wives and children. During these colder months the smaller groups spread out across the forest areas and the grassy plains beyond the rivers, hunting small mammals, which were dug out of burrows, as well as wallabies, kangaroos and emus, which were caught in nets and traps. A variety of tubers and seed foods replaced the high protein diet of the coast and river estuaries.

One technique of hunting emus was described by an early settler who lived among the Ngemba of the central Darling River. Emus were drawn close to the hunter by a decoy horn made from a piece of hollow eucalyptus tree rubbed with stone until quite thin. One end was plugged with gum, leaving a small circular hole. The sound produced by blowing across this hole attracted emus from long distances. As they approached, they were driven by a party of hunters toward a large net strung up between trees. Another technique, devised by ingenious Aboriginal hunters, capitalised on the natural curiosity of emus. On the plains the inquisitive birds were drawn close to a hunter who lay on his back waving

Emus were once hunted widely by Aborigines and are still an important meat source. Skilful mimics took advantage of the birds' natural curiosity to entice them towards the hunters.

his legs in the air. When the emu was close enough another hunter quickly caught it and clubbed it to death.

To the west of the Darling River lie the great grasslands of the more arid regions of New South Wales. Although now affected by grazing, this area was once part of a wide belt of grassland that swept across the north and down through the east of the continent. Here the seed-gathering economy of the Bagundji of the Darling River basin thrived. This native millet (*Panicum*) was gathered and heaped in piles. When the seed fell to the ground, it could be collected in bundles and was threshed by being pounded on a log or trampled in a hole. Dust and dirt were separated by winnowing in long bark dishes. The seed was stored in skin bags and one report records a quantity of portulaca seed wrapped in grass and coated with mud. Throughout the western area of New South Wales and Queensland large grindstones were once found on every property, testifying to this widespread seed-eating economy. The desert tribes still store seeds.

In the southern part of the continent the seasons have never been defined in any way other than spring, summer, autumn and winter. Nevertheless, Australia's climate and vegetation continue to frustrate as year after year expectations of wet, cold winters and dry, hot summers, mild springs and brisk autumns are confounded. Aboriginal seasonal perspectives from Arnhem Land and Cape York may explain why. Perhaps we should be looking for the season of the flowering plants, the winds and flattened grasses, the season of rain and the season of the great fruit harvest. We can only mourn the profound loss of knowledge of the environment once held by every Aborigine and value the understanding that remains as a vital part of Australia's heritage.

Yellow-billed spoonbills.
PHOTO: REG MORRISON/WELDON TRANNIES

PHOTO: LEO MEIER/WELDON TRANNIES

THREE

PEOPLE, PLANTS AND ANIMALS

Aborigines have an extensive and intimate ecological knowledge of the Australian landscape. Contrary to the common view of Aboriginal culture before the arrival of Europeans, people did not constantly wander the continent in search of food in order to survive in a harsh and desolate land. The country was not exploited continuously. Each clan or language group lived in a well-defined area that it owned according to ancestral law or Dreaming. Each had a detailed knowledge only of the resources of its own area and a limited knowledge of surrounding areas. There is some evidence to suggest that, even if the climate changed drastically—in drought years, for example, or during heavy monsoons in the north— people could develop different strategies for survival.

USING FIRE

Perhaps the most important single way in which Aborigines related, and still relate, to the plants of their environment is through the use of fire. Although they are not strictly 'farming', Aborigines are able to alter and manage their land and thereby, to some degree, control the source of food by using small fires in well-defined areas. They know that country that is

Above: Goanna, northern Queensland.

Young mother Christine Garangar and her baby Derek at Yathalamara , central Arnhem Land.

43

PHOTO: LEO MEIER/WELDON TRANNIES

not burned for a significant period is poor as a food resource. The general pattern, both in central Australia and in the north, is to burn patches of land and then to perform totemic increase ceremonies so the plant foods will multiply. Many important Aboriginal plant foods appear in the early regenerative phase following burning and particularly in north Australia, species such as cycads actually increase following fire. In the north it is a common practice at the close of the dry season to burn patches of country as people travel. Aborigines say this is the way they 'look after the country'. Fire is also used to signal from one group to another and to clear ground. It is important in hunting animals of the grassland plains.

Although many fires are lit, they seldom extend over large areas. The traditional Aboriginal pattern of fire management produces small areas of landscape which, as it changes, offers various plant communities at different stages of recovery from fire. Large-scale wildfires, now so common in the southeast of Australia and in Cape York, are not prevalent with this traditional management of small-scale fires.

Rhys Jones coined the phrase 'fire stick farming' to describe the relationship between Aborigines and their environment using fire.[1] Jones lived for some time with the Gidjingali in Arnhem Land. The Gidjingali have two words for fire: *bol* for a hearth or domestic fire, and *mindjongork*, which relates to a fire in the bush. Jones found that at the main burning season people fanned out from their camps eager to taste new foods, burning the tall grass as they went to clear the ground for walking and to expose the game. In one afternoon 50 kilograms of goanna and 10 kilograms of long-necked turtle were obtained by a small group of people. By the end of the dry season most of the country within half a day's walk from the camp had been burnt, with the most extensive burning on the grasslands and open savannas though eucalyptus forests had also been burnt. Jones admired the skill of the fire stick farmers and commented that:

> People used their fires accurately, aiming them into a natural break such as an old fire scar or swamp, timing the fire so that predictable wind changes later in the day would blow them back into their own trap, or so that the evening dew would dampen them down.[2]

Jones' research indicates that the use of fire was probably essential for Aboriginal survival. The Tasmanian rainforest, with its closed canopy, contained little food that could have been used by Aborigines. However, after repeated burnings the rainforest was replaced in part by a 'complex mosaic of wet scrubs, heaths and small plants', which was the richest habitat of all in terms of edible plants and animals. An important coloniser of newly burnt forests, both in Tasmania and southeast Australia, is the bracken fern (*Pteridum esculentum*), the tuber of which was an important staple. Although it is clear that Aboriginal people adapted to the Australian environment, it is also true that to some degree they adapted the environment to themselves.

Women return to Ramingining carrying the sheets of paperbark and turtles
back to the camp across recently fired plains. Systematic firing of the bush
increases food supplies.

PHOTO: LEO MEIER/WELDON TRANNIES

ACCIDENTAL FARMING

Conservation in its generally used sense of environmental preservation cannot strictly be applied to Aboriginal management of land. Nevertheless, Aborigines indirectly conserve the resources of the land by taking only food that can be consumed immediately and not tolerating waste. In times of drought, they harvest an available supply of food and store quantities for some time. Some myths explain the common practice of replanting portions of yams and other root vegetables to ensure a continual supply of food.

The custom of leaving a little of a tuber in the ground is maintained on Bathurst Island and in Arnhem Land and Cape York. Among the Tiwi on Bathurst Island some of the yam is always put back in the ground to placate the yam spirit and young children learn these principles as they accompany the older women gathering yams. One woman told her children: 'When you dig up yam, you must all time leave little bit end of that yam in ground… if dig it all out, then that food spirit will get real angry and won't let any more yam grow in that place'.[3]

The small yam daisy, or *myrnong*, which was a staple in Victoria and New South Wales, was once harvested intensely. In 1909-1910 Isaac Batey referred to his observations of Aboriginal people in the mid-nineteenth century when he was a young boy.[4] He spoke of myrnong mounds, particularly a large area of a sloping ridge at the lower end of what was originally known as 'Sideline Gully' in Victoria. There were many mounds with short spaces between each at right angles to the ridge's slope. Batey regarded this as conclusive evidence that they were plots where Aborigines uprooted the soil to harvest myrnong. He considered this to be 'accidental gardening' and assumed that 'The Aboriginals were quite aware of the fact that turning over the earth in search of yams, instead of diminishing that form of food supply, would have had a tendency to increase it'. Batey commented further:

> Young as I was on that station [Glen Junction], I have a vivid recollection of seeing lubras with bunches of myrnongs that had been washed, and if that operation removes the thin outer skin, the things are beautifully white. They have an agreeable taste, are crisp, but are watery.

This 'accidental gardening' phenomenon was also commented on by Rhys Jones, who observed the relationship of Anbara camping sites with the occurrence of fruit trees.[5] When Jones and Betty Meehan were living with the Anbara in Western Arnhem Land, a particular sweet red apple *(Syzygium suborbiculare)* was gathered to be eaten under a tree at the beach. Their large seeds, the size of eggs, were thrown to the side of the cleared area and accumulated in the litter of the casuarina tree needles. Four months later the anthropologists again camped under the tree and noticed that many of the seeds had germinated. The Aborigines remarked

Banduk Marika washes long yams in the creek near Yirrkala.

that the fruit had been eaten before and that soon the discarded seeds would be bearing fruit, just as a garden would or, in the local vernacular, 'all the same gardny'.

Over the decades, during which Aboriginal people have observed local teachers, administrators and other supportive staff living in their communities, they have obviously learned the rudiments of gardening, if not farming. Dick Kimber noted that when travelling through the desert with a group of Pintubi men he observed the joy they had in finding particularly important fruit trees at one sacred site.[6] One man brought back the fruit of one of these trees and planted it close to his camp at the settlement. Kimber astutely suggested that it was not necessarily the fruit that the old man wanted close to him, but the essence of the site itself. The fact that the tree had grown at the sacred site was very important and he was, in a sense, bringing some of his spiritual connections with the land closer to home.

Children's sharp eyes quickly find small edible berries while on bush hunting trips with their mothers.

PHOTO: REG MORRISON/WELDON TRANNIES

RULES AND TABOOS

To Aborigines, there are no relationships between people, plants and animals that do not also involve the spirit world. Customs, rules and traditional law determine all practices associated with the gathering, cooking and eating of foods throughout Aboriginal Australia. Whether these have arisen as a means of controlling resources in an environment where food is difficult to obtain, or whether some food taboos have a basis in Aboriginal medical lore, has not been fully explored.

In the desert there is, of course, a great taboo on spilling water. This incurs severe consequences, but has a very practical basis. In drought years in pre-European times, people often had to carry water in precarious coolamons on a head ring for up to 25 kilometres back to base camp. Even in the north today, I noticed that a group of women from Weipa bringing fresh water from a billabong to the beach carefully ensured that none of the precious liquid spilled from their billies by placing a layer of leaves across the top. Leaves serve to slow down the splashing action of the water as they walk and also 'keep the water sweet' by preventing flies settling on the surface.

Many rules concerning food are taboos on eating certain types of meat. Such taboos occur, for example, during the initiation of young boys, at a girl's first menstruation or during pregnancy, childbirth and lactation. The taboos on food are generally said to have been made as law in the Dreaming, and songs and legends support belief in the dire consequences that will befall people if they break these taboos. On Bathurst Island, among the Tiwi, the immediate relatives of deceased persons are declared *pukumani* or taboo, and they may not touch food until certain mortuary ceremonies are completed. At this time they must be hand-fed by those who are not *pukumani*. Taboos such as these, with their basis in traditional law, are still important to modern Aboriginal communities.

The principal rule when walking through Aboriginal land is that only the people themselves know which areas are 'open hunting' and which areas might contain secret or sacred foods. In the Top End, throughout Arnhem Land, the jungle is thought to be the home of special and malevolent spirits and women do not often go into certain areas. Sacred yams grow in many places, having been placed there by the creation ancestral women. The *Djankawu*, creator ancestors of eastern Arnhem Land, travelled from Yirrkala across to Ramingining, putting their digging sticks into the ground as they went. The songs relate how as they did wells appeared and sacred trees grew. They also placed emblems in the soil, now known as 'sacred yams'. These are like the yam tuber in form, with an attached feathered string resembling the vine and foliage of the yam. According to the legend, the men stole the sacred emblem and knowledge from the women. Therefore women today are not permitted to see these emblems and there are many penalties if they should inadvertently dig up the sacred yams.

Just as the early European settlers trespassed on many areas that were sacred to Aboriginal people around the towns, it is still quite common for roadmakers, travellers and unthinking visitors to trespass on sacred places in traditional Aboriginal land. These may be areas where totemic ancestors are resting or places where some of the ancestral spirit himself is present in the form of plant or animal. One of the essential rules when visiting another person's land is that permission must be sought. Aboriginal people always hunt on their own land where they know the dangerous places as well as the safe hunting areas.

Almost all the techniques of butchering and cooking animals, as well as sharing the flesh, have been decreed by legends from the Dreaming. In the southwest, the Kulin have a story about Kurburu, the koala:

The ancestral koala, Kurburu, was greedy, stole the water from the Kulin, and climbed to the highest branch of the gum tree.

> The ancestral koala, Kurburu, was exceptionally greedy and continually stole the water and gum drink from the Kulin people. On one particular occasion they had gathered a large quantity of gum and mixed it with water in their wooden dishes or tarnuks. Kurburu stole the tarnuks and climbed to the highest branch of a eucalyptus tree and as he climbed the tree grew higher and higher, accounting for the great height of eucalypts in Victoria. Bunjil the eaglehawk, the creator spirit, was summoned to help and, having dispatched two of his messengers to bring back the water and kill Kurburu, then gave the law to the Kulin about cooking Kurburu in future. He told them always to cook koalas with their skin on, never to remove the skin at any time. He also told them to break the koala's legs before cooking so that he would not be able to climb a tree, taking the tarnuks with them.[7]

The division of meat, especially kangaroo, into particular sections is an important part of traditional law. This is very much 'men's business' and is part of the delicate meshing of the relations between the sexes.

A young boy being initiated in Cape York is not allowed to eat the meat of small marsupials such as possums. The following legend acts as a strong deterrent to boys tempted to touch forbidden food:

> An initiate and another smaller boy went out hunting. They found possums—the initiate wanted to eat them, but the little boy said 'It's bad food, you have just come out from the initiation ceremony, we must not eat it.' The older boy replied, 'That does not matter, you and I will eat anything, I am hungry.' So they sat down and ate the food. Suddenly the singing of the Rainbow Serpent was heard. The boys tried to run away, but the Rainbow Serpent ate them and the Rainbow Serpent remains at that place to this day.[8]

Another vital rule is that food must be conserved and shared. That greed and lack of sharing food can sometimes be a problem becomes apparent from the following story from Yirrkala:

> Two Ancestral beings, Djirid the kingfisher and Damala the eaglehawk, were preparing for a fishing trip. The small son of Djirid was looking for crabs and fish at the water's edge. He caught many and in his hunger and eagerness quickly made a fire and cooked them. His father and Damala asked him for some but he refused and ate all the food himself.
>
> The two older men were silently furious, and when they returned from their fishing did not give any of their catch to the young boy. The boy pleaded and cried out for food and began to scratch himself strangely. As he did so his body sprouted feathers and he changed into a kingfisher. The two men also changed into birds and followed the small boy into the sky.[9]

In Creation times the kingfisher was a young boy who sprouted feathers and changed into a bird.

PHOTO: LEO MEIER/WELDON TRANNIES

49

PHOTO: JENNIFER ISAACS

FOUR

COOKING TECHNIQUES

Aboriginal cooking techniques seem so deceptively simple that popular accounts of Aboriginal culinary expertise provide little insight into the range of procedures used or the suitability of each process for particular foods. General accounts talk of 'throwing the animal whole on the fire and eating the meat near-raw' or 'cooking the damper on the coals'. In reality there are different techniques for preparing and cooking each food. The most common methods are roasting on the coals, cooking in the ashes, steaming in a ground oven and boiling. Some foods, such as turtles, stingrays and sharks, are cooked by a process unique to themselves.

ROASTING ON HOT COALS

This is basically a technique for cooking flesh. Foods roasted on the open coals of a fire include most meats, fish and small turtles. Meat is usually cooked this way when it has to be eaten quickly, though most Aboriginal people agree that it is better cooked in a ground oven. Occasionally the fast-roasting technique is followed by a slower process in which the food is covered with coals and ashes to cook the flesh through.

Above: Catfish cooking. Fish are gutted, then laid on their backs on the coals.

Damper is cooked in hot ashes which have been
cleared of coals. It is baked on one side, then turned
and covered again to cook through.

51

PHOTO: JENNIFER ISAACS

Goannas are placed whole on the red hot coals and turned occasionally to crisp the skin. Then they are cooked through in the ashes.

PHOTO: REG MORRISON/WELDON TRANNIES

Ada Andy Napaltjarri and others from Papunya wait to enjoy goannas and a leg of kangaroo which has been freshly cooked in a ground oven.

PHOTO: REG MORRISON/WELDON TRANNIES

A freshly killed animal—kangaroo or rabbit, for example—is generally first thrown on to the flames of a fast-burning fire. The fur singes quickly and the animal is turned over to remove all fur. After ten minutes or so, when it is bloated, the animal is taken off the fire, the intestines removed and the fur scraped off with a sharp implement. Then the animal is returned to the fire, which by then has subsided to form a bed of hot coals. After around twenty minutes it is turned over and cooked on the other side. If large animals such as wallabies are cooked by this method, the result is near-raw or red meat in which the blood still runs, though it is warmed through. This warm, partly cooked blood is a delicacy drunk by men and rubbed on weapons for greater efficacy.

Small long-necked turtles, snakes, goannas and fish are also cooked this way and are quickly cooked through. Meats of snakes, goannas and turtles are well done, whereas kangaroos are more commonly eaten rare because of their size and the hunger of the hunters. When combined with slow cooking in the coals, the roasting method produces very juicy cooked meats which, because of the initial high flame, have a hard skin. The flesh of the game stays chewy—considered by Aboriginal gourmets as a reason for their excellent teeth. Other foods, particularly shellfish, are cooked briefly on the coals at the side of the fire, not over the flame.

BAKING IN THE ASHES

All manner of dampers, seed and nut breads, as well as tubers, corms and root vegetables, are cooked in the hot ashes. It is important to select good wood for this cooking fire; many Australian native bushes have slightly irritant properties and some ashes are never used by Aborigines for cooking. Acacias are safe and fast burning.

Some foods such as witchetty grubs are simply rolled in the hot ashes; some, such as damper or goanna, are placed on the hot ground beneath the ash and covered with more hot ash. Sometimes small hollows are dug under the ashes and lined with ash and coals. Yams and small vegetables such as bush bananas are placed in these hollows and covered with another layer of ash and coals. This technique is like a small ground oven.

Shellfish are often cooked briefly on the coals at the side of the fire. When the liquid inside begins to froth they are quickly removed.

PHOTO: JENNIFER ISAACS

STEAMING IN A GROUND OVEN

Aboriginal cooks have developed a range of ground ovens with distinct regional variations. The people who lived along the Murray, Murrumbidgee, Lachlan and Darling rivers used ground ovens very similar to those found in Arnhem Land and Cape York today. Beveridge described 'blackfellows' ovens' in the mid-nineteenth century as follows:

> When they reach the spot selected for the purpose they begin with a will to excavate a hole about 3' in diameter and nearly 2' deep; during the digging of the hole any pieces of clay, which they chip out, in size similar to ordinary road metal, are placed carefully on one side with a view to their future use. When the hole has been dug sufficiently deep it is swept or brushed out with some boughs or a bunch of grass; it is then filled to the top or a little above it with firewood, which the Lyoors [women] have previously collected and prepared for that purpose. On the top of the firewood the selected pieces of clay are carefully placed, the wood is then ignited and, by the time it is all burnt, the clay nodules have become baked until they are exactly similar to irregular sections of well-burnt brick; of course they are red hot.

Beveridge went on to explain the use of these red-hot stones:

Thancoupie supervises the removal of hot food wrapped in foil from a cup-mari, the Cape York ground oven.

PHOTO: JENNIFER ISAACS

> Hot clay is removed quickly from the hole with two sticks held in one hand, like a pair of tongs. The ashes are quickly swept out and a thin layer of moist grass is then placed in the bottom. Possums and other game are then put on the grass and covered with more damp grass, which is then packed tightly down with the red-hot clay lumps. Over this the fine earth, which originally came out of the excavation, is spread so that no steam can escape.[1]

Beveridge commented that the possums were so well cooked that they might have come out of the most perfect kitchen range. In the southeast ovens were often reused, just as they are today, and in many places the old oven sites now form dome-shaped mounds that stand above the level of the plains.

In Arnhem Land, ground ovens are the preferred method of cooking large game. The oven is prepared close to where the catch has been made. The remains of many ground ovens are found along sandy banks of creeks or under shady trees by the beach. Usually people head for these known 'cooking places' where there is a leftover supply of smooth rocks or broken fire-hardened antbed. Along the way they peel off large strips of paperbark

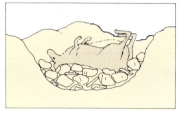

Traditional ground oven for cooking large meats in Arnhem Land. The heated stones and hot coals fall into the pit and the steam from the meat is sealed with sheets of paperbark covered with soil.

The large soft leaves of the spear tree (*Macaranga tanaris*) are used to wrap food for the cup-mari in Cape York.

PHOTO: JENNIFER ISAACS

for the ground oven covering. A pit up to sixty centimetres deep is dug and the fire set balancing over it. The stones or antbed lumps are placed on top of the fire. As the fire burns, the red-hot stones fall into the pit, along with ash and coals. The ash and coals are quickly swept out, leaving, as far as possible, a clean bed of hot stones lining the pit.

Meat, vegetables, fish and turtles are all cooked this way. Sometimes food is wrapped in paperbark bundles; sometimes it is placed straight on the stones. The steam from the food must be instantly sealed in, so the pit is covered with paperbark, then earth. The oven is tended by several people who watch for escaping steam. If that happens the hole must be quickly sealed off with soil. A successfully cooked meal is moist, well done and clean; earth fallen from the lid of the oven is regarded as a sign of poor cooking technique.

Although the procedure for earth oven cooking seems straightforward, variables such as the size of the game or vegetables determine the size of the pit, the number of stones required and the cooking time. As well, the fire used initially must heat the stones or antbed right through. Once the pit is opened it is very hard to extend the cooking time if the food is not done, as the steam has by then escaped. Judgment, experience, skill with fire and some strength (for digging and for moving wood and stones) are therefore required: in fact, this experience and knowledge very much resemble the skills needed by our grandmothers to manage fuel stoves.

Stones are used near watercourses and along the shore shellfish are often cooked in ovens made of beds of old shells heated on the fire. When cooking in the open forests and grasslands, lumps of antbed are broken up and used in place of stones.

In many areas these purely traditional techniques are improved with twentieth-century additions. At a recent ceremonial gathering at Hay Point, near Weipa in northern Queensland, a large quantity of food had to be prepared for more than thirty people. Thancoupie, Joyce Hall, Thelma and Gertrude prepared a *cup-mari*, the traditional Cape York ground oven. They were cooking the fresh fish they had caught along the beach and vegetables from the shore—yams and sweet potatoes. All traditional practices were observed except that the food was first wrapped in aluminium foil. Fortunately, the wraps were imperfect and the fish and vegetables tasted pleasantly of the leaves and smoke of the pit.

First, the women dug two pits around 45 centimetres deep and 60 centimetres square. A fire the size and depth of the pit was set of light wood topped with heavier sticks around nine centimetres in diameter. Lumps of rock—bauxite from the beach—were put on top of the pyre. As the fire grew hot, the rocks also heated and the wood burned away until only coals and rocks remained. Then quick action was necessary. The pit was lined with the rocks and ash was swept away with leaf switches. The fish and vegetables were placed on the stones and coals; the pit opening was covered with sheets of paperbark, weighted to keep them flat; and

Cape York cup-mari. Although the traditional paperbark
or leaf wrappers have given way to foil, the ground oven is still
the preferred cooking method for large gatherings.

A large fire over a pit has reduced itself to coals and red hot stones,
in this case lumps of beach bauxite.

The pit is cleared of fire debris and timber. Then the wrapped food
is placed on the hot stones and covered with coals.

Sheets of paperbark quickly cover the pit and seal the steam within.

Hot sand or soil is shovelled over the paperbark and tended
carefully in case steam begins to escape.

The cooking time varies with the food. Vegetables and fish require
only half an hour to cook thoroughly; large meats take several hours.

PHOTOS: JENNIFER ISAACS

warm soil was shovelled over the whole bark 'lid'. If steam escaped, the hole was quickly sealed. The fish and vegetable *cup-mari* took only twenty minutes, though large meats would take hours and require a larger pit and many more stones.

This ground oven technique of cooking is well known throughout Oceania and is used by other indigenous people, including Torres Strait Islanders, Maoris, Pacific Islanders and Papua New Guineans. In both Arnhem Land and Cape York some sort of herb is often added, though such culinary herbs are not numerous. Joyce Hall described the practice of placing the meat on she-oak or casuarina leaves in the *cup-mari* 'to taste it, like pepper and salt'. At Yirrkala there are special 'ground oven leaves', called *djilka,* which are put in the oven with the meat and also used to flavour turtle.

Food from the *cup-mari,* or ground oven, is served on leaves or paperbark plates. In Cape York the huge, flat, soft leaves of the spear tree, *ar-rem-i (Macaranga tanaris),* are occasionally used to wrap the food before it is put in the ground oven; they also serve as plates. The outer bark from the stems of saplings is stripped to use as ties for the parcels of food; other 'ties' include the binding on the ends of stringybark troughs.

The same care is taken in choosing serving leaves as in selecting wood. Custom has established which leaves are suitable, the criteria being proximity to food source, flatness and, one suspects, taste. Women know the possible toxicity of leaves not customarily connected with food and choose only known varieties.

Billies are used for boiling all foods, as well as for copious amounts of tea.

PHOTO: REG MORRISON/WELDON TRANNIES

BOILING

In most Aboriginal communities the local store sells billies, large aluminium boilers and pannikins, and these have made possible the boiling of large quantities of meat and other foods. Consequently ground ovens are not made as frequently and daily meals are now more commonly provided from the boiler. Some seemingly incongruous sights can be seen on north Australian beaches. In Yirrkala the author shared meals of boiled dugong meat (half a kilo of flesh carved off an animal that had been boiled in sections in old tin drums), boiled turtle eggs and wild ducks plucked and boiled with their feet and heads intact. Kangaroo legs are often boiled; the sight of the bent foot and claws over the edge of the pot is perhaps one of the most common in outback camps. Shellfish are also occasionally boiled.

The advantage of boiling for large families is that the meat or seafood juices can be utilised in big rice stews. This common dish is made by putting vegetables and rice into the boiling liquid with the meat. The resulting mass is often kept on the fire for twenty-four hours, to be eaten by young children and the rest of the family whenever they return to camp. The advent of this cooking technique has not altered preferred traditional cooking techniques, but is often used by large settled communities, a fair proportion of whose diet comes from store-bought foods.

In Arnhem Land vegetables and meat are wrapped
in paperbark and cooked in a ground oven.

PHOTO: LEO MEIER/WELDON TRANNIES

PHOTO: JENNIFER ISAACS

FIVE

FRUIT

Hundreds of varieties of fruit are found on native Australian trees, bushes, shrubs and vines. Some of these form a staple part of the diet of Aboriginal communities at different times of the year, but most occur only intermittently and seasonally. In some years many varieties of fruits are simply not available at all because of drought, too much rain or other environmental factors. In north Queensland, for example, the nonda plum, which is widespread and bears huge quantities of fruit, is eaten as a staple when in season, while in the desert the quandong forms a staple in the diet of several groups including the Pitjantjatjara and the Pintubi. The children usually have the greatest knowledge of where to find fruits as on their daily adventures with the family they are free to roam widely, exploring creeks and gullies outside the main food-gathering grounds. It is still common to find children bringing back quantities of fruit to the camp with a wide range of small and large berries. Often the fruit forms a kind of entrée that adds taste, sugar and excitement to an otherwise fairly bland diet. Frequently fruits are picked while on the hunt for goannas or during the arduous task of gathering enough seed in the hot desert to make bread. The green plum of Arnhem Land, which is now known to have an

Above: Wild mistletoe berries are valuable on long walks as they have a high water content.

Davidson plum, brown pine plum, lillypilly and red monkey nuts. Semitropical and temperate Australian bushfruits and nuts are grown widely in parks and gardens.

PHOTO: LEO MEIER/WELDON TRANNIES

Wild peaches *(Terminalia carpentariae)*. They taste like a drier version of their namesake.

PHOTO: LEO MEIER/WELDON TRANNIES

Apple berries *(Billardiera scandens)* grow freely in open woodlands of southeast Australia. If gathered when they drop from the vine, they are sweet and palatable.

PHOTO: JENNIFER ISAACS

extremely high vitamin C content[1], is commonly picked on the hunt because of its 'refreshing' quality, and is highly thought of in many places not so much as a food but more as a pick-me-up medicine.

A survey of the vast number of fruits on the Australian continent indicates that there are relatively few that can be described as sweet or tasty when compared to the array of pulpy and very sweet fruits to which we have become accustomed. There is no equivalent of a mango, pineapple or pawpaw in the native Australian array. To appreciate native fruit, we need to adjust our sense of taste so that we can accommodate a range of flavours that have always been acceptable to the Aboriginal palate: bitterness, sourness and a high degree of acidity. Native fruits are seldom extremely sweet and many contain a large quantity of seeds that add a nutty or crunchy texture. Despite this, even the early explorers still managed to praise many of the native varieties.

Australian fruits quickly became colloquially known by familiar European names and now there are a confusing number of wild 'plums', 'peaches', 'cherries' and 'apples' so named because of colour or shape, though unrelated to their European namesakes. Many fruits in the southeast of the continent are suitable for making preserves, jellies and nutritious summer drinks.

While not advocating the wholesale harvesting of the native fruits of Australia, a knowledge of the qualities of Australian foods gathered and eaten by Aborigines enables many of us to feel that we could at least survive in otherwise difficult circumstances in the bush and, perhaps belatedly, overcome our inability to adjust to the Australian environment, an inability based on our heritage of the European landscape and its fruits and foods.

Children gather wild figs on a bush food excursion from Yipirinya school, Alice Springs.

PHOTO: HAROLD WELDON/WELDON TRANNIES

Flower of the wild quince of the north, a large tree which bears numerous small fruit known as cocky apples.

PHOTO: LEO MEIER/WELDON TRANNIES

Shirley Muyku at Yathalamara outstation near Ramingining. Wild quince flowers, known as *dhangi*, are popular for making necklaces or headbands.

PHOTO: LEO MEIER/WELDON TRANNIES

COCKY APPLE; Wild quince   *Planchonia careya*

These elegant trees are found throughout the open forests of Queensland and the Northern Territory. The trees bear huge quantities of long ovoid fruit, yellow to green when ripe and with a fleshy pulp over several seeds. Known as *jungara* or *dhangi* at Ramingining, the blossom-like flowers have numerous radiating stamens that are sometimes threaded on strings to make ornaments and personal decorations for young girls. Cocky apples taste a little like quinces.

WILD PLUM   *Buchanania obovata*

These green fruits, called *munydjudj* at Yirrkala, are only 1-2 centimetres in diameter and are eaten raw after discarding the seeds. This is an important north Australian fruit, which ripens in clusters from November to January. It is occasionally stored like dried prunes and when required, reconstituted with water.

WILD PLUM   *Santalum lanceolatum*

The wild plum, as it is colloquially known in central Australia, is smaller than the quandong and, though it passes through a red stage, is dark purple when fully ripe.

This is the sandalwood tree, found widely over Australia and used in some areas for 'smoke medicine' because of its aroma. In desert regions the trees seldom reach more than a metre or so, though in mulga scrub close to creeks they can grow to 2 metres. In the desert the trees do not have the characteristic sandalwood scent. Among the Warlpiri they are known as *mukaki*. The fruits have been found to have a good water content, some protein and fat.

Many fruit trees have multiple uses. The bark of the wild peach (*Terminalia carpentariae*) is used as a medicine at Yirrkala.

PHOTO: JENNIFER ISAACS

WILD PEACH *Terminalia carpentariae*

This large tree is found throughout northern forests. The green ripe fruit look somewhat like withered peaches before they ripen; the taste resembles a very dry peach. The local term for this fruit at Ramingining is *mardunggudj*.

FINGER CHERRY *Rhodomyrtus macrocarpa*

This fleshy red fruit is particularly dangerous as a fungus on the flesh can cause blindness. Aborigines once ate this fruit often but knew the time to harvest so that they felt no ill effects. Because of the reported dangers it is not recommended that anyone try the finger cherry.

WILD PLUM *Terminalia ferdinandiana*

The small fruit of these trees is common from northwestern Australia to eastern Arnhem Land, where it is termed *murunga*. Recently it has been drawn to attention as possibly the richest natural source of vitamin C in the world. Research carried out at the University of Sydney's Human Nutrition Unit, headed by Dr Jennie Brand, has confirmed that this fruit has more than fifty times more ascorbic acid than citrus fruit. Terminalia are tall slender tropical trees with light green leaves and grow to 10 metres in height. The green fruits are about 2 centimetres long and 1 centimetre in diameter and contain one large pip. Brand's team has commented that the fruit looks and tastes like an English gooseberry.

The tart fruits are not a staple food for which Aborigines might go out on a special trip, but are devoured when in season by Aboriginal children. They are also eaten by adults on hunting trips for quick energy and refreshment and to quench thirst. The people of central Arnhem Land regard the fruit more as a medicine than a food, obviously with good reason.

The green plum *(Terminalia ferdinandiana)* is possibly the richest natural source of vitamin C in the world. These tart fruits are not staples but are regarded more as medicine or refreshments in the bush.

PHOTOS: VIC CHERIKOFF

Wild grapes
(*Ampelocissus acetosa*).
PHOTO: VIC CHERIKOFF

Apple berries (*Billardiera scandens*). The overripe fruit is sweet tasting.

PHOTO: JENNIFER ISAACS

Small fruit of the dodder laurel, a pervasive parasitic vine of southern and eastern Australia.

PHOTO: JENNIFER ISAACS

WILD GRAPES   *Ampelocissus acetosa; A. gardinera*

The wild grape is found throughout the north of Australia. It is common in Arnhem Land, the Gulf of Carpentaria and Mornington Island, where it bears fruit during the early part of the wet season. The vine grows in open forest, jungle or near beaches and appears annually from perennial roots. Clusters of grape-like fruits can be eaten when ripe; when the vine itself has withered and dried the roots are dug up and roasted. Among the Lardil the roots are called *dabum-dabum*.

APPLE BERRY   *Billardiera scandens*

This is one of the many twining climbers of the southeastern states that have edible fruit. It grows in forests and bears cream tubular flowers followed by fleshy edible fruits up to 2 centimetres long. The cylindrical berries are green or yellow, holding many small seeds in a sweet pulp. As the fruit ripens it falls from the bush, so that edible fruit is mostly found on the ground.

DODDER LAUREL   *Cassytha melantha*

The slender stems of this widespread parasite twine around their support in tight masses, often killing the host. When the stems have parasitically established themselves on the host by means of adhesive cushions, the plant becomes detached from the ground.

Dodder laurel produces small fruits crowned with the remains of the calyx. The flesh, surrounding a central stone, is very aromatic and tangy. A slightly reddish green variety found in the Hawkesbury area of New South Wales is quite delicious and refreshing. Another common name is 'devil's twine'.

Dodder laurel (*Cassytha melantha*) growing in the Hawkesbury area of New South Wales.

PHOTO: JENNIFER ISAACS

Cherry ballart. The species below is a yellow variety (*Exocarpus latifolius*). Opposite *Exocarpus* sp.

PHOTOS: VIC CHERIKOFF

Desert tomatoes. Fruits of many *Solanum* species are eaten throughout arid areas. They are known colloquially as 'sultanas', 'tomatoes' or 'raisins' depending on whether eaten raw or dried. Some fruits are poisonous so it is wise to ask local Aboriginal people before tasting them.

PHOTO: LEO MEIER/WELDON TRANNIES

CHERRY BALLART   *Exocarpus cupressiformis*

One of the most widely known Aboriginal fruits in southeast Australia is the cherry ballart, which derives its colloquial name from similar Aboriginal names given to the fruit—*ballee* and *ballat* in Gippsland, *pallert* at Lake Condah and *balad* as far south as Wilson's Promontory.

The tree occurs widely in eucalypt forests and grows between 3 and 7 metres high. Young trees resemble weeping cypress trees with thin, leafless branches that hang as the tree grows. The fruits are small and distinctive, each small seed being supported on a large, swollen fleshy stalk that appears itself to be the fruit. The fruits eventually turn deep red or pink, when they become sweet and palatable.

BUSH TOMATOES, RAISINS, SULTANAS   *Solanum* spp.

Sultana	*yakajiri*	*Solanum ellipticum*
Raisin	*kampurarpa*	S. *centrale*
Green tomato	*wanakidji*	S. *chippendalei*
Green tomato	*ngaru*	S. *petrophilum*
Yellow fruit	*albaraji*	S. *cleistogamum*
	yipirntiri	S. *cleistogamum*
Yellow fruit	*(southeast Australia)*	S. *esuriale*

The many species of solanum are related to the 'deadly' nightshade and some contain the toxic alkaloid solanine, which is found in green potatoes (also of the nightshade family). Many solanums are extremely important desert staples.

66

Desert raisins or *kampurarpa* (*Solanum centrale*). These may be eaten as dried fruit or ground into a seedy paste, formed into balls and dried.

PHOTO: REG MORRISON/WELDON TRANNIES

Desert raisins and tomatoes of various *Solanum* varieties are extremely valuable staple foods.

PHOTO: HAROLD WELDON /WELDON TRANNIES

Two species of solanum are commonly eaten by the Pitjantjatjara people: *kampurarpa,* desert raisin (*Solanum centrale* or *S. ellipticum*) and *ngaru,* desert tomato, (*S. petrophilum*). When ripe the fruits of both these solanum species look like small green tomatoes; however, *ngaru* is slightly more bitter. The advantage of these fruits to Aborigines is that they ripen at different times of the year—*ngaru* from December to January, and *kampurarpa* from July to August. *Ngaru* eventually rot on the bush, whereas *kampurarpa* dry on the bush and can be found at any time of the year looking like dried raisins. They are gathered both fresh and dry. *Ngaru* is simply picked ripe from the bush, but the *kampurarpa* bush is shaken until the fruit drops on to the ground. The *ngaru* must be cleaned of seeds and this is done with a small sharpened stick about 15 centimetres long, flattened like a spatula. A single deft wrist motion is enough to separate the fruit from the seed, leaving only the thin flesh and skin. Many *ngaru* skins are eaten on the hunt; others are brought back to camp.

The dry *kampurarpa* desert raisins are often prepared by the Pitjantjatjara in a manner similar to that of the Warlpiri further north, who make them into round balls of fruit. The desiccated *kampurarpa* are

Pale violet flowers of the bush tomato (*Solanum chippendalei*).

PHOTO: LEO MEIER/WELDON TRANNIES

ground with water on a flat stone with a very hard grindstone. A dark brown seedy mush results, which is then formed into a ball. This can be dried in the sun and kept indefinitely. The *ngaru* are also eaten raw but can be dried near the fire or in the sun. *Ngaru* are one of the main foods stored by desert people. They are strung on sticks and either kept in caches in trees or carried while on long expeditions looking for food. When not stored, the dried *ngaru* seed is ground and made into balls, similar to *kampurarpa*.

Further north in the arid zone, among the Warlpiri, *wanakidji* (*S. chippendalei*), or bush tomatoes, are eaten raw and dried, but in the raw state the black seeds are thrown away. The skins are also dried in the sun and stored on strings to be eaten when fruits are out of season.

The fruits of *Solanum centrale* are particularly prevalent after fire. These plants tend to grow in large numbers in confined and well-known areas that are 'looked after' by Aboriginal people, not only by firing but occasionally by damming watercourses after heavy rain so that the run-off services patches of fruiting vegetation. The various solanum fruits are still gathered by desert women whenever they move from base camp, though most, except for bush tomatoes, are now eaten during the foraging expedition, with only a few being brought back to camp.

In the more arid regions of Victoria, the yellow berries of a similar plant, *Solanum esuriale*, were eaten raw or cooked.

The solanum fruits so far analysed have good amounts of carbohydrate and varying amounts of protein, with vitamin C and thiamine.

Plums of north Queensland forests. *Planchonella australis* has a crimson centre and dark purple skin. The fruits are tart and must be overripe before they become sweet.

PHOTO: VIC CHERIKOFF

Wild desert orange bush, *Capparis* sp.

PHOTO: JEANNIE DEVITT

Desert fruit known as *alurra (Capparis lasiantha)*.

PHOTO: JEANNIE DEVITT

WILD DESERT ORANGE   *Capparis mitchellii*

This small desert fruit, which grows on a large shrub, is much admired by desert people but is found only infrequently in summer. It offers moderate energy, water and carbohydrate compared with other fruits, but is a good source of vitamin C and thiamine.

BURDEKIN PLUM   *Pleiogynium timorense*

This spreading tree of the mango family grows to 20 metres. The purple-black fruit are about 5 centimetres long, rather like small pumpkins. They are frequently seen growing in Brisbane gardens, and at Cairns and Yorkey's Knob. The fruit is edible only when completely ripe and even better when kept for a few days after picking. Aborigines keep the fruit until it is ready to eat by burying it in sand for up to two weeks.

When ripe, desert figs *(Ficus platypoda)* turn a rich deep red.

PHOTO: REG MORRISON/WELDON TRANNIES

Cluster figs from a small patch of rainforest near Ramingining, Northern Territory.

PHOTO: LEO MEIER/WELDON TRANNIES

Wild fig trees *(Ficus platypoda)* are always found on rocky outcrops usually in association with a watercourse or waterhole. These bushes are growing near permanent water at the base of Ayers Rock.

PHOTO: DIANA CONROY

FIGS   *Ficus* spp.

Most Aboriginal people eat some kind of native fig. Although all figs are theoretically edible, several are more readily eaten because of their better taste and texture. Some figs appear as small pairs at the base of the leaf; others appear in clusters on leafless branches. They vary from pea size to around 5 centimetres in diameter.

The Moreton Bay fig, well known on the east coast, has small fruits about 2 centimetres in diameter that are just palatable when dark purple. 'Sandpaper' figs, more common in the north, have much better flavour. The leaves of this species *(Ficus opposita)* are very rough, hence the common name, and were once used by Aborigines to smooth spear handles and boomerangs.

The desert fig *(Ficus platypoda)*, or *wijirrki* in Warlpiri, is a much more appetising fruit loved by Aborigines in arid regions from Western Australia to New South Wales. It grows mostly in rocky outcrops in crevices where water and soil debris collect, or at the base of rocks where water run-off ensures fertile soil. Individual trees may be quite large and bear thousands of fruits. The figs are yellow in their immature stage and turn red, orange or brown when ripe. They are usually eaten raw, straight from the bush. Food analysis shows that they have a good protein and fat content and some trace elements. The sandfig *(Ficus superba)* abounds in northeastern Arnhem Land. The fruits may be up to 2 centimetres in diameter and are eaten green, though they are sweeter when brown and fully ripe. The trees grow in sand close to beaches and fresh water.

Another *Ficus* variety commonly termed cluster figs *(Ficus racemosa* var. *glomerata)* is found in forests in north Queensland and the Northern Territory. The fruits grow in heavily laden bunches on branched stalks hanging vertically from the trunk. Although eaten by Aboriginal people wherever they occur, they are not as sweet and tasty as other varieties and are not prized as food. *Ficus racemosa* has a high water content, with traces of protein and fat.

At Ramingining in central Arnhem Land a large tree in the jungle beneath a spreading banyan tree carried numerous cluster figs. Elsie Ganbada pointed them out and said: 'This one ngatha food. Old people used to eat these long time ago. We eat them only if we are very, very hungry, starving.' One of the men, Charlie Djota, however, remained sceptical and said, 'Whoever ate those figs must be a "devil-woman".'

KONKLEBERRY   *Carissa lanceolata*

Konkleberries are large perennial shrubs that set fruit quickly after rain in desert areas. The small fruits last only a few weeks, though they may also be gathered dry. Known by various Aboriginal names, including *marnikiji*, they are a valuable food adjunct.

The desert banana, *(Leichhardtia australis)*. Young green pods are eaten raw, along with flowers and leaves. Mature brown pods are roasted lightly under the coals and taste like a mixture of zucchini, pumpkin and beans.

PHOTO: LEO MEIER/WELDON TRANNIES

LADY APPLE   *Syzygium suborbiculare*

Small lady apple trees, with their distinctive shiny red and green foliage, are prevalent along rivers and coastal cliffs of northern Australia, particularly Cape York. Along with black fruit they are eaten for variety in the diet, particularly by children, during the monsoon months from December to February.

DESERT BANANA   *Leichhardtia australis*

This variety of bush banana found in central Australia is called *yuparli* by Warlpiri people. The small vines climb young trees or grow in rock crevices close to dry riverbeds in spinifex country. The fruit resembles small dry chokos. The *yuparli* are cooked before eating if they are mature, though young pods are eaten raw along with flowers and leaves. The fire is scooped aside, exposing the dry ground beneath the ashes, and the bananas are baked together with other vegetables by covering them with coals. They taste somewhat like stringy zucchini with echoes of pumpkin and beans. The green flesh is eaten as well as the seedy pulpy centre, which lifts out intact when cooked. When raw, the inside looks like kapok.

The edible fibrous interior of a cooked desert banana.

PHOTO: LEO MEIER/WELDON TRANNIES

Cooking desert bananas. The pods are placed on the hot sand to be covered by coals. As the fruit splits the central pulp lifts out whole. All parts are edible.

PHOTOS: LEO MEIER/WELDON TRANNIES

Ulpundu gathering emu berries from the small shrub *Grewia retusifolia* in the open grassland near her home at Yirrkala.

PHOTO: JENNIFER ISAACS

A handful of emu berries. These taste like very seedy tamarinds or figs.

PHOTO: JENNIFER ISAACS

EMU BERRY   *Grewia retusifolia*

This small upright shrub grows in shaded grassy areas of open forests and has many uses for Aborigines. It bears small dark red or orange double fruit with a very small amount of reddish pulp surrounding the seeds. The taste is pleasant, a little like that of seedy tamarinds or figs. This fruit has been known to Europeans since the explorations of Ludwig Leichhardt, who reported gathering large quantities and making refreshing drinks by boiling the fruit; 'The beverage was the best we had tasted on our expedition', he wrote. The plant has medicinal uses as well.

On a recent bush tucker expedition the children, in particular, leapt from the vehicle to gather the berries and ate them immediately.

BLACK FRUIT   *Terminalia muellen; T. melanocarpa*

Black fruit are found all over Cape York, most frequently along the northern beaches of Cairns. The tree bears many small blue-black fruit about the size of a fingernail and in Thancoupie's words are always eaten 'just for pickings; kids on walkabout would eat them. Good if no water'. Black fruit appear at the height of the monsoon period when vegetables and fruits are hard to find. Before the advent of store goods, they provided a welcome if small source of fresh fruit.

Guninyi or cheese fruit (*Morinda citrifolia*).

PHOTO: REG MORRISON/WELDON TRANNIES

MORINDA; CHEESE FRUIT   *Morinda citrifolia*

This small tree is known throughout Arnhem Land for the yellow dye that can be extracted from its roots and used by women for weaving pandanus.

The large, squashy fruit is an important medicine and is also edible. It fills the palm of the hand and can be broken into segments of swollen translucent flesh. It is greenish white, and has the strong smell and taste of Roquefort cheese. Local names for the fruit in eastern Arnhem Land include *burukpili* and *guninyi*.

Red apple of Arnhem Land, *Syzygium* sp.

PHOTO: DIANNE MOON

Ripe red quandong fruits and seeds form a litter beneath the quandong tree in central Australia.

PHOTO: JENNIFER ISAACS

Quandong trees are parasitic on the roots of other species. This tree has a 'ladder' placed against the trunk to help gather the fruit.

PHOTO: JENNIFER ISAACS

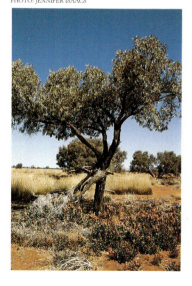

WILD RED APPLE   *Syzygium* sp.

This large red 'apple' is abundant from the end of the dry season. It has a very large stone and is a favoured food in Arnhem Land.

QUANDONG   *Santalum acuminatum*

Quandongs stand alone among desert fruits because of their pleasant taste and texture and the size of their bright red fruit. The trees usually appear in open spinifex and mulga country as single specimens or in small stands. The large, globular fruit are so loved by desert people that it is uncommon to find a tree, whether in fruit or not, that does not have a 'ladder' against it—a broken branch of another tree leant against the trunk halfway up to aid climbers. Even domestic quandong grown in Alice Springs gardens are well known and frequented by Aboriginal visitors to the town.

The ripe red flesh of the quandong is dry but sweet and is eaten straight, though it is also dried and stored for future use. Small collections of the fruit are always brought back to camp to give to older people or to the family.

The distinctive textured seeds are strung and worn as body ornaments or necklaces and the fruit of some trees have a tasty kernel that is extracted when it can be heard knocking inside the stone. These oily kernels are either eaten raw or pounded so the oil can be removed and used as a cosmetic to smooth the skin of face and body, much as almond and apricot oils are used in European cosmetics. Aborigines know which trees have fruit with 'good' kernels and which might be toxic.

The fruit is rather acid and contains appreciable amounts of carbohydrate. It is high in protein compared with most fruit. Among some desert tribes it is considered such a valuable food that the CSIRO is investigating the possibility of commercial production.

Quandong fruits *(Santalum acuminatum)*.
PHOTO: LEO MEIER/WELDON TRANNIES

Lillypilly fruits (*Syzygium* spp.) may be pink, white or purple. The pink and white varieties were a popular Aboriginal food in the southern regions of Australia.

PHOTOS: VIC CHERIKOFF

LILLYPILLY   *Acmena* spp., *Syzygium* spp.

This large group of trees and shrubs has been known to Europeans since their earliest encounters with new flora, possibly even from the first visit of James Cook when Joseph Banks recorded a small red fruit. The clusters of berry-like lillypilly fruits may be cream with pink tints or deep pink to purple and are thick and pithy, sometimes slightly sour. They are eaten raw. The berries were also used for jellies by early settlers, and trees can be found in many suburban gardens.

In Victoria lillypilly occurs mostly in the gullies of East Gippsland, as far south as Wilson's Promontory. In New South Wales, it is common on the edge of the rainforests of the north coast near Lismore. The trees can grow to 20 metres, though they are usually smaller.

Native raspberry (*Rubus* sp.)

PHOTO: JENNIFER ISAACS

NATIVE RASPBERRY   *Rubus parviflorus*

The small red fruits of the native raspberry, common in wet sclerophyll forests of Victoria and New South Wales, are gathered and eaten raw. These are never a staple as the fruits are not plentiful, but their agreeable taste probably adds some interest, as well as useful vitamins, to forest travellers on hunting and gathering expeditions.

DAVIDSON'S PLUM   *Davidsonia pruriens*

This small rainforest tree grows to 12 metres and has pinnate leaves with slightly irritant hairs and small flowers. The fruits are purple, about 5 centimetres long, and very acid. The large plum-shaped fruits are purple on the outside, scarlet inside, and highly prized for jam.

NONDA PLUM   *Parinari nonda*

Nonda plums of north Queensland are well appreciated, the Aboriginal name *nonda* being incorporated into the botanical name. The tree itself is large and has a weeping habit. The fruit is very important because it once sustained whole communities in September and October. The honey-brown coloured plums are usually gathered after they have fallen to the ground. When still firm the flesh leaves a bitter, unpalatable sensation on the tongue, like an unripe banana, but after a few days of sun-ripening the fruit are soft and mildly sweet, though surprisingly dry.

The nonda were one of the main fruits dried and stored for long periods by Cape York Aborigines and the trees are still carefully tended close to settled communities. The nonda kernel gives highly nutritious milk when crushed and strained. According to Thancoupie and her sister, Joyce Hall, Weipa women always gather and keep nonda fruit for children who are being weaned. This 'nut-milk' forms an admirable milk substitute in a culture where animals are not milked, but in which young infants are occasionally superceded on the breast by a new baby a little too early.

The nonda fruit are dried thoroughly until they resemble hard dry plums, then cracked between stones so that the white kernel is crushed. The pulverised fruit is compressed, squeezed and soaked in water in a bark trough. The milk that results is strained through fine grass baskets and given to babies and old people.

Pulverising nonda plums with a stone.

The kernels squeezed with water to make nut milk.
PHOTOS: JENNIFER ISAACS

Nonda plums (*Parinari nonda*) of north Queensland. This widespread fruit once sustained whole communities. The plums are either eaten fresh after falling to the ground, or they are stored. When dry they are pounded and the mashed plums and kernels are soaked to make a thin white nut milk, popular as food for babies.

PHOTO: JENNIFER ISAACS

PHOTO: LEO MEIER

SIX

NUTS

Delicious nuts are found throughout the Australian continent. By far the largest number of nut-bearing trees occur in forests and rainforests, particularly in Queensland, where more than ten nuts are collected, processed and eaten by Aboriginal people.[1]

Candlenut tree	*Aleurites moluccana*
Bunya nut	*Araucaria bidwillii*
Yellow walnut	*Beilschmiedia bancroftii*
Moreton Bay chestnut	*Castanospermum australe*
Cycad and zamia nuts	*Cycas*
Queensland almond	*Elaeocarpus bancroftii*
Black walnut	*Endiandra palmerstonii*
Matchbox bean	*Entada phaseoloides*
Ivory silky oak	*Hicksbeachia pinnatifolia*
Macadamia nut	*Macadamia*

Many of these are slightly toxic and require lengthy preparation by pounding and washing of the meal. Some of the more common nuts, such as macadamia, are harvested and then processed on stones specifically

Above: Bunya nuts, macadamias and quandong seeds.

Ancient cycad nut palms form an understorey
in the schlerophyll forests of Arnhem Land.

PHOTO: LEO MEIER/WELDON TRANNIES

Monkey nuts
(*Hicksbeachia pinnatifolia*).

PHOTO: VIC CHERIKOFF

developed for this purpose. These large nut-processing stones with delicate incisions for holding the nuts, as well as accompanying hammer stones, have been found throughout Queensland when clearing forests, poignant reminders of the once vibrant culture of the people who inhabitated the rainforest areas.

In Arnhem Land the four most commonly used nuts are:

Pandanus nut	*Pandanus* spp.
Cycad nut	*Cycas armstrongii*
Kurrajong nut	*Brachychiton paradoxum*
Bush peanut	*Sterculia quadrifida*

In the southeast of the continent the macrozamia palm bears poisonous nuts which, like the related cycads of Arnhem Land and Cape York, have to be soaked and processed before being eaten.

In the northwest Kimberley area of Western Australia the unique boab tree has the largest nut of all, a single nut the size of an emu egg.

BLACK BEAN; Moreton Bay Chestnut   *Castanospermum australe*

The Moreton Bay chestnut tree bears large seeds that are processed to yield a saponin-free flour. The trees are found in Queensland rainforests and, though not relished, provide some protein, fat and fibre in the traditional Aboriginal diet. The nuts are soaked, pounded and made into cakes, after which they are roasted.

Moreton Bay chestnuts
(*Castanospermum australe*).
These must be roasted, sliced and leached thoroughly to remove toxins before being eaten.

PHOTO: VIC CHERIKOFF

Arnhem Land cycad palms
(*Cycas armstrongii*).
PHOTO: LEO MEIER/WELDON TRANNIES

When ripe, the nuts hang
beneath the fronds and drop to
the ground. Baked ceremonial
cakes are made after pounding,
leaching and fermenting the
kernels into nut meal.

PHOTO: JENNIFER ISAACS

MATCHBOX BEAN   *Entada phaseoloides*

Like the Moreton Bay chestnut the matchbox bean, or *dhapul* as it is called
at Weipa, has to be processed to remove toxins. The seeds or nuts from
this open forest tree are available in all seasons. First the hard brown shells
are cracked open and the white kernels removed. These are roasted, then
grated or pulverised, after which they are soaked for several days before
cooking again. When the nut meal is soaking in string bags it is frequently
squeezed to remove the water. According to Joyce Hall, 'Old ladies would
sit on those bags of dhapul to make them ready'.

A favourite recipe is mixed cake of *dhapul* and *n'omb* (mangrove radials
of *Bruguiera gymnorrhiza*) wrapped in leaves and baked in a *cup-mari*.

CYCAD   *Cycas armstrongii*

Stands of cycads are found in the dry open woodland of northwest
Australia, Cape York and Arnhem Land. They are low plants, each
producing twenty to thirty large seeds that radiate on stalks beneath palm-
like branches. They are easily harvested. Usually several women gather,
crack and pound them as a communal activity. The cycads are particularly
interesting in that their yield increases dramatically after fire and the
practice of burning off large areas of grassy woodland in Arnhem Land has
ensured their large numbers. They are a favoured food because they can
be stored.

The nuts are highly toxic in their unprocessed state. Virtually every group of explorers in Australia from the early nineteenth century onward suffered the effects of poisoning from eating the tempting nuts of the cycad tree. The nuts are also poisonous to cattle, which suffer a form of nervous disease called zamia staggers if they graze in cycad country. The toxin, macrozamin or cycasin, produces tumours of the liver, kidney, intestine and brain after a period of a year or more. Zamia staggers is associated with degeneration of the spinal cord. In humans, eating untreated cycad nuts causes such intense vomiting and diarrhoea that it is virtually impossible to eat sufficient to produce zamia staggers. Cattle seem able to eat the food without immediate sickness and so the toxin can accumulate.

It is quite remarkable that Aborigines have developed the processing and cooking technology necessary to render the seeds of cycads edible. Cycads grow in groves and bear very large quantities of fruit: one report indicated that 13 kilograms could be gathered in a 10 x 20 metre plot.

The method of removing poison from cycads varies throughout the country, but generally involves pounding the nut kernels, soaking them for a considerable period in still or running water, then mashing the fermented nuts into a paste that is made into a damper and cooked in the ashes. In north Queensland and at Yirrkala the kernels are roughly pounded, dried for three to four hours in the sun and put in string bags in a running stream for four or five days, followed by still water for another

Brilliantly coloured zamiad nuts form a pineapple-shaped cone. The dwarf palm is found in the southeast of Australia. These were an important Aboriginal food but the nuts must be processed before being eaten.

PHOTO: VIC CHERIKOFF

Cycad palms in central Arnhem Land. These regenerate well after fire management, increasing their yield of nuts.

PHOTO: LEO MEIER/WELDON TRANNIES

three or four days. The nuts have then fermented into a bubbling, smelly mass. This is squeezed and compressed to remove the liquid, then pounded between stones and reduced to a paste. Each woman has her own special grinding stone for cycad nuts, often left at the grinding site until the next time the nuts are needed.

The paste that results from the grinding is extremely thick. It is wrapped in small bundles of paperbark bound with strips of pandanus. The parcels are cooked in a small depression scraped out beneath the hot ashes. The cycad meal cooks slowly. When ready, it is removed from the ashes and the paperbark is peeled back to reveal the food. Cycad bread can be kept for many months, but in central Arnhem Land must not be eaten by women or children unless the older men give their permission. It is a special food prepared by the women only for men participating in sacred ceremonies. No reports seem really sure just how the poison is destroyed during this cooking process, if indeed it is all destroyed.

Aboriginal people are highly aware of the poisonous nature of the cycad nut. During the dehusking process the women's hands become covered with a grey substance that has to be washed off periodically. Great care is always taken to ensure that it does not fall into any unattended cups of tea around the camp or contaminate drinking water.

BURRAWANG NUTS   *Macrozamia spiralis; M. miquelii; M. communis*

A small group of zamias occurs in the Macdonnell Ranges in central Australia (*Macrozamia macdonnellii*). These are the only cycads not eaten by Aborigines.

The dwarf zamia palm, found in the rainforest belt in the southeast of Australia, has fruit somewhat like a pineapple. The seeds or nuts were eaten after leaching and cooking.

Pandanus tree with ripe cone.

PHOTO: JENNIFER ISAACS

PANDANUS   *Pandanus* spp.

The postcard sunsets of tropical Australia invariably use the silhouette of a pandanus tree as a symbol of the paradise of northern beaches. This distinctive branched, spiky-leaved 'palm' remains a very important plant of multiple uses to Aborigines. There are several pandanus species, often hard to identify by sight though *Pandanus spiralis* is the most important. The nuts or kernels from the large cones are eaten both raw and cooked. The fleshy basal part of the ripe fruit is also scraped or soaked and eaten. The soft white inner part of new leaves is eaten, as well as being stripped and woven into baskets that are essential for collecting and straining foods.

The heavy, hard, woody fruits, up to 20 centimetres in diameter, are made up of many individual segments, each of which contains seeds or 'nuts'. The seeds are removed from the plant only after the fruit has turned red and dropped in segments to the ground. This is extremely arduous work, requiring an axe or tomahawk to split the woody surround. It takes

Pandanus trees are of multiple uses to Aborigines and form distinctive silhouettes along the tropical Australian coast.

Pandanus seeds are embedded in the woody casing and must be prised out.

considerable physical effort to produce a small pile of nuts, and because of this many writers have wrongly assumed that pandanus are not important items of Aboriginal diet. In fact, pandanus kernels are eagerly eaten by Aborigines and the nuts are regarded as a luxury. During the fruiting season pandanus is a daily dietary component, though never a staple, and in order to collect enough nuts they are harvested and chopped almost every day.

The fruit of the pandanus is utilised fully. The base of the nut has a semi-fleshy fibrous mesoderm, which is chewed to extract the starchy pulp. The nut is also broken open and the kernels eaten. In Cape York, if the fruit is slightly unripe it is roasted before being eaten. This cooking process helps to reduce the mild throat irritation that can occur from eating the basal part of the drupe. The pulp of the drupe is also soaked in water to produce a sweet drink. It is interesting to note that more than 140 years ago Ludwig Leichhardt observed a variety of pandanus debris in an Aboriginal camp. Following the example of the Aborigines Leichhardt scraped the soft end of the drupe with a knife and boiled the pulp. The resulting infusion was pleasant and 'did not affect the bowels'. Leichhardt mentioned in his diary that the natives seemed to live principally on the seeds of *Pandanus spiralis*. In their camp the pandanus was covered in hot ashes, roasted drupes were soaking in water-filled coolamons, and roasted soaked drupes had been put back on the coals.[2]

When gathering food, no opportunity is lost to collect materials for craftwork. Green pandanus leaves are woven into bags, mats and strainers for leaching food.

PHOTO: LEO MEIER/WELDON TRANNIES

Among the Lardil people, now settled on Mornington Island in the Gulf of Carpentaria, the leaves are knotted as a sign of ownership to deter others from stealing the fruit. If footprints show that the signs have been ignored, the owner digs a spear into the footprint. This is a form of punishment-sorcery to ensure that the thief will be harmed in some way.

When analysed at the University of Sydney, pandanus nuts were found to be very high in protein (between 24 and 34 per cent) and fat (44 to 49 per cent).

PEANUT TREE *Sterculia quadrifida*

Known in eastern Arnhem Land as *balk-balk,* the bush peanut is one of the most delicious native nuts and requires no preparation before eating.

The nuts grow on small trees in thick, leathery pods about the size of a 20-cent coin. Each pod contains four or so large, shiny black nuts. The pods are initially green but turn bright orange or red when ripe, then darken to brown. The oval nuts may be gathered at any stage. The black skin of the nuts is removed with the fingernail and they are eaten raw by men, women and children out hunting. Banduk says these nuts are never a staple, always just for 'pickings'.

Bush peanuts *(Sterculia quadrifida)* known as *balk-balk* at Yirrkala. These are delicious small nuts which do not require processing.

PHOTO: JENNIFER ISAACS

BUSH CASHEW NUT *Semicarpus australiensis*

Called *ganyawu* in eastern Arnhem Land, these nuts grow on large shade trees of the Arnhem Land forests. The sap is very irritant and Aborigines prevent their children climbing up the trunk and branches as the skin can develop allergic itchy patches on contact.

The nuts are attached to hard, yellow jelly-like matter, which must be removed and safely discarded away from children. They are encased in a 'skin' that is also poisonous and must be burnt off. Banduk described the preparation of *ganyawu* as follows:

> Build a fire away from camp because of the smoke. Spread the coals, put all the ganyawu in and cover them with more coals, then leave them for about fifteen minutes. While it's cooking sit right away from it so the wind can't blow the smoke in your face or your face will dry up and crack and peel off like a bad burn. When the nuts are cooked take them out and remove the skins without touching them or the same thing happens to your fingers. They are really delicious and taste a bit like hard uncooked cashew nuts. These nuts are also occasionally pounded after cooking so they can be eaten by people without teeth.

Mothers have to wash their hands carefully after preparing *ganyawu* before they touch their babies. The traditional way is to rub them with cuttlefish and water, then rub some bush passionfruit leaves into a lather and use it as soap.

BUNYA PINE   *Araucaria bidwillii*

The bunya pine is an enormously tall tree, up to 80 metres high, from the mountains of southeastern Queensland and northern New South Wales. It bears huge cones full of nuts. Although they fruit each year, they are particularly plentiful every three years. In the past, up to three hundred Aborigines gathered from different tribes to feast on the nuts. Descriptions of the bunya feasts are in many ways similar to those of the bogong moth gatherings of the alpine area in that observers described the Aborigines as living on a diet of nuts and emerging from the feasts and ceremonies 'sleek and fat'. Constance Petrie in her book about her father's memories, *Tom Petrie's Reminiscences*, says that the pine is wrongly pronounced 'bunya'. It should be 'bon-yi', the 'i' being sounded as an 'e' in English, which was the way the Aborigines used to pronounce it.[3] Tom claims that his grandfather, Andrew Petrie, discovered the tree, but when he gave some specimens to a Mr Bidwill, who forwarded them to England for classification, the tree was inadvertently named after him.

The cones are gathered by a man slinging a vine around the trunk, tying the rest of the rope around his waist and hoisting his body upward by clinging to the tree with his feet. Notches are sometimes cut into the tree trunks to help the ascent. The nuts are eaten both raw and cooked and were feasted upon until the season was over. The gatherings to feast on bunya nuts were times for ceremonial exchange, when different communities coming together would pass on songs and dances. These great ceremonies, which culminated when a particular food supply was plentiful in one area, were the means by which rituals and song cycles were transmitted from one part of the country to another.

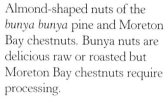

Almond-shaped nuts of the *bunya bunya* pine and Moreton Bay chestnuts. Bunya nuts are delicious raw or roasted but Moreton Bay chestnuts require processing.

PHOTO: DIANA CONROY

The bunya pine forests of southern Queensland were once nut feasting areas for hundreds of Aboriginal people.

PHOTO: WELDON TRANNIES

The nuts of many species of kurrajong are delicious but require great care in processing. Seedpod and flowers of the red kurrajong of Arnhem Land (*Brachychiton paradoxum*).

The yellow kurrajong nuts must be treated carefully as the hairy packing in the pods is an irritant.

KURRAJONG   *Brachychiton* spp.

Red kurrajong	*Brachychiton paradoxum*
Desert kurrajong	*B. gregorii*
Black kurrajong	*B. populneum*

Tall, distinctive kurrajong trees grow all over the country and most of the seeds were once gathered and eaten by Aborigines.

In Arnhem Land, Cape York and Western Australia the red kurrajong bears distinctive single red flowers when the leaves have fallen, and the nuts that follow are still relished throughout the north. Although delicious, great care is needed. The nuts can be harvested either when the pods are green and mature or when they are brown. When green, the pods are collected in large quantities and baked in the ashes. When they are opened the whole of the pod contents, the seeds and their packing, are peeled out. The nuts pop easily out of the packing and can then be eaten. The packing, however, is very poisonous and must be thoroughly removed and the hands washed.

When the pods are a dull brown, the seeds inside are bright yellow. To prepare the nuts at this stage of maturity the packing and nuts are extracted and baked together. The fire tenders must sit with one side to the fire so that no smoke blows into their eyes. When baked, the sandpapery packing is rubbed off the seeds between the hands. The wind blows the poisonous 'hairs' away, leaving the clean seeds, but again, the workers must sit so that the wind cannot blow the debris into their faces. According to Banduk, blindness can result; she lost a baby sister who ate some of these nuts in their casing.

In central Australia the desert kurrajong, *Brachychiton gregorii*, replaces the red kurrajong of the north as a source of nuts. The people of the desert have an ingenious way of avoiding the toxic hairs and pith of the seed cases by gathering the nuts from the droppings of crows around waterholes— already cleaned of hairs and pith, but requiring cooking and dehusking. The nuts are baked in the ashes, removed from their 'skins' and pounded into a type of damper.[4]

Another variety of kurrajong, *Brachychiton populneum* or black kurrajong, grows widely on rocky slopes in New South Wales and Victoria and is grown by farmers as drought fodder for stock. Southern people once gathered and ate these seeds which, when analysed by the University of Sydney team, were shown to have 25 per cent fat and 18 per cent protein, a most sustaining food.

BAOBAB NUT   *Adansonia gregorii*

This tree is usually called boab tree in the Kimberley region of Western Australia. It is distinctive for its huge bulbous trunk and large 'nuts', the size of emu eggs. The nuts must be harvested when mature but before they become hard.

The seeds and pith are eaten by Aborigines either raw or, after being dipped in water, sweetened with honey. Old reports say that the seeds and pith were also pounded and cooked into bread. The dry pith tastes like sherbet.

The distinctive boab tree of Western Australia bears huge nuts the size of emu eggs which contain a pithy substance tasting like sherbet.

PHOTO: JENNIFER ISAACS

Boab nuts are engraved with totemic animals and designs and, when dry, are used as rattles for dances.

PHOTO: REG MORRISON/WELDON TRANNIES

SEVEN

ROOTS, TUBERS, CORMS AND BULBS

The underground parts of many Australian plants and trees are dug, processed and eaten by Aboriginal people. In particular, yams of many varieties form a large part of the diet. In the southeast orchids with edible bulbs or corms, as well as other tubers such as the *murrnong* or yam-daisy, were once important foods.

In Arnhem Land the long yam and round yam (*Dioscorea* spp.) are staples and in the central deserts the most frequently eaten tubers are *yala* (*Ipomoea costata*), bush potato (*Vigna lanceolata*) and bush onion (*Cyperus bulbosus*). Roots and tubers have similar food values to potatoes and carrots, though the wild foods have a higher proportion of trace elements.

The digging of a yam takes skill and determination, particularly if the leaves are no longer visible and the dead parts above ground are simply dried, twining tendrils. Patience is needed to track the plant, particularly in rocky areas as it winds through the rocks and goes underground. Often the tuber itself may not be found where the vine enters the ground but some distance away. Aborigines know exactly where to dig: usually at an angle to the tuber so that the hole, which may be a metre or more deep, meets the tuber at an acute angle. It is important that the tuber itself is not

Above: Corms of the spike rush or water chestnut (*Eleocharis dulcis*),
a delicious staple food.

Banduk Marika washes *ganguri* or long yams,
(*Dioscorea transversa*) at First Creek, Yirrkala.

91

damaged and even a large yam must be dug out intact, though a small upper section attached to the vine may be separated and left in the ground. Often it is of ritual significance that the tuber is left whole. Of more practical importance is the fact that yams are cooked in the coals or ground oven and an intact skin keeps the moisture in the vegetable, retains the juicy flavour and prevents the yam becoming dry and floury.

A story from the Gunwinggu in western Arnhem Land highlights the pride felt by Aboriginal women when they have successfully gathered yams. A group of women went out with their digging sticks to gather a long yam, one of their favourite foods. These yams were around 45 centimetres long and 10 centimetres round; they were very sweet and eaten either raw or cooked. The women dug quite deeply. Some were lucky and others were not. As the day waned they all came back to camp, but some were empty-handed. As they were cooking and sharing the yams, the unsuccessful women, shamed and miserable, said that they would leave the camp and go up into the sky. The other women said generously, 'We want to live up in the sky, too, where people can see us—we will join you there'. Then all the women were transformed into stars. The Gunwinggu say that when you look into the sky at night some stars are twinkling and some are not. Those that twinkle are the women who found the yams; the motionless stars are those who came back to camp without any yams.[1]

LONG YAM   *Dioscorea transversa*

Long yams, known as *ganguri*, are washed and placed on a paperbark plate before cooking in a small ground oven. They have a slightly sweet, potato-like flavour.

PHOTO: JENNIFER ISAACS

This species of yam, commonly known in eastern Arnhem Land as *ganguri*, once formed the most important source of carbohydrate throughout Arnhem Land and Cape York. The yams of this twining vine grow up to a metre underground and may be as slim as a pencil or multi-pronged and as long as a person's forearm. Small yams can be eaten raw, though they are usually cooked. In the early dry season the long yam can be recognised by its net-veined, heart-shaped dark green leaves; in the latter part of the year, when the leaves have turned yellow or dropped, it is recognisable by the seeds that hang in groups of dry, brown winged capsules.

Digging yams is still women's work. Groups of related women head into the bush with string bags and digging implements—crowbars flattened at one end, machetes or long, strong digging knives. In Arnhem Land the traditional wooden digging stick is now seldom used, though women will often quickly cut and sharpen a suitable implement from the stem or trunk of a young tree if a good food patch is found. The first places checked for yams are the most easily dug; loose-soiled sandy areas relatively close to camp. In northeast Arnhem Land women know from experience where the yams will be. Areas of open forest close to roads have long been harvested and people return to the same patches when they think the yams will be sizeable again.

In dense forests the presence of long yams is detected by vines bearing heart-shaped leaves, or, in the dry season, by the brown-ringed seed capsules.

PHOTOS: JENNIFER ISAACS

With acute and trained vision the women follow the vines until they disappear in the grass, then feel for the point at which they enter the ground. Pushing the tall grass out of the way, they dig a narrow hole with their sticks, machetes or knives, beginning 60 or so centimetres away and at an angle to the presumed position of the tuber. But they can be wrong and some tubers are so far underground that it is not worth going on. On one recent trip my *yapa* (sister in law) Dhuwandjika, her daughter Mararu and sister Banduk dug a section of open woodland near Nhulunbuy airport and found 15 kilograms of tubers in half an hour. When the yams are removed from the ground the women leave the vine stem and a small section of tuber in position and often push the earth back in the hole so the yams will form again.

The *ganguri* are washed and dried before cooking and some of the hairs on the skin are gently rubbed off. To cook yams the women build a small ground oven 30 centimetres deep and the diameter of a suitable saucepan for the quantity of yams they have found. They line the hole with coals, on to which the yams are placed and covered with ashes, coals and warm earth. The yams are lifted out after twenty minutes, put on a platter of leaves and given to everyone to peel and eat. These yams are quite firm and delicious and have a flavour rather like a slightly sweet potato.

In Cape York the same yams are eaten, though Thancoupie was more specific in describing just when the tubers were ready to be dug. She grows them in her backyard in Cairns and never digs until the leaves are yellow when, she says, 'the water is out of the yam'; otherwise, she says, 'they taste horrible'. Another way to tell that yams are ready is 'when the grass seeds burst, that's the yam digging time. So this way animal spirits look after food and tell the tribe right time'.

DESERT YAM   *Ipomoea costata*

The desert yam or *yala* is one of the staple foods of central Australia. The yam, sometimes difficult to locate, grows up to 90 centimetres underground and is distinguished by runners, or dormant stems, when growing. The tubers can be very large when close to creeks and water supplies. The rounded tubers are 12-20 centimetres long and 5-18 centimetres wide and a single plant may have up to twenty yams.

The tubers are cooked under the coals. The hot coals are brushed aside and the yams placed on the warm earth before being covered with ashes for twenty minutes or so, depending on the size of the vegetable. When cooked the yams are peeled, though even the discards can be eaten and are chewed by the children. This outer skin is tasty, rather like very stringy sweet potatoes but not as sweet.

The yams have a considerable percentage of moisture, with some protein and a little fat.

Long yams of the desert region, known as *yala*, are staple foods. Taproots of some sapling trees are also eaten.

PHOTO: LEO MEIER/WELDON TRANNIES

Wendy Napananga digs for yams in a sandy creek bed of the western desert.

PHOTO: LEO MEIER/WELDON TRANNIES

Heart-shaped leaves of the vine of *Dioscorea bulbifera*.

PHOTO: VIC CHERIKOFF

The round yam (*Dioscorea bulbifera*) of Arnhem Land and Cape York has many fibrous roots and requires cooking and leaching before being eaten. It has a slightly hot taste.

PHOTO: VIC CHERIKOFF

ROUND YAM   *Dioscorea bulbifera*

The round yam grows either in jungles or in very sandy soil. This yam, known as *jitama* in eastern Arnhem Land, is somewhat round and fat and is covered with numbers of fibrous roots. It requires more preparation than the simply baked long yam.

The round yam is either boiled or roasted in the ashes, then peeled, grated, pounded and soaked in running water for at least a day. The 'cakes' that result are 'hot' food. It 'picks you up', said my friends as they ate them for breakfast.

CONVOLVULUS   *Ipomoea* spp.

The common native convolvulus is harvested by Aborigines for its edible taproot. The vines of a number of species bear distinctive purple, mauve or pink flowers and can be seen on beaches in all parts of Australia. The thick taproots of *Ipomoea gracilis* and *I. brasiliensis*, for example, are gathered and roasted in the hot ashes.

The roots of *I. graminea*, or grass-leaved convolvulus, are high in energy and water with good levels of carbohydrate and protein and some fat and trace elements.

Dhuwandjika Marika gathers the delicious nutty corms of the spike rushes *(Eleocharis dulcis)* that grow in profusion on swampy land in northeast Arnhem Land.

PHOTO: JENNIFER ISAACS

SPIKE RUSH; Water Chestnut   *Eleocharis dulcis*

This thin rush grows profusely in swamps across the tropical north. The corms or chestnuts grow beneath the heavy dark soil of the swamps. The plant grows vigorously during the wet season and the first corms are dug out at the end of May or early June when the swamps are drying out. They are a delicious food still gathered in Arnhem Land where they are known as *rakay*. In Cape York they are called *ganj* and to the Lardil people of Mornington Island they are known as *panja*.

Good *panja* areas are traditionally 'owned' by the Lardil. To indicate ownership, clumps of the long rushes are tied into knots in a custom called *goobal*. The food provided by *panja* extends over long periods of the year.

Older, dark-coloured corms are roasted; younger, light corms can be eaten raw. After pulling them from the ground, the women collect the corms in bark containers, rinse them, bake them in the ashes for a few minutes and rake them out with a stick. The corms are then rubbed between the hands to remove the husks. Pounders and stones for grinding such foods were developed in Cape York where cakes of *ganj* were kept for up to two weeks.

limbuk or *gingin*, the bush potato *(Vigna lanceolata)* of central Arnhem Land.

PHOTO: LEO MEIER/WELDON TRANNIES

BUSH POTATO   *Vigna lanceolata*

Among the Guparbingu people of central Arnhem Land, the *limbuk* or *gingin* are cooked in the ashes all year round. This small, thin tuber has a sweet potato-like flavour. The plant has oval leaves in clumps of three.

Vigna species are also commonly eaten yams of the central desert regions. Here, the species is a low-growing plant that favours fine, relatively moist sediments, often occurring along watercourses. It has a thin taproot up to 20 centimetres in length, eaten raw or roasted. Food analysis shows it to have a high water content, some protein and carbohydrate and many trace elements, like the cultivated sweet potato.

BUSH ONIONS   *Cyperus bulbosus*

This is a small onion sedge with corms on shallow roots the size of shallots. To the Warlpiri it is known as *janmarda;* to the Arrente, *yelka;* and to the Pitjantjatjara it is *nyiri.* Eaten raw or cooked, the corms may be kept for a period in underground storage. They have a tough husk that is removed before eating. In some areas the corms are placed on flat ground and spinifex is burned over them until the corms crack. Sometimes they are put in hot sand and the husks rubbed until the skin cracks. When the rains come all underground vegetables begin to shoot and are not harvested again until a month or so after the rains have ended and the tubers have matured. Women say the onions are not good to eat when they are in the early growing phase after rain.

Bush onions, or *yelka, (Cyperus bulbosus)* may be eaten raw or cooked after removing the hard casing.

PHOTO: HAROLD WELDON/WELDON TRANNIES

Mirna anularra, by Kubatji Ngwarrayi. This contemporary Anmatjera painting from Utopia records the bush potato dreaming. All foods have religious significance.

PHOTO: LEO MEIER/WELDON TRANNIES

This tasty bulb is interesting in that the Pitjantjatjara have named paper and books *nyiri* because of paper's resemblance to the skin of the onion bulb. It has a high water content, good protein levels and some fat and trace elements.

BUSH CARROT   *Abelmoschus moschatus*

This small pointed tuber looks like a miniature parsnip and tastes like a carrot, hence its colloquial name. In the Djinang language of central Arnhem Land it is called *marrakangalay*. Although infrequently eaten, it is nevertheless admired for its taste after being cooked in the ashes or, with other vegetables and yams, in a ground oven.

Bush carrot (*Abelmoschus moschatus*) of central Arnhem Land.
PHOTO: LEO MEIER/WELDON TRANNIES

Elsie Ganbada holds aloft a long bush carrot at Yathalamara, central Arnhem Land. The soil must be dug with a strong digging stick, sometimes over a metre deep, to extract the tuber intact.
PHOTO: LEO MEIER/WELDON TRANNIES

YELLOW LILY YAM   *Amorphophallus glabra*

This vegetable, called 'yam' by local Aboriginal people, is really the corm of a yellow lily found on the edge of dark patches of jungle in Arnhem Land. It can be dug during the dry season as the upright dried lily stems make it easily recognisable. The corm is large, round and squat, about the size of a fist, but its taste is not really admired.

The plant figures in the paintings of David Malangi, who owns large tracts of land on which the lily grows freely near Ramingining in central Arnhem Land. The bulb, called *kanawarangi* or *lowiya* in the Djinang language, must be cooked in a ground oven or on the coals for a whole night or, Malangi warned, 'It makes mouth sore, can't talk'.

The first scientific expedition to Arnhem Land in 1948 described the cooking of *Amorphophallus* as follows:

> The normal procedure [at Melville Bay and Port Bradshaw] was to make an oven early in the morning. A large layer of hot stones was covered with large green leaves, then the roots were put on top, then another layer of stones, more green leaves and finally paperbark and sand to close the oven. The oven was not opened until the following morning... Until it has been sufficiently cooked this corm has a very sharp flavour and leaves an unpleasant burning feeling in the mouth.[2]

Bark painting of edible tubers. Milingimbi, Northern Territory.

PHOTO: REG MORRISON/WELDON TRANNIES

YAM DAISY   *Microseris scapigera*

The yam daisy is a native perennial, similar to a dandelion and between 10 and 30 centimetres in height. The fleshy roots were once eaten by Victorian Aborigines as a staple food. The plant was dug widely along the rivers, especially the Yarra, Murray and Maribyrnong, where it had the common name of *murrnong* among Aboriginal people. The white milky tubers were either washed, scraped and eaten raw, or washed and roasted in fibre baskets. It is rather sweet with some seasonal bitterness.[3]

Although no longer commonly seen in settled areas, the yam daisy is still found in the bush in some areas of southern Australia.

YAM   *Dioscorea* spp.

In the north of Western Australia there were once plots of a yam known as *ijecka*. The tubers grew in such abundance that Aborigines erected bark huts during harvest time. The yams were very large and the people dug patches of ground thoroughly to collect them all.

In 1850 some of the state's early pastoralists, Thomas Brown, the Berger brothers and A.C. Gregory, were herding their flocks to the area south of Geraldton when they came across 200 Aboriginal men, women and children harvesting *ijecka*. They fiercely defended their territory. However, the settlers, carrying double-barrelled shotguns, were not deterred and by 1856 the *ijecka* groves had disappeared.

ORCHID

The small underground tubers of many species of terrestrial orchids are eaten in all Australian states, including species of the following genera: *Caladenia, Cryptostylis, Diuris, Dipodium, Geodorum, Glossodia, Lypernathus, Microtis, Prasophyllum, Pterostylis* and *Thelymitra*.

The Queensland tree orchid, *Cymbidium canaliculatum*, also provides food. The 'fruit' or pseudo-bulbs are eaten raw or grated and boiled. The thick starch gives this food the common nickname of native arrowroot.

Rock orchid.

PHOTO: VIC CHERIKOFF

Tree orchids of the cymbidium variety offer food in times of hardship as the false bulbs can be eaten raw or boiled.

PHOTO: DIANA CONROY

WILD ARROWROOT   *Tacca leontopetaloides*

The explorer Ludwig Leichhardt may have given this species its colloquial name of arrowroot when he wrote in his journal:

> I tried several methods to render the potatoes, which we had found in the camps of the natives, eatable, but neither roasting nor boiling destroyed their sickening bitterness; at last I pounded and washed them, and procured the starch, which was entirely tasteless, but thickened rapidly in hot water like arrowroot, and was very agreeable to eat, wanting only the addition of sugar to make it delicious—at least, so we fancied.[4]

Although this tuber grows throughout the Top End of the Northern Territory, it is harvested and processed with elaborate skill only in Cape York. The tuber itself is not eaten but its starch is extracted, set and cooked in cakes. The processing of this food is perhaps the closest Aboriginal equivalent to the techniques of the horticulturists of Papua New Guinea.

Alice Mark of Weipa holds the double tuber of an arrowroot plant.

PHOTO: GEOFF WHARTON

The plants can be found in semi-shade relatively close to water. At Weipa they occur along sandy ridges around a kilometre from beaches. The plant has a double tuber, one old and dried, the other white and fresh. Only the new tuber is removed; the other is replaced to grow again. This harvesting takes place after the wet season, when the green growing time has passed. Indeed the tubers can be collected right through the Dry when a bare brown stem is the only visible evidence of the plant.

The people of Weipa and Aurukun on the west coast of Cape York do not often harvest arrowroot today, but they talk with pleasure of great arrowroot feasts after weeks of harvesting and communally processing large quantities.

Usually the women collect net bags full of tubers over several days. They wash the dirt off and leave the vegetables in the sun to dry. The tubers must be soaked because of their intensely bitter taste, so the work always takes place close to running water, usually a freshwater stream.

The arrowroot is first grated into a receptacle with the sharp edge of a shell or knife. In traditional times a trough made from stringybark was used; today it is more probably an enamel bowl. The grated arrowroot is then sieved from one bark trough to another through a grass mesh basket or through layers of unworked grass which have first been cleaned of seeds and debris. As the fibre collects in the sieve the white, starchy water passes through to the trough below and settles. This process is repeated and the fibrous matter squeezed to release all the starch.

As the starch settles the water is tasted. It will be changed several times until no bitterness remains. When the water is 'sweet' it is drained off and the powdery starch left to dry in the sun until it can be removed with a shell and formed into cakes or balls about twenty centimetres in diameter.

The technique of cooking these starch balls is surprising. They are not cooked whole, but roasted on the coals. The outer part of the ball is quickly wet in a shell filled with water, then the ball is thrown on the coals. The outer skin is browned on both sides, turned after about ten minutes and removed. The browned part forms a 'skin', which is removed and eaten immediately. Then the inner starch ball is wet again and put on the coals to repeat the process.[5]

Waterlily seeds, stems and corms of the *Nymphaea* species are all edible.

PHOTO: JENNIFER ISAACS

Waterlily corms are collected by women from the mud, then washed in hand-woven pandanus sieves. Cooked for a short time in the coals, they are then peeled and eaten as a delicious meal. They can also be ground into cakes for children or the elderly.

PHOTO: LEO MEIER/WELDON TRANNIES

Opposite: Lotus flower *(Nelumbo nucifera).* These elegant plants of the billabongs of western Arnhem Land have edible rhizomes.

PHOTO: LEO MEIER/WELDON TRANNIES

WATERLILY BULB *Nymphaea* sp.

Throughout Arnhem Land there are three types of waterlilies in swamps and billabongs. The underground corms are gathered and roasted in the ashes. The blue waterlilly is termed *wak wak* at Yirrkala, the pink is *dhatum* and the white is *burpa*. The women wade into the billabongs or swamps and dig with their fingers and feet in the mud under the plants to get the corms. As Banduk says:

> That means we are in the water most of the time, but that's fun for everyone because the woman is mostly the food collector. The children are mostly with us unless they are back home with a relative, like a grandmother or aunt. You have to feel your way around under the water in the mud to get them. You wash the mud away so that you then see the 'nuts'. You cook them under the coals, wait about ten to fifteen minutes and rake them out. Sometimes after cooking you can pound them all together into a flour dough and eat it. Usually this is a good food for children or for old people that can't chew.

The processed corms are high in carbohydrate and fibre, and contain a significant amount of protein as well as water, fat and trace elements.

SACRED LOTUS *Nelumbo nucifera*

The lotus differs from the waterlily in that its leaves are suspended on the stem above the surface of the water. The large pink flowers are followed by distinctive brown seed capsules.

The rhizomes of the lotus plant are used as food, particularly in western Arnhem Land. They have a high fibre content with good energy and carbohydrate levels and are sweet and palatable.

CORAL TREE *Erythrina vespertilio*

The fibrous roots of the seedlings of the *ininti* tree, *Erythrina vespertilio,* are sometimes eaten by the Warlpiri, Pintubi, Alyawara and related groups of the desert. This large tree grows up to 10 metres high along desert water-courses.

Erythrina roots, along with other desert tubers such as *Leichhardtia australis, Clerodendrum floribundum* and *Boerhavia diffusa* are roasted, then scraped or pounded with rocks to separate the flesh from the fibrous inner core, which is discarded. Only the skin and flesh are eaten.

Erythrina or *ininti* trees are always pointed out by western desert women on bush food expeditions, not so much for the tubers of the saplings but for their bright red seeds. These are gathered and strung into necklaces, headbands and chest ornaments to be worn by women and children when dancing. The root is an occasional food only and is collected infrequently.

NATIVE GINGER   *Hornstedtia scottiana*

Native ginger is a much loved Aboriginal food, offering a pungent lift to the senses. This aromatic plant is found in swampy areas and small heart-shaped fruiting bodies at ground level contain the seeds. The small seeds appear to be wrapped up in little packets, which are sucked. They are very sweet.

BRACKEN   *Pteridum esculentum*

The common bracken fern has become a pest in some country areas and

Bulrushes (*Typha* sp.) are common throughout Australia. Large quantities of the cooked rhizome were once eaten seasonally by Aborigines.

PHOTO: DIANA CONROY

is often the first plant to regenerate after fire. The thin, starchy rhizomes are edible from late summer to autumn, but must be processed to avoid possible ill effects. Some Aborigines pound the rhizomes to extract the starch, which is cooked in cakes as the rhizomes alone are very fibrous.

BULRUSH   *Typha* spp.

Common bulrushes grow in shallow water of creeks, rivers and swamps. The rush grows prolifically in warmer months, reaching a height of 2.5 metres.

The glutinous rhizome was roasted and provided starch, sugar and a considerable amount of fibre to the people of Victoria and New South Wales. According to the explorer Thomas Mitchell, bulrushes were the principal food of Aborigines of the Lachlan River. He observed them wading through the swamps gathering large bundles and carrying them in net bags on their heads.

PHOTO: LEO MEIER/WELDON TRANNIES

EIGHT

SEEDS AND DAMPER

In the central desert damper from the seeds of native grasses, shrubs, herbs and trees still forms an important part of Aboriginal diet, though local stores provide both plain and self-raising flour. The seeds of up to forty-five plant species were once used for food in the centre. Although food grasses and trees occur in Arnhem Land, Cape York and coastal regions, fewer were used because of the availability of other foods, including fruits and seafood.

Grinding seed and utilising native grasses is an ancient survival technique of Aboriginal people. Grindstones at Lake Mungo in western New South Wales (a site now on the World Heritage List) have been dated to around 15 000 years ago. Even older examples have been found in Arnhem Land and the Kimberley region.

The origin of seed food can be found in mythology. Two old men of the Katherine area in the Northern Territory gave a very interesting description of the mythological base of the gathering and processing of wild sorghum (*Sorghum intrans* and *S. plumosum*) in their area. These men from the Tagoman and the Wardaman tribes were assisting agricultural research officer Arndt, who was working for the CSIRO in Katherine at

Above: Two of the edible desert acacia seeds.

A family at Mt Liebig is making wild seed damper in the ashes. The cooking is done inside the tin shelter to prevent twigs and coals from being blown into the paste.

PHOTO: LEO MEIER/WELDON TRANNIES

Painting of the mulga seed totem
on Ayers Rock.

the time. Arndt recorded his discussions with the men and the myths associated with the gathering of sorghum in the area:

> The morkul, or 'tucker of the long grass', was given to the people by a spirit known as Morkul-kau-luan. He was a man with a slightly crouched figure and a long sharp nose. He moved through the long grass unseen—only his long nose was occasionally glimpsed, which looked very much like the awns of the grass. He kept his eyelids almost closed to keep out the sharp grass. He wore a broad human hair belt and had a voice with a humming sound, which could sometimes be heard as the wind blew through the grass.[1]

A painting of this spirit is on a sandstone outcrop at Katherine. In common with great ancestor paintings on rock in other parts of the Australian continent, this is where the spirit of Morkul-kau-luan came to rest.

Many species of wattle trees have edible seeds. These are generally collected when they are fully ripe, with brittle pods still hanging from the branches. In order to separate the seeds from the pods the women either pluck the seeds directly from the bushes or pick whole branches and pile them on top of each other on a patch of clear ground or on a blanket. They are beaten heartily with a stick until the seeds fall from the branches into piles. The pods themselves are then beaten with the stick to release some of the seeds and both the pods and remaining seeds are winnowed in a curved wooden dish or coolamon. Any green pods that remain are removed because they are difficult to work with and the seeds generally stick inside them.

Grass seeds are much smaller and, though only a few are staples, there are many possible food sources. The most commonly used grasses of the Pitjantjatjara and Jankuntjatjara people are the millet (*Brachiaria* sp.) and woollybutt (*Eragrostis eriopoda*). Another commonly gathered seed-bearing grass is *Panicum decompositum* or native millet, known to the Pitjantjatjara as *kaltu kaltu*.[2]

Grass seed is generally tiny: the largest, arm grass millet seed, is no more than 2 millimetres in diameter and most are smaller. The smallest seed of all is that of the portulaca, comparable in size with grains of gunpowder. Acacia seeds are usually collected from October to December; grass seed is ripe for harvesting later, from January to March. This, however, is never predictable and depends entirely on the pattern of previous rainfall in the area.

Grass seeds are collected by stripping the seed heads or flowers by hand and beating them into a coolamon with a stick. One interesting practice of Aboriginal women is to collect seeds from the debris around ants' nests. Some desert ants collect fallen seeds, eat part of the surrounding case, and deposit the seeds at the entrance to their underground nests. These seeds can be collected with a little of the soil from around the nest and winnowed to remove the grit from the husked seeds. At times when grasses are not bearing seed, women often look for ants' nests to find small deposits.

The outer glumes of all seeds must be removed. For some species, including *Panicum decompositum* and *Eragrostis eriopoda,* this can be done simply by rubbing the seeds between the hands so that the wind winnows the husks away. For harder seeds, however, the process is more elaborate. A hole is dug in the sand beneath a tree and the husks and grain are poured in. Holding the tree, women stand on the grain and grind the husks away by rotating their feet from side to side. The grain and husks are then winnowed in a dish.[3]

Most seeds are ground before eating. Depending on the seed type, they are either dry milled or wet ground: hard acacia seeds, for example, are dry milled while grass seed is wet milled. In the hard seed dry milling technique, fire is often necessary to prepare the seeds for processing. The hard seeds are roasted in the ashes, then winnowed, sprinkled with water and ground on a grooved grinding slab. Even harder seeds must first be cracked with a hammer stone after burning in the fire. Only after cracking can they be ground. Softer seeds are simply ground with water into a paste and eaten raw or made into bread, commonly called damper.[4]

Ripe black waterlily seeds *Nymphaea* sp. are enjoyed by children as well as adults.

PHOTO: LEO MEIER/WELDON TRANNIES

109

Distinctive grey-green mulga
trees *(Acacia aneura)*.

PHOTO: DIANA CONROY

Simpsons Gap, central Australia.
Acacia trees, including witchetty
bushes *(Acacia kempeana)* are
widespread in desert regions,
offering a bounty of edible seeds.

PHOTO: DIANA CONROY

MULGA   *Acacia aneura*

Although as many as twenty desert species of acacia have edible seeds, by far the most common and important food sources are mulga bush, *Acacia aneura,* and witchetty bush, *A. kempeana,* both of which form dense stands close to each other in the central desert region. Mulga bushes seed prolifically only when rainfall is reasonable and the mulga looks 'green', not its usual dull grey. On a mulga seed gathering trip Maude Peterson, from Mt Liebig in the MacDonnell Ranges, scanned the horizon and said, 'When we go for tucker', we look for green mulga'.

Mulga trees carry pods from 2.5 to 3.75 centimetres long, containing three seeds. The pods are collected from the tree, threshed and winnowed to separate them. Some accounts indicate that mulga seed is soaked or roasted before being ground and eaten, whereas a recent report from the Ashburton area of Western Australia indicates that *wintamar,* as acacia seed is known in this region, is ground up and eaten without cooking.[5]

Among the Pitjantjatjara and related peoples further south the mulga bush is known as *wanari.* Here the ripe seeds are ground into coarse flour, mixed into a paste and eaten raw. The trees are also useful for their many small waxy red growths *(wama)* found on the twigs. These are gathered, pounded up and infused in water, to be drunk as a sweetish tea. The process obviously varies from one group to another.

Throwing the mulga seeds into the air allows the wind to winnow the seeds from pods in the coolamon.

PHOTO: LEO MEIER/WELDON TRANNIES

Mulga seeds and pods (*Acacia aneura*).

PHOTO: LEO MEIER/WELDON TRANNIES

Among the Warlpiri other acacia seeds, such as *A. cowleana*, are winnowed, cooked in piles on hot ashes and winnowed again, after which they are ground with water into a sweet-tasting porridge.[6] Among the Pitjantjatjara, other sources of seeds and seed foods include *A. estrophiolata*, the ironwood tree, the seeds of which are crushed and mixed with water as a sweet for children, and *A. ligulata*, the umbrella bush or *watarkas*, the seeds of which are treated like mulga seeds. Some very tough seeds need to be roasted first before being ground. Among these are *A. murrayana* or *tjuntjula* and *A. tetragonophylla* or *wakalpuka*.

All acacia seeds analysed for their food content by the University of Sydney proved strikingly rich in nutrients with higher energy, protein and fat than crops such as wheat and rice, and even higher than some meats.

The yellow-tipped seeds of *Acacia tetragonophylla* must be roasted before being ground into flour.

PHOTO: LEO MEIER/WELDON TRANNIES

Molly Nungarai gathers edible seeds from witchetty bushes along the road from Papunya to Mt Liebig.

PHOTO: LEO MEIER/WELDON TRANNIES

Ripe brown witchetty bush seeds (*Acacia kempeana*).

PHOTO: LEO MEIER/WELDON TRANNIES

Delicious green beans from wiry wattle are known as *irkilli* (*Acacia coriacea*) to the Pintubi.

PHOTO: LEO MEIER/WELDON TRANNIES

WITCHETTY BUSH   *Acacia kempeana*

Witchetty bushes are smaller and more spreading than mulga trees and are commonly found on spinifex plains. Their name stems from the presence of the favourite desert food in their roots.

Seeds of *Acacia kempeana* are treated in the same way as mulga seed. Among the Pitjantjatjara they are known as *wintalka*. They are ground into a paste, mixed with water and eaten raw.

WIRY WATTLE   *Acacia coriacea*

This hardy plant is known as *irkilli* to the Pintubi and *pankuna* to the Warlpiri of the western desert. *Acacia coriacea*, bearing the *irkilli* beans, grows to 3-4 metres high with a heavy crop of pods as long as 30 centimetres, each containing twelve or so large green seeds with an orange cap. The seed pods are gathered green and can be opened and eaten raw like green peas or cooked in the ashes. They have a delicious flavour like sweet beans. On the day we found them, the car was full of young children who stripped the tree as quickly as possible and sat on the road devouring the seeds with great enjoyment. As the green beans appear during the dry season between September and November, they are a highly rated moist vegetable in Warlpiri and Pintubi country.

If the *irkilli* are to be cooked, they are lightly roasted in the fire and eaten. The cooked vegetable tastes rather like a chestnut, though it remains crisp. The Pintubi women explained that when the *irkilli* are dry, they are roasted, mashed up and mixed with water to form a porridge. The dry black seeds can also be harvested and ground into a paste.

The wiry wattle has a distinctive formation and regenerates after fire. It offers a bounty of green beans or seeds.
PHOTO: HAROLD WELDON/WELDON TRANNIES

The *irkilli* seeds can be cooked fresh or dry. When fresh they are rolled gently in their pods through the ashes and flames; when dry, they are roasted, mashed and made into a porridge.
PHOTO: LEO MEIER/WELDON TRANNIES

In spinifex areas these seeds are a staple food as they are highly nutritious. The green beans have a high water and protein content, some fat, carbohydrate and fibre and good trace elements. When black and dry they offer very high energy levels, high protein, very high carbohydrate and fibre, some fat and water and good trace elements.

GRASS AND HERB SEED   *Panicum* spp.; *Brachiaria* spp.; *Eragrostis* spp.

In addition to seeds obtained from trees and bushes, Aborigines utilise many nutritious seeds from grasses, herbs and succulents, most of which are short-lived and favour disturbed ground or a consistent fire regime to encourage fruiting.

Grasses of the *Panicum, Brachiaria* and *Eragrostis* genera seem to predominate and are common throughout the centre, particularly along watercourses and in floodplains or mulga areas. Although most seeds are very small, each grass bush bears heavily.

Armgrass millet, *Brachiaria miliiformis,* bears seeds 2 millimetres in diameter with a slight lustre; woollybutt grass (*Eragrostis* sp.) or *wangunu,* a staple of the Pintubi, is somewhat smaller. Both are wet milled and poured into the ashes to make damper.

MITCHELL GRASS   *Astrelba pectinata*

This seed-bearing grass was named after Major Thomas Mitchell, who explored western New South Wales and opened the way for pastoralists to settle in the area. Mitchell travelled along the Bogan, Darling, Lachlan and Murrumbidgee rivers and commented on the intense 'farming' of this grass by Aborigines. In 1835 he observed racks of the grass drying in the sun along the Darling River and noted that the grass grew saddle high as far as the eye could see. These were the stores of the Bagundji people, who had a remarkable seed-collecting economy. The seeds were gathered, ground and made into damper. Large quantities of stored seed were found long after the local people had been displaced.

When pastoral properties were established and the Bagundji stopped firing the grasslands, the grass crops soon failed. Scattered around most outback stations are the remains of this great seed economy—flat, well-worn grinding stones left at specific places until next season's visit because they were too heavy to carry. Many were left never to be used again.

PIGWEED   *Portulaca oleracea*; *P. intraterranea*

The prostrate portulaca herb is widespread from the coast to the inland desert, where it grows along sandy riverbanks. This succulent plant has opposed fleshy ovate leaves about 2 centimetres long. The stems sprawl along the ground. Small yellow flowers appear in summer, followed by

Linda Sideek of Papunya collects a small plant of the *Portulaca* species.

PHOTO: JENNIFER ISAACS

Portulaca, or pigweed, grows widely throughout Australia. Both seeds and leaves are edible

PHOTO: VIC CHERIKOFF

capsules containing large numbers of minute kidney-shaped black seeds which, when piled in a heap, look like black sand. Each plant bears a large quantity of seeds and many can be collected quickly as whole plants are gathered and upended on sheets of bark or skin. The seeds fall out after some time and may be used fresh or stored for a considerable period.

Grass and herb seeds are stored for indefinite periods in desert areas, providing a predictable and safe supply of food in times of drought.

WILD RICE *Oryza sativa*

After the wet season wild rice grows extensively on the swampy plains around the Gulf of Carpentaria. Aborigines process the grain by soaking it, then removing the chaff by rubbing the seeds in bark troughs. Alternatively, the grain is often burnt and the seeds removed from the ash, ground, mixed with water and baked. The grains are very like smaller brown rice. Wild rice is also eaten in western Arnhem Land.

NARDOO *Marsilea drummondii*

Nardoo *(Marsilea drummondii).* The seeds make a damper eaten as a staple during drought.

PHOTO: REG MORRISON/WELDON TRANNIES

Nardoo is a type of fern found in all states of Australia. It sometimes grows in the dry ground at the edge of lakes, though more usually it is aquatic with leaves like four-leaf clovers floating on the water's surface. The spores, produced in sporocarps about the size of a pea, were once gathered for food. Nardoo bread is mentioned in the journals of explorers Burke and Wills as being somewhat unpalatable, though it satisfied their hunger.

Nardoo is no longer gathered and eaten, but accounts describing its use indicate that Aborigines ground the spores between stones and removed the black husks. The remaining yellow powder was mixed with water for damper. Clearly it was a food for hard times, a hunger mollifier rather than a sustainer.

OLD MAN SALTBUSH *Atriplex nummularia*

A perennial shrub, the saltbush can grow to 3 metres in height and has bluish-grey leaves with brittle stems. The prolific seeds are ground into flour and made into damper in the drier inland areas, including Victoria and western New South Wales.

DAMPER

The memory, smell and taste of home-cooked damper brings to mind thoughts of home, family and the bush to Aboriginal people all over Australia. Damper is prepared in many different ways throughout the country. In northern Australia, for example, nut cakes are more common than the seed damper of the desert, though wild rice is occasionally used.

Since the beginning of the European colonisation of Australia, settlers have been trading flour, sugar and tea with Aborigines. This practice has deservedly been strongly criticised. Particularly in desert regions, the availability of white flour, which makes a light and palatable damper, has had profound effects. In areas where people once had to walk long distances in search of a small quantity of seed, the trading of flour encouraged a more sedentary life close to the new food supplies. Recent research by the University of Sydney has confirmed that seed from native acacias and grasses have strikingly high nutritional value, far higher than the processed flours that have largely replaced them. As a consequence, the health problems of Aborigines are now severe. Obesity, inadequate nutrition and poor general health are all matters for concern.

As lifestyles changed and settled Aboriginal communities developed close to country towns, people maintained their own tradition of cooking bread or damper though the grain had changed. Dampers are now cooked in the ashes in camp ovens, on hotplates and in the oven.

DESERT SEED DAMPER

For the Pitjantjatjara women, with whom Winifred Hilliard lived for many decades at Ernabella, several seeds provided the basis of different breads. The portulaca plant, known as *wakati* to the Pitjantjatjara, as well as various grasses, in particular *Panicum* species, were considered to be delicious seed for bread. Winifred Hilliard describes the process of making the damper as follows:

Wendy Napananga of Mt Liebig enjoys the dark brown wild seed damper.

PHOTO: LEO MEIER/WELDON TRANNIES

The tiny seeds are ground with water into a thick paste. The mixture is poured on to the hot ashes. Glowing sticks 'toast' the upper surface until the loaf can be turned, covered with ashes and coals, and cooked through.

PHOTOS: LEO MEIER/WELDON TRANNIES

Many species of wild grass seeds are ground for damper.

PHOTO: LEO MEIER/WELDON TRANNIES

Cleaning and winnowing of the seeds gathered are carried out by a deceptively simple process known as *kanini*. The seed is poured on to a digging dish, which is then held at both ends and given a slight flicking movement. Immediately, the seed begins to separate from the grit and moves to one end of the dish, while the impurities move to the other to be thrown away. The grass seeds need to be winnowed as well as separated from the impurities, and this is done by pouring the seeds from a dish held at about 45 centimetres from the ground into a lower dish while the husks blow away. The grass seed can also be cleaned with water poured over the seed in a dish before flicking.

When the seed has been cleaned the *wakati* is mixed with a little water and ground with a small round stone on a larger flat one and the paste thus produced is ready to eat. With the grass seed, it is also mixed with a little water and ground in the same manner, and can be either eaten as a paste or the paste may be formed into a small loaf and cooked in the coals. When the fire has burned long enough to make the ground hot for cooking the coals are pushed aside and tiny twigs of mulga are placed on the spot and burnt into a fine white ash on to which the loaf is placed. More tiny twigs are set on top of this loaf and these too are burnt to fine ash which is spread carefully over the upper surface. The whole is covered with hot coals and left to cook for half an hour.[7]

The process by which the Pintubi cook a similar traditional seed bread is slightly different. Molly Nungarai, an elderly woman considered the local expert on making seed damper, prepared some for us on a recent trip to Mt Liebig. She winnowed the seed, not by pouring it from a dish but by

tossing it into the air so the wind blew the husks away while they were airborne. When the seeds were thoroughly clean, Molly cleaned her grinding stones—the flat base and the round grinder—by rubbing them carefully together with water to remove most of the surface sand. The seeds were placed in a small heap in the centre of the flat stone. Dribbling water on to the seeds, Molly then ground the seeds into a slushy paste. As this mass flowed toward the edge of the stone it dripped over into a waiting coolamon below. The thin paste was pooled on to the hot ashes of the fire so that it formed a disk-shaped loaf.

While the dough cooked from below on the ash, firewood was balanced over the bread, but not touching it, so the coals of the sticks above could harden the upper surface of the bread as though it were under a griller. When a firm crust had formed on the upper surface the damper was turned over. Using a stick, Molly scraped the ashes off the surface, made a groove around the now hard loaf and deftly turned the loaf over with two sticks. It was piled with fine ash again and then with coals so that the interior could bake through.

When the bread was cooked it was dark brown in colour and very tasty, rather like rich rye bread but, considering the amount of sand that had entered the dough paste during the grinding process, quite gritty. A jam tin half full of seeds about the size of small bird seed or alfalfa seed had produced a damper approximately 2 centimetres high by 11 centimetres in diameter.

PLAIN FLOUR DAMPER

Jean George of Weipa pats the ash off a delicious white damper, lightly browned.

PHOTO: JENNIFER ISAACS

Wendy Napananga made plain white flour damper at Mt Liebig in the western desert in a similar way to the technique employed by Dhuwandjika at Yirrkala. Wendy heaped the flour in her coolamon, added water into a 'well' in the centre and gently tossed the flour over the water from the sides of the heap until she had a very sticky dough. She added flour to the outside of the dough until it could be lifted, formed into a flat loaf and placed in the ashes. The dough was not kneaded to any great extent, just enough to mix the grain and water through while not de-aerating the dough.

Dhuwandjika substituted a tin for the coolamon but her cooking technique was similar. The coals were swept to one side and the ashes brushed lightly to reveal a bed of hot clean fine ash. The dry dough (unlike the wet sludge of wild seed dampers) was placed on the white ashes. Allowing a minute or so to harden the dough a little, the ashes that had been moved to one side were heaped back on top of the damper and the whole was covered with hot coals. After fifteen minutes or so, depending on its size, the loaf was turned and covered again. Dhuwandjika also makes the same type of damper adding milk powder to the flour or using wholemeal flour.

Wendy Napananga rests after a
long walk and cooks a fresh
damper in the ashes. The damper
is delicious eaten as slabs with
golden syrup and black tea.

PHOTOS: JENNIFER ISAACS

To test whether the damper was baked, the cooks uncovered the loaf
and tapped the upper surface with a stick, listening for the right sound. If
the inside is still moist, the sound is very dull, whereas a good fresh light
damper with a hard skin gives a higher pitch when tapped. This sound is
usually accompanied by appreciative noises from the hungry family
gathered around.

Women told me that the wood used for the fire is most important.
A quickly burning wood is preferred, and one that provides a not-too-
astringent ash. Hardwoods are sometimes used, but the pieces must be
small in diameter and quite dry, so that no sap runs into the damper. The
ash from some native timbers is very irritating to the skin and these trees
often have medicinal value. The ash of *manyarr* trees, *Avicennia marina*,
for example, is used as an ointment for scabies.

'Stockman's damper' is not cooked in the ashes. A dough is made in the
usual way and small flattened balls are thrown directly on to the coals, then
turned to cook quickly.

In the settled life of missions, many women prefer to cook 'clean'
damper over a hot slab of iron mounted on a stone hearth. The Cape York
women like to use a teaspoon of baking powder to make the dough rise,
and in many places in Queensland, coconut milk is used if available instead
of water. When cooked on a metal tray, the fire must be at the perfect
temperature or the skin of the damper will blacken. A low, slow heat is
preferred. The damper hardens and browns and is turned over until it
makes the hollow sound that indicates it is ready.

Recipes for damper and Johnny cakes have appeared in colonial
cookbooks since the earliest days of European settlement. It is still true
that damper, preferably with some bush honey (replaced with golden
syrup by the newcomers) and billy tea offers the most archetypal relaxing
Australian bush meal for both Aborigines and Australians from many
other backgrounds.

PHOTO: JENNIFER ISAACS

NINE

GREEN VEGETABLES

Although Aborigines living on bush food eat relatively few fresh uncooked vegetables or plants, several foods in each area provide variety in the diet and valuable nutritional components. One of the principal 'greens' of coastal and forest areas is the growing tip or inner core of various palms, including *Livistona* species, tree ferns and bangalow palms. The stems, new shoots and corms of reeds and rushes are eaten in coastal areas and the tropics, and sometimes flower buds or new leaves of plants such as the desert banana are eaten in the desert. Some seeds are eaten green as beans, including those of *Acacia coriacea* and *A. farnesiana*.

'Green vegetables' is very much a European definition, separating as it does the growing stems and leaves from the fruits, seeds or roots, which are discussed elsewhere in this volume. Nevertheless, a survey of some of these vegetable foods is instructive and shows the commonly held view that Aborigines have no green vegetables to be wrong.

Above: Janita Motton of Weipa collecting
waterlilies for their edible stalks.

Tree ferns at Carnarvon Gorge, Queensland. The growing tips of many palms
are edible including *Livistona* species and common tree ferns of *Dicksonia* species.

Bulrushes *(Typha* sp.*)*. The new white shoots of these common aquatic plants are edible.

PHOTO: DIANA CONROY

BULRUSH   *Typha* spp.

The bulrush is an easily recognised aquatic plant as it has a flower spike shaped like a brown rod protruding well above the water. The very new white to green shoots of these rushes are gathered and eaten raw or cooked by Aborigines of the marshlands of south western Australia and the Murray–Darling system of New South Wales.

NEW ZEALAND SPINACH   *Tetragonia tetragonoides*

This green-leafed plant was once eaten by many of the southeastern Aboriginal communities, particularly along coastal areas. The stems and triangular leaves have greenish yellow flowers and crisp stems. The young shoots may be eaten as a green vegetable, cooked or raw. Joseph Banks took this plant back to England in 1772 where it became known as Botany Bay greens.

PIGWEED   *Portulaca oleracea*

Although the seeds of portulaca are well known as a staple Aboriginal food made into damper, the leaves and stems also provide an important source of green vegetables. The plant grows widely in all states and has long been used in inland areas. It is a succulent plant containing a reasonable amount of mucilage.

When on a bush hunting expedition with the Pintubi we collected several portulaca plants. The whole plant, stems and leaves were ground on a flat stone to form a thick green mush. This was then rolled into balls and eaten immediately. Wendy Napananga told us that it could also be dried and reconstituted later by soaking in water. This food is rather acidic and bitter to the taste.

Portulaca plants are found along dry desert riverbeds.

PHOTO: JENNIFER ISAACS

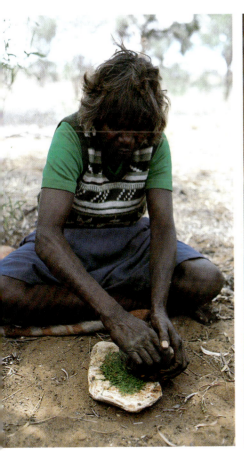

The leaves and stems of portulaca are ground into an edible paste by Linda Sideek of Papunya. The green mixture may also be rolled into balls and dried.

PHOTOS: LEO MEIER/WELDON TRANNIES

GRASS TREE   *Xanthorrhoea australis*

This distinctive Australian grass tree—or blackboy as it is sometimes called by white Australians—was once a multiple source of food to Aborigines, especially in Victoria and New South Wales. The flower nectar, basal leaves and shoots were eaten.

Grass trees grow mainly on sandy heathlands at the edge of forests such as the Grampians in Victoria and the Hawkesbury area in New South Wales. The crown of spiky narrow leaves may grow either directly from the ground or from a short or long trunk. The age of the plants can be determined by the height of the trunk. Early photographs of Aborigines show them scaling *Xanthorrhoea* 'trees' twice the height of a human. Today such specimens are extremely rare.

The flowering spikes of *Xanthorrhoea* were soaked in water to make a sweet drink and the soft basal part of the leaves was eaten. The growing tip of the stem could also be eaten, though this destroyed the plant altogether. The tall straight stems of the flower spikes, up to 150 centimetres long, made excellent light spear shafts. They were attached to the lower end of spears to extend their length and, therefore, range. The section of the spear closest to the tip was of harder wood that could withstand impact.

These beautiful plants are now protected species and cultivated examples are used as features in many landscape gardens.

TREE FERN   *Dicksonia antarctica*

Tree ferns and many similar ferns are found in gullies and rainforests throughout Australia. The soft pithy tissue near the top of the trunk contains a lot of starch and can be eaten either raw or cooked. Removing the pith, however, destroys the plant. Another tree fern once eaten is the *Cyathea* genus, with eleven species common in moist gullies in south-eastern Australia. The trunk was split open and the starchy pith eaten raw or roasted. In many areas, the 'fiddleheads' or unopened fronds were a staple. They had to be roasted to remove shikimic acid.

Tree ferns in the Grampians, Victoria. The new fiddle shoots were eaten after being roasted to remove poisonous shikimic acid.

PHOTO: REG MORRISON/WELDON TRANNIES

PALM HEART   *Livistona benthamii*

There are two common *Livistona* palms in Arnhem Land: *Livistona humilis,* known as 'emu tucker' and called *dhalpi* in Yirrkala, and *L. benthamii,* called *gulwirri.* The latter is harvested for 'heart of the palm', one of the main vegetable foods eaten in bulk in north Australia. This harvesting kills the plant, though only palms of a certain height are harvested so whole stands are not wiped out. The palm may be eaten raw or cooked. It is crisp and clean with a delicious nutty flavour.

In the southeast of the continent the cabbage tree palm, *Livistona australis,* was once harvested and the unexpanded leaves of the tufted heads eaten raw.

Grass trees (*Xanthorrhoea* sp.), South Australia. The flowery spikes were once made into a sweet drink and the soft basal parts of new leaves were eaten.

PHOTO: REG MORRISON

Above and right: David Malangi's family from Yathalamara harvests several new palm trees (*Gronophyllum ramsayi*) from a grove on their traditional lands in central Arnhem Land. The delicious core of the trunk is relished by all.

PHOTOS: LEO MEIER/WELDON TRANNIES

CUT-LEAFED PALM   *Hydriastele wendlandiana*

In northern Australia the top of the trunk near the fronds and the growing shoots of this palm are cut, the outer layer peeled and the heart eaten raw. In some areas this palm grows in swampy places so it is generally gathered in the dry season.

ALEXANDER PALM   *Gronophyllum ramsayi*

Aborigines collect the heart of this palm—known as *bulmurrk* – in monsoon jungle areas from Yirrkala to western Arnhem Land. In central Arnhem Land, Malangi's family and I walked some seven kilometres from the camp at Yathalamara to a patch of jungle that had developed around a sacred banyan tree. On the edge of this jungle was a healthy stand of palms, though there was some evidence that they had been harvested occasionally as there was palm litter between the outer stands. Elsie Ganbada set about gathering some palm heart with a machete. She indicated that the only palms to be harvested were those around 2-3 metres tall. Smaller and larger palms were not to be touched.

The trunk is severed about half a metre from the ground and the leaves and outer pith cut off. The central core of the trunk is exposed and cut into sections. The pithy end is discarded but the middle core or heart of the palm is eaten on the spot by all present. Children in particular love this fresh delicious vegetable and munch it like an apple. When I showed some concern that the palms would disappear if harvested continuously in such a small patch of jungle, Elsie reassured me that the family did not gather them very often and that people always 'look after bush tucker'. She said that every time one palm was cut down more would spring up 'same banana tree'.

WATERLILY   *Nymphaea* spp.

These vigorous water plants grow throughout Australia on swamps and billabongs. The way in which Aborigines, children especially, harvest them has been photographed frequently, epitomising for many the romantic view of a people at one with a tranquil landscape and enjoying the fruits of the billabong. Waterlilies may be white, pink or blue in Arnhem Land. The stems of all three are eaten as well as the fresh seeds from the flower bud and the corm. Seeds are eaten direct from the capsule, though the raw stems must be peeled before eating. Stems are often carried back to camp in dillybags or chewed along the route as they are full of water and good for quenching thirst. The black seeds taste somewhat like poppy seeds and the stems take on the taste of the billabong itself, with a distinctive stringybark swamp smell of mulch and vegetation.

Waterlilies are not only foods; they are considered to be the morning star itself. In eastern Arnhem Land the spirits of the dead follow the light

of Barnambirr, the morning star, on their way to the island of Baralku. The waterlily is the symbol of this star; its stalk is the path of the star across the sky, its flower the bright glow.

MANGROVE   *Bruguiera gymnorrhiza*

The hypocotyls of some mangrove trees are eaten, particularly in Cape York. During the wet season when people are confined to smaller areas and foods are hard to find, beaches offer a source of unusual food. Thancoupie explained, 'We would go along beaches in wet season and look for food that tide chuck up, like *n'omb* [*Bruguiera gymnorrhiza*] and *dhapul*, matchbox bean [*Entada phaseoloides*]'.

Bruguiera gymnorrhiza is a medium to tall tree that grows on intertidal sand and mud along tropical shores. It has rough, dark grey bark, knee-shaped pneumatophores and buttress roots. The distinctive flowers have rigid reddish green bell-shaped calyx lobes, which are found among tidal debris. The seed germinates while on the tree and the green hypocotyls or roots (looking like small thin okra) fall from the tree and are washed up. These are gathered and eaten after complicated preparation. The plant contains a high proportion of tannin and must therefore be leached. Quantities of *no'omb* are first baked in a *cup-mari* and the skins discarded. The food is then pounded into a pulp and soaked in water. The mass is strained through a grass bag to remove excess water, then cooked again or mixed with cooked *dhapul* and eaten.

WHITE MANGROVE   *Avicennia marina*

On Mornington Island in the Gulf of Carpentaria, fruit pods from the canoe-making tree are buried in hot ashes for around an hour. They are then peeled and soaked in water overnight before being eaten.[1]

This food was once probably eaten by most coastal people with mangrove areas within their tribal lands.

Mangroves, Hinchinbrook Island, Queensland.

Edible mangrove hypocotyls must be processed. These are *Bruguiera gymnorrhiza*, known as *n'omb* at Weipa, and are often eaten combined with matchbox bean paste (*Entada phaseoloides*).

Mangrove-lined salt waterhole, Western Australia.

Dhuwandjika Marika and her grand-daughter, Ulpundu, collect waterlilies from a paperbark swamp in their homelands near Yirrkala, eastern Arnhem Land.

PHOTO: LEO MEIER-WELDON TRANNIES

TEN

HONEY, GUM AND NECTAR

SUGARBAG HONEY

Across the north of Australia, with the end of the dry season in about September or October and the coming of the warm southeast winds, Aboriginal people look for signs that the wild bees' nests are ready to be drained. The appearance of stringybark gum blossoms, wattle blossoms and the lovely pink Darwin heath (*Calytrix* spp.) are signs that honey can be found in abundance, and hunting parties leave in great excitement to gather the delicious sweet food. Sweet nectar and honey is as much a delight in Aboriginal cuisine as a French cake is in the European. Although not a staple food, it nevertheless provides high energy and is eagerly sought, not only in northern Australia but throughout the continent. Even in arid lands grevillea, hakea and banksia flowers are drained of their nectar to make watery sweet drinks and 'honey ants' are uncovered from nests a metre deep to be drained of the honey stored in their abdomens.

Honey is imbued with such desirable qualities that its gathering and continued supply were explained in mythology and controlled through ceremony and custom. In eastern Arnhem Land kinship laws divide the people into two halves or moieties, *dhuwa* and *yirritja,* and all the plants, animals and creatures of the environment also fit into this classification. In

Above: Marinka Nungala Marshall enjoys the sweet nectar from the desert grevillea *(Grevillea juncifolia).*

Rachel Yunupingu has gathered bush 'chewing gum', the resinous globules that exude from wild plum trees of Arnhem Land.

131

PHOTO: JENNIFER ISAACS

When looking for bush honey, Aborigines follow the tiny bees to their nests high in hollow trees. David Malangi selects a likely site to begin chopping.

PHOTO: LEO MEIER/WELDON TRANNIES

northeast Arnhem Land from Yirrkala to Maningrida, the bush-honey ancestor of the *dhuwa* moiety, Wuyal, found the first 'sugar bag', and paintings, songs and ceremonies record his activities, forming the basis of present-day hunting, harvesting and sharing of honey. The 'sugarbag people' of the Dreaming hunted kangaroo on their journeys, chopping down large trees in their search for honey. The fallen trees became today's rivers and creeks.

There are six main native bees in Arnhem Land, two *dhuwa* bees and four *yirritja*, varying both in temperament and in the quality of their honey. Hives may be made in the top of eucalyptus trees, in mangroves and even in termite mounts. One particularly vicious *yirritja* bee, *niwuda*, sometimes attacks eyes. The honey of *niwuda* is slightly sweet but not as sweet as that from the *yarrpany*, the small, quiet bees. Two other *yirritja* bees have very sour honey: *milnhirri*, which build their hives in *manyarr* mangrove trees, and the yellow bees, *barnggitj*, which build hives close to the ground, sometimes in termite mounds.[1] The *dhuwa* bees are *yarrpany*, a small gentle bee that nests high in trees, and *lirrawar*, a slightly larger bee whose hive is much smaller. Both *dhuwa* bees give very sweet honey.[2]

Honey must always be shared. In some communities the hunter cannot eat any, but must rely on the good fortune of other relatives to give him or her some of their cache.

A great degree of skill and very sharp eyes are needed to track the wild bees to their hive. All the techniques used require specialised knowledge of the habits of particular bees in particular hives. Dick Roughsey wrote in his autobiography of the 'very good fun' to be had getting bush honey:

> We call the bee Wongabel, and the hive sugar-bag because of its sweetness. The bees can be seen going in and out a small hole in a hollow tree. Sometimes the entrance is a small tunnel made of wax and shaped like a funnel. It looks exactly like a nostril and we call it the nose of the sugarbag. When looking for honey, people watch for a small black lizard which often lives in a honey tree and waits by the entrance to catch and eat bees as they come back to the hive. When the tree is knocked the bees make a deep humming noise. If the moon is seen in the sky during the day it is no good going hunting for honey, because bees do not leave the hive to gather food at this time.
>
> When a honey tree is found it is usually cut down. But if it is a very big tree a hole is cut just under the place where the bees can be heard humming inside. A stick is then poked into the hive and stirred about until honey runs down the stick into the bark bucket.[3]

The technique of trailing the bees to their hive is especially cunning. The hunters attract the bees in some way, perhaps by cutting the bark of a tree so that the fresh scent draws them. When the bees gather a small piece of white feather or a long tail of spider's web, which is easy to see, is attached to a bee's abdomen. When the bee returns to its hive, the hunters follow.

Mararu strips off some paperbark to form a honey container.

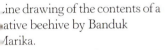

Line drawing of the contents of a native beehive by Banduk Marika.

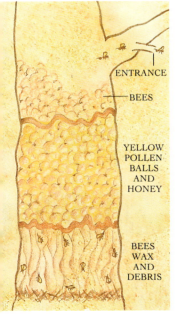

ENTRANCE

BEES

YELLOW
POLLEN
BALLS
AND
HONEY

BEES
WAX
AND
DEBRIS

The honey is gathered in paperback carriers quickly fashioned on the spot. Usually people have a good feast in the bush, especially children accompanying their mothers. Damper cooked in the coals and dipped hot into fresh honey is a delicious meal.

Throughout the Kimberley in northwestern Australia Aborigines have always had more access to sugar in the form of honey than anywhere else. One writer remarked that the poor condition of the people's teeth, in comparison with those who lived in the centre, showed that they ate sugar frequently.[4] Anthrolopogist Kim Akerman has identified three species of bees in the northern Kimberley area recognised by the Ngarinjin and Worora people: *namiri*, *narra* and *wanangka*. *Namiri*, which have thick treacle-like honey, build hives in the ground, under boulders, in antbeds and in hollow trees. *Wanangka* bees produce slightly runny honey, described by Aborigines as 'cool jam', and this is found in trees. *Narra* honey is very fluid, 'very cold and runny'.

In the Kimberley honey is a staple food, not just a luxury, and its importance is reflected in mythology, art and ritual life.[5] In the past it was an important item in trade and beeswax had essential uses such as joining the seal on a bark bucket and helping attach a stone axe to its handle.

Honey is gathered in earnest for ceremonies and on these occasions people get up early before the heat has made the bees more mobile. Acute vision and 'knowing what you're looking for' enable hunters to spot hive entrances high in the trees, or to notice bees around a knot or hole. Ground hives can be opened easily and the honey pots picked out carefully.

Two implements are unique to gathering honey in the Kimberley and their equivalents are also used in Arnhem Land. To ensure that honey loss from a ruptured hive is minimal, a *jirgam*, a wad of fibre or 'mopping rag' is put beneath the opening to soak up spilt honey. It can also be used to wipe out the empty hive. In thick hollow trees, a honey mop, or *katjin*, is used. This is a long stick pounded at one end until it becomes a frayed mop, termed *bongbirrdi* or *lawarr* at Ramingining. It is poked up the hollow tree into the hive. The honey is released and flows on to a *jirgam*, out through the entrance and into a bark bucket, the unique Kimberley utensil used for carrying water and honey.

Bark buckets are not used in Arnhem Land but tightly woven pandanus bags termed *binba* or paperbark troughs serve the same function. The *jirgam* can be drained of its honey later by being soaked in a container of water and squeezed out to make a sweet drink.

Bees and hives are depicted in Kimberley cave paintings and the rules for gathering and sharing of honey are told in myths. One Dreaming story from this area tells of the original Namiri and Wanangka ancestor bees who came to the Kimberley chased by a mob of flies. They could not agree on where to camp, stopping at different trees and leaving their wax there. Finally they settled at Larinjam where a Bee Dreaming painting is now found. These paintings mark places where the ancestors stopped for a

'Bush honey' bark painting by Ray Munyal of Ramingining. The origin of bush honey is an important aspect of religious knowledge. Different types of bees and their honey are owned by the clans and represented by sacred honey patterns symbolising features like the honey-soaking stick, the hive itself and its compartments, bees, axes and the great ancestral honey hunter himself.

PHOTO: REG MORRISON/WELDON TRANNIES

time, where they 'put themselves'.[6] Usually the paintings show the hive in cross-section with entrance, pollen pots, honey pots and wax plugs.

Honey is never cooked or added to other foods, but must always be eaten raw. This is laid down in another Dreaming story:

> The Spotted Nightjar had obtained a quantity of fine honey. While he was making a spear the Owlet Nightjar saw the honey and decided to cook it. He wrapped it in bark and put it in a steam oven. By the time the Spotted Nightjar realised what was happening the honey had all run off leaving tasteless wax. In his anger at the stupidity of the Owlet Nightjar he beat him badly with his club and drove him off. He had wasted and spoilt the honey, which now must be eaten raw.[7]

In the Kimberley, as in Arnhem Land, honey is important socially. Honey, meat and fat are given as gifts by the 'promised' husband to his future wife's parents and gifts of honey are given when one group visits another. It is very bad manners not to give and share honey, and the elaborate exchange and trading patterns of the Kimberley included honey in these transactions. Women belonging to the home group have the special duty of collecting honey before the arrival of visitors. 'They will go out each day and store up in bark buckets, gallons of this delectable food'.

Among the more mundane aspects of the 'honey culture' is its use as a medicine by many Kimberley tribes. People 'clean their guts out' by eating large amounts of honey or by drinking vast quantities of pollen mixed with water. Honey eaten in large quantities makes one feel very thirsty and the effects of large quantities of honey or pollen and water are quite remarkable.

Bush honey. All the contents of the hive are collected: honey, wax, yellow pollen balls and dead bees.

PHOTO: JENNIFER ISAACS

Bush honey can be easily carried back to camp in a quickly made paperbark trough, folded and tied at either end.

PHOTO: JENNIFER ISAACS

Mararu's daughter, Ulpundu, eagerly tastes the bush honey, one of the most delicious and highly prized of bush foods.

PHOTO: JENNIFER ISAACS

Nectar, Edible Gum and Beverages

Accounts by early European settlers tell of many beverages being made in the southeast of the continent, of nectar gathered or sucked from flowers, and of manna or lerp taken from eucalyptus leaves. The large white gum of Victoria and Tasmania was termed manna gum by the settlers as it yields a considerable amount of manna, which was described as 'a curious saccharine mucilaginous substance'.[8] It is secreted on the leaves by insects, especially cicadas and appears as irregular, rounded small white masses. It was eaten in lumps or mixed with water to make a drink. Another manna, described as the *lerp* manna, is found on the leaves of *Eucalyptus dumosa* in the Mallee regions of Victoria, New South Wales and South Australia.

The pupae of several species of insects appear beneath masses of tiny pale yellow domes, giving the leaves a white appearance. The manna was simply rubbed off the leaves, collected and eaten or mixed with water and drunk.

NECTAR

Nectar-bearing flowers are common in spring in bushlands throughout Australia from the coast to the desert. Aborigines gather bottlebrush, grevillea, banksia, hakea and the grass tree and suck them for their sweet taste. A type of liquor or drink is made in many parts of the country by immersing nectar-bearing flowers in water. When the diet is relatively monotonous, sweet nectar provides a pleasant lift to both taste and scent. In Queensland, when the dew is still on the grass and plants and the air perfumed and fresh, men and women gather nectar by going from flower to flower, dipping them up and down in a container of water until it becomes sweet.

Grevillea sp. Numerous nectar-bearing flowers from species of grevillea, hakea, xanthorrhoea and banksia were sucked or drained to make sweet drinks.

PHOTO: JENNIFER ISAACS

Nectar-rich *Grevillea eriostachya* at Ayers Rock.

PHOTO: DIANA CONROY

Thelma Minor Djambijimba, like many other children of the desert, sucks the sweet grevillea nectar on food-gathering trips with her mother.

PHOTO: LEO MEIER/WELDON TRANNIES

Honey from the blossoms of the corkwood trees (*Hakea suberea*) is gathered by women of central and western Australia. The flowers are collected and kneaded in a coolamon. After the flowers have been removed, water mixed with the sweet residue makes a sweet drink.

In Victoria, *Banksia marginata* is a good source of nectar. It can be obtained by sucking the nectar directly from the spiky flowering cone or soaking the flower in water. *Banksia dentata* and *Grevillea pteridifolia* are similarly drained in Arnhem Land.

GUM

The resins that exude from ironwood, acacia and allocasuarina trees are a source of carbohydrate and may be eaten straight from the tree in balls like pliable toffee or melted with warm water to form a jelly. Although some are tasteless, casuarina gums are sweet and children enjoy these treats, leaping from vehicles when the globules are sighted on hunting trips in the north. Edible gums can be found all over Australia.

Edible gums exude from many native trees throughout Australia. Rachel Yunupingu finds some by the swamp at Yirrkala.

PHOTO: JENNIFER ISAACS

The sweet crystalline exudates of some desert trees are called 'bush lollies' by the children of Papunya.

PHOTO: LEO MEIER/WELDON TRANNIES

Charles Mountford recorded a ceremony in the Mann Ranges, in the north of South Australia, at the sacred place of Malili, a woman ancestor of the Pitjantjatjara.[9] This ancestor camped in earlier times and, after eating various species of edible gum, left some lumps on the ground that subsequently turned into rounded rocks. Each of these rocks is now the life essence of a particular gum and in ceremonies observed by Mountford, the rocks were rubbed with a stone while a song was sung to blow the life essence of the gum in the form of rock powder to other places so that the gum would be plentiful in seasons to come.

In the southeast there are hundreds of species of wattle in many different habitats. As soon as summer was over, Aborigines cut notches in the bark to allow the gum to exude. It was often soaked in water with a sweet substance like honey, manna or flower nectar. The people of many traditional northern homelands maintain this technique of making drinks and the author enjoyed a similar drink at Yirrkala in 1985. Dhuwandjika explained that, after mixing up the gum with water and honey, the liquid sets and forms a jelly that can be kept in the camp and eaten later.

Often, after a hunting trip, when the meat is cooking and the wait seems long, young children look around for what desert people term 'bush lollies' and climb trees to pick off the gum to stave off their hunger.

ALCOHOLIC BEVERAGES

It is commonly believed that Aborigines had no alcoholic beverages among their traditional drinks. It is well known, of course, that the nectar of various flowers was gathered and soaked in water and then drunk, but reports of settlers also suggest that some techniques of using nectar and gum produced a state of euphoria.

At Bunbury in southwest Australia, a drink called *mangaitj* was made by soaking the flower heads or cones of grass trees (*Xanthorrhoea* spp.) in water in bark troughs. This mixture was allowed to ferment for several days and was reported to make people excited and voluble.[10] Basedow refers to the people of Roper River fermenting pandanus in order to make an intoxicating drink.[11] *Pandanus spiralis* was prepared by beating the fruit between heavy stones and soaking the pulp in water for some time to 'extract as much of the palatable ingredient as possible'. The infusion was left up to several days so it could ferment. 'A refreshing toddy' similar to a mildly intoxicating cider was produced. On ceremonial occasions the drink was prepared some time earlier and the people had more than usual, which produced in them 'a condition of indubitable merriment'.

Grass trees in the Washpool rainforest, New South Wales. The flower heads were sucked for nectar and, in some areas, the nectar was fermented to make a mildly intoxicating drink.

PHOTO: LEO MEIER/WELDON TRANNIES

ELEVEN

LAND ANIMALS

Hunting game, particularly large animals such as kangaroos, wallabies and emus, has always been important to Aboriginal men. Their capacity to bring back meat for the camp enhances their status enormously.

Meat is a significant part of Aboriginal diet. In discussing animals as food in the Australian environment it is important to realise that most species are now protected. Although Aborigines in traditional situations are still permitted to hunt, this is never done indiscriminately. All animals are part of the interconnected system of life and are related to human beings. All are descended from the great creation ancestors and, in fact, each Aborigine regards some animal species as relatives. These they call their 'totems'. Few totem animals are ever killed or eaten. Thus, one Aboriginal community will happily hunt a large goanna, while a few hundred kilometres away, where the animal is considered a sacred totem, it is protected. In many communities the importance of being able to hunt and kill a kangaroo is emphasised as the first ordeal that must be undertaken by a young man at a certain stage of manhood training. At Papunya in 1980, four men showed me a ground design of the Bush Onion

Above: Echidna, Northern Territory.

Almost all animals were occasionally eaten by Aborigines. In the north, flying foxes are a favourite meat in the flowering season, when their flesh is sweet and scented from the blossoms on which they feed.

141

PHOTO: LEO MEIER/WELDON TRANNIES

Walter Pukutuwara brings a kangaroo to his waiting family in the vehicle. The animal has been ritually cleaned and trussed. The procedure for killing and cooking kangaroos or *malu* is determined by strict religious laws.

PHOTO: REG MORRISON/WELDON TRANNIES

Bark painting depicting a kangaroo by Barrbuwa from western Arnhem Land. The artist has shown some important internal organs in the x-ray art style and the dotted divisions roughly correspond to the division of the meat after cooking.

PHOTO: REG MORRISON/WELDON TRANNIES

Dreaming and told how a young initiate must bring a kangaroo back to camp and place it on such a design. This would be the first game he has single-handedly caught for the community.

Hunting animals is, therefore, inextricably entwined with religion and custom. Procedures for killing, preparing, cooking and sharing all meats are set down according to laws established by the creation ancestors and are varied only at an individual's peril. Today some of the young people in Aboriginal communities are reluctant to heed the strict codes of the elders. Even if the threatened dire punishment does not occur, the rebels are nevertheless subjected to ridicule, fights and bickering between families as a result of their disobedience, and this acts as a deterrent to breaking the traditional food laws.

Almost all animals were occasionally caught and eaten in the Australian continent. In the desert areas, as well as kangaroos, wallabies, euros, emus, dingos, lizards, possums, echidnas and bandicoots, there is scattered evidence that wombats, native cats, marsupial moles and a variety of birds including wild turkeys, parrots, cockatoos, owls, eaglehawks, magpies, ducks, crows and some snakes were once eaten.

Fresh meat is still prized though it is relatively easy to buy carbohydrates from the store in the form of flour. The significance of hunting has actually increased because of the availability of guns and the scarcity of fresh meat, the tinned variety being a poor substitute. In addition, feral game such as buffalo, cattle, pigs and, in the desert, rabbits, are hunted as food and in some months can account for up to 20 per cent of food caught in the bush. A recent study of western Arnhem Land revealed that wild animals comprised 90 per cent of the diet of one outstation.[1]

As is well known, wild game is usually much lower in fat than domestic stock. Analysis has shown that the Aboriginal custom of consuming the liver, heart and other offal of game added substantial amounts of vitamin A, B group vitamins, folic acid and a heat-resistant form of vitamin C (found in liver and not destroyed by cooking) to the diet.

KANGAROOS, WALLABIES AND EUROS

In remote parts of Australia it is inevitable that living and working with Aborigines will entail going on a kangaroo hunt. On one such expedition I went bush for the day with Walter Pukutuwara and his family to get kangaroo meat for the family and, from my point of view, to gather sinews in order to make and photograph weapons. The short trip looking for one kangaroo turned into a day's epic drive. We set out from Amata in the northwest of South Australia early in the morning and having gone on an enormous loop to within sight of Ayers Rock and back, arrived in Amata again at 10 pm.

Admittedly this was an unusual trip, but it highlights the enthusiasm that remains in Aboriginal hunters when they have a car, a gun and a quarry in sight. The haul was around seven kangaroos, enough to feed

A hunter with spears and woomera ready waits while others drive the kangaroos towards him.

PHOTO: REG MORRISON/WELDON TRANNIES

most of the community that night. Despite my feelings of nausea at the carload of dead kangaroos, it was clear that the men approached the animals with reverence and that the procedures they followed were of great ceremonial importance and 'men's business'. Although they shared the meat back in camp, the women took little part in the kangaroo hunt, preferring to head off and dig for rabbits when the truck stopped.

When hunting kangaroos silence is usual, though sometimes whistles and signals communicate intentions from one man to another. People often work as a group, one man acting as a decoy while the startled animal stands motionless, staring. The others close in and freeze as the animal looks again. When speared or shot a wounded kangaroo is finished off immediately with blows to the neck. The animal is disembowelled the moment it is killed through a small incision made in the abdomen. The incision is then neatly skewered with a stick and bound in a figure-of-eight with the cleaned-out small intestine. The legs are dislocated and the carcass is either carried home on the hunter's head or, more frequently, taken to the waiting vehicle.

One interesting variation occurs in the Kimberleys, where at this stage the stomach, lower intestine and liver are removed, cleaned and boiled. The empty stomach is filled with fat and blood and rolled into a kind of black pudding. It is cooked in the earth oven with the kangaroo. The animal is tossed on to a blazing fire and turned several times until the fur has been singed and blackened. It is then removed from the fire and scraped so that the flesh is clean. The tail is usually cut off and placed beside the animal when cooking, though it can be left intact.

To prepare the oven a rectangular hole is dug about the size of the kangaroo to be cooked. A hot fire is made with plenty of wood in order to make a good supply of hot coals. The kangaroo is put on its back in the pit and the tail placed beside the body. The flesh is completely covered with hot coals, then with earth so that only the feet protrude. Cooking time varies depending on how hungry people are, and can be from three-quarters of an hour to four hours. If the hunters return late at night, the meat may be left in the pit overnight; in this case it is very well done.

When the animal is removed from the pit, the men gather to cut up the meat ritually. Women remain in the background waiting for pieces to be handed to them by their male relatives. This has been described as 'men's time'.[2] In the desert the belly is opened and the rich blood soup is carefully drunk or poured into a billy and shared. The kidneys, heart and lungs are also shared. The meat must then be cut up by the hunter, each section going to an appropriate relative depending on his or her relationship with the hunter. It is quite common for the hunter to get very little himself. He must rely, in turn, on the success of a relative if he is to have one of the best sections of meat.

This success depends not only on skill but also on the capacity of the hunters to deceive their quarry. Aborigines are brilliant mimics, both verbally and physically, and imitate the calls of birds, people's voices and movements. Emus are caught by preying on their inquisitive nature as hunters imitate other emus visiting from parts far off. Geese are brought down by hunters imitating their 'honk, honk, honk' in high branches and are then attacked with stones and sticks. Hermit crabs can be brought out of their shells with the high-pitched 'drrrrrr' sound of the tongue against the palate; the sound of a snake from a hunter's mouth will cause a bandicoot to leave a hollow log. Hand signals are an additional aid and the elaborate sign language recorded by people such as Walter Roth in northern Queensland at the turn of the century meant that, without speaking, hunters could communicate extremely well over large distances without alerting their quarry.[3]

Hunting magic is frequently employed to ensure a successful hunt and the weapons themselves are often smeared with blood from a kangaroo. Many weapons are carved or painted in an act of ritual and faith. The decoration is not purely superficial but associates the weapons visibly with the ancestral spirits and gives them greater power and accuracy. Spear-throwers and spears may also be 'sung' to ensure that they do not fail.

Apart from simply spearing kangaroos, Aborigines use other, more ingenious, hunting techniques. Hides are constructed at waterholes and the animals speared when they come to drink. Brush fences are

Dotted lines indicate the ritual division of kangaroo meat into portions.

144

constructed, behind which hunters can conceal themselves near a frequently used animal track. Other men, or more often women and children, beat the bushes to drive the game into the ambush.

This technique is sometimes used to catch euros, the lovely rusty red wallaroos that live on the rocks in the desert and leap about skilfully. Kangaroos are afraid of the rocky outcrops and will not mount them but the speed with which euros hop from one rock foothold to another makes it impossible for men or their dogs to run them down. The Pitjantjatjara hunt euros by utilising knowledge of their migratory pattern from one rocky outcrop to another. Euros fear the open plains and choose the shortest route between hills. Aborigines know these paths and conceal themselves behind trees along the track. Other men beat the animals to the concealed hunters or occasionally light bushfires that drive the euros ahead of the flames until they can be speared.

On the raised beach platforms of the Gulf of Carpentaria similar drives were once organised to catch wallabies. The beaches of the Gulf are covered with a modified jungle that forms relatively narrow belts of cover with open country on either side, kept so by regular burning off in the dry season. Wallabies could easily be seen feeding at night and early morning on the grasses of the plains, hiding in the jungle during the day. Hunting parties imitate the hunting call of the dingo and flush the wallabies out toward hunters hidden in specially constructed hides.

EMUS

Emu near Birdsville, Queensland. The large birds are sought after by Aborigines for their delicate flesh and huge green eggs.

Emus are highly thought of as bush tucker because of the quantity of their meat and the delicacy of their flesh. Emu eggs are also sought and eaten, each mother bird laying several beautiful large deep green eggs. One of the most common techniques of hunting emus is to stun them by putting narcotic leaves in their waterholes. The poison most frequently used by northern desert people is *Duboisia hopwoodii*. As the stupefied bird walks slowly from the waterhole as if drunk, it is ambushed by the hunters from a brush fence. Other poisons including *Prostanthera striatiflora* are used in the desert. At Mt Liebig, Maudie Peterson explained that the waterholes remained poisoned until the next rains, after which they were fit to drink from again.

Another very old technique for trapping emus was described by Spencer and Gillen in 1927. Pits were dug near the feeding grounds and covered with branches, and the unwitting animals were driven into them. Occasionally a pointed spear was placed upright in the bottom of the pit to ensure that the animal could not jump out again.

Emus are usually cooked in a similar way to kangaroos, but after plucking and gutting, blood is often wiped over the skin. When cooking birds the ground oven may be lined with herbs or leaves and hot stones may be placed within the body cavity. Among the Pitjantjatjara, however, an ancient method of cooking the emu was to skin the bird completely and cook the skin separately, stuffed with feathers like a pillow. This extra-ordinary practice was common at least until the 1950s.

Preparing and cooking an emu in the traditional Pitjantjatjara style was a lengthy process. After killing the bird, the legs and head were tied together so that it could be carried effectively on the shoulder of the hunter. A pit was made as for a kangaroo and the body was prepared for cooking. To keep it clean it was laid on green leaves and branches. First it was plucked, then completely skinned through a narrow aperture cut along the legs and behind the anus. The skin was pulled off the body as though it were a jumper. This skin was then turned right side out and stuffed with grass and feathers. The opening of the skin was closed with two pointed sticks and it was rolled in the flames to stiffen and brown.

The body was prepared for cooking by cleaning out the intestines and filling the space with a wad of emu feathers or sticks. The head of the bird was pushed into the body cavity through a hole in the neck and the whole bird, together with its stuffed skin, was cooked in a ground oven for half an hour or so depending on its size. The feathers used as stuffing were, of course, removed and discarded before the meal began.

When out in the bush on Aboriginal hunting trips it is interesting to watch how people ensure that flies are kept, as much as possible, at a distance. The discarded intestines are thrown five or six metres from the camp and this mass of offal and blood attracts swarms of flies away from the picnicking party. The flies prefer the offal to anything else being prepared and eaten, and the camp is relatively free of flies, at least for a short time.

POSSUMS, BANDICOOTS AND ECHIDNAS

Small marsupials are usually cooked quickly. They are gutted and roasted directly on the coals. Care is taken to avoid overcooking so that the precious fat will not escape.

Bark painting of an echidna by Maralwanga, a Gunwinggu artist from the Maningrida area, Northern Territory.

PHOTO: REG MORRISON/WELDON TRANNIES

Bandicoots can be enticed from their hiding places or hollow logs by imitating the hiss of a snake and possums are hauled from trees with the aid of long hooked sticks. Echidnas are dug from the ground, their spines burned and pulled off and then cooked in the coals. These spines were once kept to use as awls for piercing possum skin rugs.

FLYING FOXES

Flying foxes are eaten by Aborigines throughout the north. Large colonies can be found in deep jungle areas of the forests and in the mangroves. Flying foxes feed on the blossom and fruits of certain trees and, depending on the season, the flesh of the animal takes on the taste of these flowers and fruits and becomes aromatic and sweet.

Flying foxes are usually beaten from their roosts with long sticks; occasionally a fire will be lit beneath the tree and they will be smoked out,

Bark painting from Maningrida of a glider possum, one of the many marsupials once widely trapped and hunted for food.
HOTO: REG MORRISON/WELDON TRANNIES

Western desert goanna.
HOTO: REG MORRISON/WELDON TRANNIES

the smoke tending to stun the animals so that they drop to the ground. During the day, when they are sleepy and not alert, they can be knocked down with throwing sticks. The fur is first scorched off and the leathery wings are removed. The little bodies are then cooked quickly on the coals or in a ground oven. The flesh is soft and rather like chicken but very aromatic, with a flavour suggesting a fruit and honey diet.

GOANNAS AND LIZARDS

Goannas and lizards are by far the most common traditional game of the desert regions.

Looking for goannas is hot work. Groups of women and children, occasionally accompanied by their husbands, head off into the desert to the areas where goannas may be plentiful. Occasionally one might be found in a hollow log, but usually it's a matter of finding an inhabited burrow. Avoiding unnecessary work is always the aim of the operation. These days, women carry digging sticks in the form of flattened crowbars. The entrances are carefully examined for recently dislodged sand or tracks and any holes with debris in them are completely ignored as these were abandoned long ago.

Dragon, Gammon Ranges, South Australia. Many similar small reptiles were eaten in times of food scarcity.

PHOTO: JENNIFER ISAACS

In the mulga and witchetty bush country near Papunya, Entalura Nangala and her husband Don Jungarrai hunt goannas by digging them from their burrows.

PHOTO: REG MORRISON/WELDON TRANNIES

Children accompany parents and learn to hunt goannas by inspecting their burrows for fresh tracks or moist sand. Digging sticks are poked into the ground some distance from the entrance, and the reptile is found and dug out.

PHOTO: REG MORRISON/WELDON TRANNIES

The reptiles can dig in any direction from the entrance and are extremely quick at making an exit under the ground. To find the direction of the burrow from its entrance the women plunge the metal digging stick into the ground in an arc about a metre from the hole. As soon as the stick sinks into the ground as though into a hollow the digging begins. The entrance is widened and the animal is dug out along its burrow with a woman hunter finally reaching in and hauling the animal out by its tail. Women know when they are getting close to the burrowing animal when the sand in their hands becomes moist. As one woman explained to me, 'That's his wee wee, he's getting scared'.

Goannas and all manner of lizards caught in the desert are cooked briefly in the coals of the fire. The meat is tender, rather more chewy than chicken and rather oily. Many other reptiles are caught and eaten throughout desert regions, including various snakes, skinks and geckos.

Pitjantjatjara women like Nellie Patterson are amazingly adept rabbit hunters. When introduced into Australia these animals quickly overran the countryside. In the desert around Amata and Ayers Rock their numbers have become a problem although they provide a ready supply of meat to desert outstations.

PHOTO: JENNIFER ISAACS

Opposite page
Black-necked stork or jabiru from Northern Australia. Large water birds are occasionally hunted by outstation groups in Arnhem Land, although they are protected from harm elsewhere.

PHOTO: LEO MEIER/WELDON TRANNIES

INTRODUCED GAME: RABBITS, BUFFALO, PIGS

Since the mid-nineteenth century, when a handful of rabbits were released near Geelong, these animals have multiplied so dramatically that in many areas they have destroyed the fertility of the Australian landscape. In the desert south of Ayers Rock, hundreds of rabbits block the roads at night and can be seen in the glare of headlights. Much of the land is potholed with rabbit warrens and they have largely replaced native marsupials of similar size such as the long-eared bilby. Bilbies were a significant source of food to Aboriginal people and rabbits have now usurped them in diet as well as landscape.

Rabbits are frequently eaten by Pitjantjatjara people. The women hunt them with digging sticks and they are dug out of their warrens in the same way as goannas. With a quick twist of the neck the animals are killed, the fur is scorched off and they are cooked on the coals.

In the north the water buffalo has become another threat to the environment because of its habit of wallowing in billabongs and swamps, destroying the delicate balance of vegetation at the water's edge. Wild pigs pose a similar menace in Cape York and they are also widespread in Arnhem Land.

Although buffalo meat is welcomed in times of scarcity, it is not actively sought by Aboriginal people unless they are living on extremely remote outstations. Guns are needed and the animals are usually butchered, slabs of meat being cooked in the ground oven. Wild pigs are shot and cooked in a similar manner.

BIRDS

Aborigines traditionally hunted many species of wild birds and cooked them in the coals. In central Australia, among the Warlpiri, anthropologist Mervyn Meggitt listed thirty bird species that were occasionally eaten.[4] Of those, the prized birds were species of pigeon, including flock pigeons and crested pigeons. In northern Australia birds constituted a significant proportion of the diet, but were most commonly found close to billabongs and water sources. Particularly important were wild ducks and magpie geese. Young children were adept at catching small edible birds of the open forest with the use of catapults or shanghais. These are still used by people in the forest areas to catch birds needed for ritual feathers. These include lorikeets, Torres Strait pigeons, black cockatoos and other protected birds that are culled by Aborigines only for particularly important ceremonial rituals.

Buffalo carving in milkwood, Yirrkala, Northern Territory.

PHOTO: REG MORRISON/WELDON TRANNIES

TWELVE

MARINE ANIMALS AND FISH

CATCHING FISH

Fish are the most important source of protein and the main food of coastal and riverine Aboriginal communities all over Australia:

> Being sea people our lives were ruled by the sea and its tides. With only one tide a day we had to change from day hunting to night hunting and back as the tides changed. Our old folk knew everything about the sea and the things that live in it. They knew when and where to hunt for salmon, for the schools of mullet and moonfish, for the big fat rock cod and all the others.[1]

The importance of fish and fishing is emphasised in myths and stories. Great ancestral fish and sea animals, like their land counterparts, formed the river systems, the bays and inlets of the north. A legend from Milingimbi Island recounts the activities of a giant shark ancestor who formed the narrow sea belt between Milingimbi and the mainland. Similarly, in western Arnhem Land, the giant ancestral barramundi, in its journey along the river, carved into the sandstone gorges thus making the bends in the present river. In the southeast the legend of the giant Murray cod explains that the bends and reaches of the Murray River were formed the same way.

Above: Turtle eggs.

Giant barramundi of the north are mainly trapped or speared in inland rivers and estuaries.

Bark painting of a barramundi by Barrdayal from Maningrida, Northern Territory. This great fish is a Dreaming ancestor who made the meanders in the Liverpool River when he swam from side to side.

Before the encroachment of modern towns and cities, it is apparent that fish were much more abundant. Reports of clear waters and shoals of fish visible from sandy reefs occur in all the early settlers' records. A great diversity of fishing techniques was used and the people had an intricate array of artefacts made from wood, plant fibre and bone that they used in the hunt.

Many kinds of fish are today eaten by Aborigines. Some of the more common species in northern waters are the barrumundi, mullet, catfish, shark, groper, barracuda, sawfish, snapper, threadfin salmon, whitefish, kingfish, bonefish, sardine, bream, garfish, jewfish, rock cod, coral trout, trevally and mackerel. In the southeast Aboriginal people retain traditional knowledge of the habits of fish and many of their forefathers' fishing skills, though nets, hooks and lines are modern.

The ability of Aborigines to catch fish was much greater than that of the European newcomers. Usually the fish were driven into enclosures or speared in clear shallow water or from canoes. The spears differed according to the circumstances and locality. Most had from two to six hardened and sharpened prongs bound to a long light shaft. Canoe spears, however, had one end sharpened and hardened and the other fitted with a point of bone or wood. They were also used as punting poles.

Another technique combined diving and spearing underwater. For this the water had to be clear. When low, the Darling River lost its muddy and milky appearance. Thomas Mitchell noted that it was 'beautifully transparent, the bottom was visible to great depths, showing large fishes in shoals, floating like birds in mid air'.[2] Aborigines could once be seen

Dhabila beach, a favourite hunting and resting place for Ramingining families.

swimming to the deep part of the river and sinking feet first without a splash or noise. The fish and the hunter would then rise to the surface with scarcely a ripple. In a nice touch, Mitchell noted the lack of success of his men, who were keen fishermen, in comparison with Aborigines. He mentioned that on one occasion at Fort Bourke, an Aborigine 'perceived Mr Lama fishing unsuccessfully, upon which he approached the river bank, and, after throwing him a fish which he had caught, continued in his frail bark to float down the stream'.

This encounter between the two cultures brings to mind a more recent attempt to assess the skills of white and black in the Australian environment. In central Arnhem Land the Willesee television team sent a commando unit from the Australian army to pit their wits against a group of Ramingining people headed by David Gulpilil in an attempt to 'live off the land proceeding from point A to point B over a given time'. As was the case a hundred years earlier, the 'experts at survival', in some ways the equivalent to explorers of last century, were no match for the Aborigines.

Fish traps were once built by Aboriginal groups along the coast and river systems of southeast Australia. Complex stone structures were constructed, as well as more simple dams and weirs of brush and clay. Remarkable stone constructions still exist in many places, though others

155

The remains of the extensive Aboriginal stone fish trap network on the Darling River at Brewarrina, New South Wales.

PHOTO: REG MORRISON/WELDON TRANNIES

Ina Hall, Graham Coconut, Godfrey and Gordon, pose with the young shark they have just hooked at Hay Point beach, western Cape York.

PHOTO: JENNIFER ISAACS

Opposite page

To many Aboriginal families living along the northern coast, owning a boat is more important than owning a car. Stanley Ngakyunkwokka fishes for catfish with a simple handline along the Archer River, Cape York.

PHOTO: REG MORRISON/WELDON TRANNIES

have been completely washed away. In inland New South Wales fish traps existed on the Bogan, upper Lachlan and upper Murrumbidgee rivers. By far the most impressive fisheries were at Brewarrina. These, it is recorded, were established in the Dreaming by the great spirit ancestor, Baiame, when he showed his people how to use the trap. The area became the scene of great tribal gatherings with the bounty from the fish traps providing food, on occasions, for up to 500 people.

The fish traps were built by collecting loose stones from the bed of the river and building walls with larger stones at the bottom, tapering toward the top. Sections of the river were enclosed to form a labyrinth of pools of various sizes. As the fish travelled upstream they were trapped in the stone pens, which had their open ends facing the direction of the fishes' approach. As soon as sufficient fish had entered the trap, the entrances were enclosed with more rocks and, as the flooded river receded, the fish were removed. Large fish were instantly speared as they caused a lot of damage by thrashing about and often eating the smaller fish in their distress. Two other fish traps still exist at Arawarra, south of Grafton on the north coast, and at Point Plomer, near the mouth of the Hastings River. At high tide the fish entered the trap through an opening, which was then blocked to prevent the fish from escaping. These fish traps were used by north coast Aborigines up to forty years ago.

Nets made from plant fibre were used on all the river systems. In the southeast they averaged 3 metres wide and 1.5 metres deep with sticks at each end. Two men usually held the net while others with beaters drove the fish toward the netted enclosure where they were trapped. They could

Fish are usually carried back to camp in traditional handspun netted bags.

PHOTO: REG MORRISON/WELDON TRANNIES

then be caught by the gills or speared. Occasionally fish were driven into a shallow part of the water where smaller nets were used like scoop nets. Some nets were of a great length: the progress of Charles Sturt up the Darling River in 1830 was blocked by one that stretched 90 metres across the river. These nets were always highly valued and instantly repaired when damaged. Hinged nets were known all over the country and are still made in central and western Arnhem Land and in Cape York. In the southeast they were described as being shaped like two large kites joined down one side. In Arnhem Land they are known as 'butterfly fish nets' because their action imitates the movement of butterfly wings. They are used as scoop nets to catch small fish in the shallow waters.

Aborigines in northern Australia still possess an impressive knowledge of the habits of fish and their river, estuarine and ocean environments. The fishing economy is extremely important in the life of all traditional people. In Cape York shallow bag-like nets made from fibre from *Acacia latifolia* or *Livistona australis* are lashed to an oval frame made of lawyer vine cane. Finer versions of these are used for catching shrimps and prawns. Sometimes in northeastern Arnhem Land a moveable fence of brush, grass and leafy branches is pushed across shallow waterholes or rivers by a line of women.

In the past, log and branch fences up to 30 metres long were built across streams. Several spaces were left open in which nets were placed. Using this technique great hauls of barramundi could be caught in the right season. In northern Australia stone and mud dams and weirs were also made. A small opening was left for the water to flow through, and a fibre trough or basket was placed in the opening. Fish were caught by a platform of broken twigs, leaves and fibre placed beneath the opening.

Along tidal estuaries, fish are caught in nets. Here at Maningrida, a group of children drive small fish towards James Iyuna who is holding a folding hinged fishnet.

PHOTO: REG MORRISON/WELDON TRANNIES

James Iyuna carries a hinged traditional fishing net made of strong spun fibre. Liverpool River, Maningrida.

Hook and line fishing with hand-spun fibre lines was common in many areas. Some ingenious hooks included crescent-shaped pieces of mother of pearl, tortoise shell, sometimes with bone barbs attached, freshwater mussel shells and carved pieces of cane and wood. More unusual sharp substances used for hooks included eaglehawk talons and catfish barbs. The bait was often a grub, shrimp or worm, small crab or mussel, sometimes well chewed and tied on to the hook or barb. A technique called 'bobbing' involved tying a line of twisted spider's web to the fishing line, leaving the spider's abdomen, full of sticky solution, bobbing on the surface. When small fish bit at it, their jaws quickly stuck together.

Metal hooks in time superseded all other forms. These were often contrived from nails or other discarded bits and pieces, though the explorers quickly realised that trading in fish hooks was appreciated by Aborigines. In the Kalumburu region of the Kimberleys, and in many other places including Cape York, fishing with a line has become the task of women, while men fish with spears and from boats. Night fishing has always been significant and early accounts describe Botany Bay dotted

At Aurukun, although hand-spun fibre nets are still made, women prefer to net bait from the beaches with a modern version.

PHOTO: JENNIFER ISAACS

Fish teem in the clear waters of the Gulf of Carpentaria. Thancoupie and a group of children from Weipa fish from a jetty of bauxite boulders.

PHOTO: JENNIFER ISAACS

with canoes, the glow from the fires on the mud hearths on their bases looking like fireflies over the water. Aborigines used flaming bark torches to attract the fish to the water's surface. Incredulous white onlookers described a frail bark canoe at night with two men in it, a fire burning brightly on a mud hearth inside. As the fish rose to the light they were speared and instantly cooked, often in the canoe. This practice is still carried out by Aborigines when camping at night. Large fires are often lit on the beach to attract the fish to the shore where they are speared, netted or hooked.

The custom of throwing plants into waterholes to stun fish with chemicals was widespread over the whole of Australia and many plants were used in this way. Most of our information is about species utilised in Cape York, where poisons included *Barringtonia racemosa*. The bark was hammered between stones and put in the water. Other effective Cape York fish poisons were *Derris* and *Tephrosia* species, including *Derris uliginosa* and *Tephrosia rosea*. *Derris* stems were hammered and put in water, while *Tephrosia* roots were hammered and placed in saltwater pools with the addition of crushed green ants' nests. *Eucalyptus microtheca* branches and leaves also worked but had to be left in the pool overnight until the water became dark and strong smelling. Generally the fish were stunned by the active properties of the poisons in the leaves, bark and roots and floated to the surface or swam around disoriented, easy marks for the hunters.

Mawalan Marika tends the kingfish he has just speared at Yelangbara, watched by the Marika family. Large fish are slit, cleaned and cooked on their backs on the hot coals.

PHOTO: JENNIFER ISAACS

Women are especially good at hand-line fishing from the beaches at Weipa. Gertie Motton, cleaning a freshly caught trevally, is watched by Janita, her grand-daughter.

PHOTO: JENNIFER ISAACS

COOKING FISH

The techniques of cooking fish are much the same across the continent and depend largely on species and size. Generally, small fish are gutted and cooked whole on the coals, while large ones are slit and laid in the coals on their backs. The comments of Tom Petrie about Queensland early this century could well apply today:

> Fish were scaled with a shell and then put whole on a nice fire of red hot coals. When about cooked a finger would be shoved in below the head at the fin, and the whole inside drawn off leaving the fish beautifully clean and nice. Fish were always cooked so.[3]

Large fish are also cooked in ground ovens, sometimes wrapped in big leaves.

The technique for preparing stingray and shark is quite different. The flesh of these marine animals is considered on its own rather unpalatable, in Banduk's words 'too salty'. This is because stingrays and sharks excrete nitrogenous wastes in a manner that gives the flesh a distinct smell and taste of ammonia. A fire is built and allowed to subside so that it becomes a mass of coals. The stingray or shark is put on the fire, back downwards, and left until it begins to bloat. It is quickly removed and cleaned out. In Banduk's words:

161

Maudie Bennett spearing a stingray among the mangroves. Stingrays are delicacies but must be prepared and cooked carefully. Most Aborigines strain or knead the flesh through fresh water and then mix it with the liver to make 'fishballs'.

PHOTO: VIC CHERIKOFF

The two livers [lobes] you keep in a cool place. We dig a hole and put it in the cold sand. After you've done that, put the stingray back on the fire or coal until it is cooked, take it out of the fire, put it on a mat or whatever you have spread out on the ground. Have some fresh water ready in maybe a shell, like we do, or a pot, and then take the green thing out of the livers, we call it 'milguminy' [gall bladder]. Then you peel off the first layer of skin and then you peel the meat off and put them on the mat. When you've got all the meat together, then you mix the water with it little by little, squeezing and kneading it and tasting it as well. The water should be getting the salt out of the meat. You change the water often until when you taste it all the salt is out. Then you spread the meat out and put the two livers in with the meat and knead that into the meat. When you have done that, roll it into round balls together, both the liver and the meat. Then you spread the balls out to eat with the family.

Shark's liver and flesh are treated the same way, and it is significant that in paintings of stingrays and sharks in northeast Arnhem Land, the animal is always shown with its liver clearly visible. The livers are thought to be a source of strength and parts are given to babies and to old and toothless people. They are an excellent source of iron and vitamins A and D.

COMMONLY EATEN FISH

NORTHERN WATERS: QUEENSLAND, NORTHERN TERRITORY, NORTHERN WESTERN AUSTRALIA

COMMON NAME	ALTERNATIVE NAMES	SCIENTIFIC NAME
Barramundi	Giant perch	*Lates calcarifer*
Barramundi (freshwater)	Dawson River salmon; Saratoga	*Scleropages leichhardtii*
Mullet	Many types, including Bully, Flattail, Sand mullet (20 species)	*Mugil cephalus* (most common) *Liza vaigiensis* (Diamond-scaled mullet)
Catfish	Eel tail catfish	*Tandanus tandanus* (most common)
	Forktail catfish (8 species)	*Neoarius australis* (Blue catfish)
Shark	Many species	
Groper	6 species	*Cheilinus undulatus*
Barracuda	Sea pike	*Sphyraena barracuda*
Sawfish	Sawshark	*Pristis zijsron*
Snapper	Spangled emperor	*Lethrinus nebulosus*
Salmon	Threadfin salmon	*Eleutheronema tetradactylum*
Whitefish	Queenfish; Leathery	*Scomberoides lysan*
Kingfish	Giant trevally	*Caranx ignobilis*
Bonefish		*Albula vulpes*
Sardine	Pilchard	*Sardinops neopilchardus*
Bream	Several species	*Acanthopagus berda* (most common)
Garfish	Many species	*Hemiramphus* spp.
Longtom	Garfish	*Ablennes hians*
Jewfish	Mulloway	*Argyrosomus hololopidotus*
Rock cod	More than 20 species	*Epinephelus* spp.
Coral trout	Coral cod	*Plectroploma maculatum*
Trevally	Many species	*Caranx* spp.
Mackerel	Several species	*Scomberomorus commersoni* (most common)

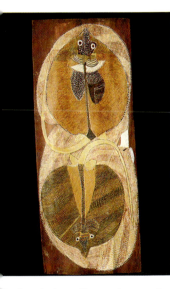

Bark painting of two stingrays by Gunwinggu artist Maralwanga, Maningrida, Northern Territory. The liver lobes, mixed with the flesh when cooked, are clearly depicted.

SOUTHERN WATERS: NEW SOUTH WALES, VICTORIA, TASMANIA, SOUTH AUSTRALIA, SOUTHWESTERN AUSTRALIA

COMMON NAME	ALTERNATIVE NAMES	SCIENTIFIC NAME
Dusky flathead	Lizard	*Platycephalus fuscus*
Bream	Silver bream; black bream	*Acanthopagrus australis; A. butcheri*
Snapper	Squire; red bream	*Chrysophrys auratus*

Catfish Dreaming site. Bark painting by Ngainmira from western Arnhem Land.

PHOTO: REG MORRISON/WELDON TRANNIES

SOUTHERN WATERS: NEW SOUTH WALES, VICTORIA, TASMANIA, SOUTH AUSTRALIA, SOUTHWESTERN AUSTRALIA

COMMON NAME	ALTERNATIVE NAMES	SCIENTIFIC NAME
Blackfish	Luderick	*Girella tricuspidata*
Mullet	Several species	*Mugil cephalus*
Tailor	Chopper	*Pomatomus saltatrix*
Jewfish	Mulloway	*Argyrosomus hololopidotus*
Salmon	Australian salmon	*Arripis trutta*
Herring	Tommy ruff	*Arripis georgianus*
Trevally	Blurter	*Caranx* spp.
Murray cod (freshwater)		*Maccullochella peeli*
Golden perch (freshwater)	Yellow belly	*Macquaria ambigua*
Silver perch (freshwater)		*Bidyanus bidyanus*
Catfish (freshwater)		*Tandanus tandanus*

MARINE MAMMALS

Aborigines generally separate scale fish and small marine creatures from large 'meats' such as sea turtles, dugongs, dolphins and whales. The language itself clearly divides these classes of animals. There are distinctive words in Arnhem Land for animals with shells and for those with twin flukes on their tails or skin. Five different kinds of turtles are harvested in the northern waters: green turtle (*Chelonia mydas*), flatbacked turtle (*Chelonia depressa*), Pacific ridley (*Lepidochelys olivacea*), hawksbill turtle (*Eretmochelys imbricata*) and loggerhead turtle (*Caretta caretta*). The dugong, a beautiful sea mammal that gave rise to the legend of the mermaid, is also hunted and eaten by Aboriginal people. Whales were relished last century along the southeast coast. When they inadvertently beached themselves along the coast, the news would spread and tribes would gather to feast.

Specific words in Aboriginal languages and dialects indicate the degree of knowledge they have about sea creatures and the distinction they make between the size of these animals at different stages of development. Two different words describe turtle eggs that have been laid in the sand and those gathered from the body of a freshly killed turtle. There is another word for a female turtle very rich in fat. Dugongs are distinguished in many ways: pregnant female dugongs in Elcho Island are called *ngarumirr*, infants still suckling have a specific name, infants who have just left their mothers have names and big old dugongs have a specific name, *warranaka*. In addition to these distinctions, *djungguwangu*, is used to describe a herd of dugong while, *djinbaypay*, describes a huge herd of dugong.[4]

According to Dick Roughsey, dugong was the best meat and tasted like pork when cooked:

> The mammals grow up to 10'. They were mostly hunted by netting or by spearing from a raft. During high tide, dugongs would come up creeks and rivers to feed on seaweed and moss and the hunters would see them going up the river, or hear them coming up for air at night and sighing softly, and the old man dugong herding them together by whistling. When there were plenty up the river men would paddle rafts to the river mouth, placing big nets made from the strong inner bark of the beach hibiscus across channels through the sand bar. These nets could be anything up to 30' long and 15' deep tied to poles at each side. Other men then, upstream, came down on rafts or canoes, beating water and making a lot of noise. The frightened dugong headed before them toward the open sea but were soon trapped in the net, which the men released from the sticks so that it wrapped around them.[5]

When dugongs were further out to sea it was more common to harpoon them with traditional harpoons. Harpoon ropes were up to 70 metres long and made from a strong, thick substance such as hibiscus fibre. Such harpoons and ropes are still made and used in Arnhem Land. Occasionally a sucker fish (remora) was used to guide the canoe or boat to prey. When a large dugong was sighted a sucker fish was tied to a mastline and dropped overboard. It made straight to the prey and the marked line indicated to the hunters how far they were from the dugong. Aboriginal harpoons never killed the dugong, but when they were lodged in its side, the long rope pulled the canoe along until the animal tired.

A permit system in Queensland allows Aboriginal people who gather at Hopevale on the west coast of Cape York to hunt dugong. The hunting takes place mainly during Christmas holidays when families move from the inland settlement to camps on the beaches north of Cape Bedford. In one recent year approximately twenty dugong permits were issued. Permission to hunt dugong is also extended to Aborigines on the coast of Arnhem Land and the Gulf of Carpentaria, but other people are not allowed to kill dugong as it is a protected species.

TURTLES

Turtles are hunted in much the same way as dugongs. Along the coast they arrive with the southeast monsoons and swim to sandy beaches to lay their eggs. As they mate, canoeists head out to sea and wait patiently until they can see them. A harpoon is hurled at the animals and the men jump over the side of the boat or canoe and quickly turn the turtles on their backs. When the turtle has·been immobilised on its back several men carry it up over the sand. Turtles are described as 'three man' turtle, 'four man' turtle and so on, depending on their size.

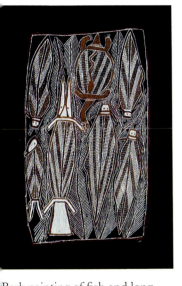

Bark painting of fish and long-necked turtle by Alex Djirrgululu from Ramingining. The fish depicted are eel-tail catfish, salmon, catfish and long tom.
PHOTO: REG MORRISON/WELDON TRANNIES

Leaves known as *djilka* in north-east Arnhem Land are used in the ground oven to flavour turtle meat.

PHOTO: JENNIFER ISAACS

Young turtles disturbed while gathering turtle eggs are helped to the sea.

PHOTO: DAVID ISAACS

Opposite page:
Spear fishing.
PHOTO: JENNIFER ISAACS

Dhuwandjika digs for turtle eggs in the white sand at Yelangbara.

PHOTO: JENNIFER ISAACS

Large turtles are cooked in a unique way. The throat is cut under the neck near the hard breastplate and the intestines, liver and fat are pulled out of the hole. A large fire is built, rather like the kind set for an earth oven with stones or lumps of antbed on top. The turtle is upended in the sand and the hot stones or pieces of antbed are stuffed into the intestinal cavity. The neck hole is fastened off by a stuffing of special turtle leaves called *djilka* at Yirrkala. The meat inside the turtle shell roasts slowly for two hours, during which time the intestines and liver are cleaned and cooked, as well as the eggs if there are any. These are roasted on the coals and eaten as 'entrées' while the rest of the animal cooks. The plastron (lower shell) is levered off and the turtle's back acts as a bowl for holding the meat and juices while they are divided. The legs are cut off at this stage and thrown back on the coals to roast.

Turtle eggs are a delicacy prized for their flavour, nutrition and thirst-quenching qualities. People follow turtle tracks along the beach to their nests. Banduk describes the hunt:

> The turtle does try to confuse people with their tracks and they make a few different false nests. One of these is the right nest with the eggs in it. They dig a hole with their two front flippers about two or three feet deep and then they lay their eggs, cover the hole up with sand, then head back to sea. When you're looking for eggs, when you feel the stick going into the sand almost like it's sinking in, you're there, that's where the eggs are.

Turtle eggs are soft shelled. When cooked, the yolk hardens but the white stays runny. Aborigines frequently 'drink' raw turtle eggs to quench their thirst while they are hunting for eggs.

THIRTEEN

SHELLFISH

Along the vast stretch of the Australian coast lie the scattered remains of shellfish meals eaten by Aboriginal people over the entire span of human life on this continent. Giant heaps of shells, known as middens, can still be found intact along many isolated beaches. Some, such as those at Weipa on the western coast of Cape York, are nearly ten metres high. Others form low layers in the sand dunes, exposed by wind and rain or the careless skid of the wheels of four-wheel drive vehicles as surfers and holidaying adventurers look for a good camp site or a secluded beach. Even on suburban beaches scattered middens are found, and the odd bone implement or stone tool is washed from the sand with the incoming tide.

Aborigines still exploit the full range of food resources of the coast. In Arnhem Land and Cape York women and children collect hundreds of varieties of shellfish from rocks and rock pools, from sandbars and from the intertidal mangrove areas where shells are dug from under the mud, picked up from the surface or prised from the roots of mangrove trees. In some northern areas, women collect shellfish from the sand beneath the sea as the tide is coming in. They locate a shell bed and 'excavate' it in the sitting position until the tide is up to their chests.[1]

Above: Giant shell mound, five to seven metres high, at Ooningan,
near Mission River, Cape York.

Giyakminy Marika collects oysters
from the rocks at Yelangbara.

169

At low tide mangrove bivalve shells litter the swamp at Aurukun. These are the remains of Aboriginal meals while out hunting.

PHOTO: REG MORRISON/WELDON TRANNIES

After excavating a heap of cockle shells, or *diyama*, at Juta Point, western Arnhem Land, Delilah fills her hand-made nylon string bag.

PHOTO: DIANNE MOON

Archaeologists have gathered valuable information on the diet of Aboriginal people over centuries by examining the shell middens. It is remarkable how similar the shell types eaten today are to those that appear at strata levels of food debris many centuries old. The huge shell mounds at Weipa are of different shapes; some circular, some long ridges. They occur behind beaches and between beaches and mangrove swamps and are mainly of cockle shells (*Anadara granosa*). The mounds mark ancient camp sites used during the wet season when tribespeople moved to the beaches to live mainly on shellfish when plant and root foods were scarce.

The observations recorded by Betty Meehan in her book *Shell Bed to Shell Midden* could be extended to cover many groups of Aboriginal women throughout the north of Australia.[2] Generally, depending on the season, the weather and the tides, two or three shellfish become the staple of any particular area. In the case of the Anbara, with whom Betty Meehan lived, the gastropod *Telescopium telescopium*, which could be found in thousands in the mangrove mud, formed one staple, but it was not as well thought of as the bivalve *Tapes hiantina*, which was excavated from the seabed at low tide.

Among Cape York women large bivalves also appear to be the most sought after shellfish. Gastropods are certainly eaten with relish, but if a supply of big mangrove oysters is found it is immediately harvested. Most people consider variety to be important, but it is more often the children or the older women who gather a range of shellfish in small quantities to add to the staples, more or less as delicacies. In Cape York, these include *Volegalea wardiana, Trisidos yongei, Placuna placenta, Conus figulinus, Hadta bipartita, Hyotissa quirites, Lioconcha sulcatina* and a variety of pipis including *Marcia liantina*.

170

Out on the sandbars, which are only exposed during what are termed 'king tides' across the north, two giant gastropods, conch (*Syrinx aruanas*) and bailer shell (*Melo amphora*), are also picked up. After the gastropods have been eaten, these shells are used as utensils. The conch shells are used to carry water; in Arnhem Land handles are made of bush string and attached to each end so that they can be easily carried. In Cape York, bailer shells are sometimes used as cooking utensils in which liquid can be heated or water boiled. Small sections of shell are occasionally chipped out to make a handle and sections of bailer are also used to form the handle of Cape York woomeras.

Shellfish are usually cooked before eating; the technique of cooking varies with the species. Heaps of empty shells are occasionally used as beds inside ground ovens on which large quantities of shellfish are cooked for ceremonial occasions. People eat large quantities of shellfish when camped at beaches or close to mangrove areas, often from half to three-quarters of a kilogram per person per day.

In places where the Aboriginal management of coastal resources has been unaffected by European activities, such as holiday usage or pollution from domestic or industrial effluents, the supply of shellfish and their continued variety and nutritive importance in the daily Aboriginal diet have not abated. This is not so, of course, along most of the southeast coastal belt. Fresh mussels, which abounded along Port Phillip Bay in the 1950s, have gone in a generation; oysters that covered the rocks of Sydney Harbour coves are greatly diminished, and those that remain are rarely eaten because of possible pollution. Many of the author's Aboriginal friends from northern Australia are, however, undaunted by this and harvest quantities of oysters when in Sydney as one of the only city sources of 'proper bush tucker'. As they cook the oysters in the traditional manner, no ill effects have been felt.

Although hundreds of Australian shellfish may be collected and eaten, Aborigines gather certain shellfish at particular times of the year, as their taste alters seasonally.[3] In the late wet season of central Arnhem Land, when plant fruits are ripe, there is an abundance of shell foods on the seashore. These include *Tapes hiantina* (up to 90 per cent in many areas). During the height of the monsoon season huge tides occasionally wash a great variety of shellfish from their beds in the deep water and small groups of Arnhem Land people on outstations have a sudden abundance of shell food, but only as long as the shellfish remain fresh as they rot quickly in the damp heat. Such bountiful winds and tides are awaited and anticipated with pleasure. The people of western Cape York today describe the years when they lived off bush food and the times when the big tides would 'chuck 'im up plenty of tucker'.

By the middle of the dry season, in June and July, though the lined nerite and *Telescopium* species are still collected from the mangroves, other varieties have replaced those collected in the Wet. Along the coast of

Bark painting by Lipawanga of Oyster Dreaming, a symbolic representation of rows of shellfish from western Arnhem Land.

PHOTO: JENNIFER ISAACS

Arnhem Land and Cape York *Telescopium telescopium* and *Terebralia palustris* are important because they can easily be collected on the surface of the mangrove mud or just beneath it. On a recent visit to Cape York, Thancoupie and I collected buckets of shellfish from the Cairns mangroves. These included the bivalve *Batissa violacea,* gastropods, *Terebralia palustris* and black nerites (*Nerita lineata*). Although resident in Cairns, and famous internationally as a potter, Thancoupie still supplements her ordinary diet with real bush food.

BIVALVES

MUD OYSTER   *Batissa violacea; Polymesoda coaxans*

These most prized bivalves lie hidden from view beneath the grey-black mangrove mud. They lurk beneath buried rotting mangrove branches and among the 'legs' of the mangroves, the branching elbow-shaped roots that reach into the mud to support the mangrove colony in heavy tides. Sometimes the women find one shell on its own. Others are found in groups. The women walk slowly, heads down, bodies bent forward, feeling in the mud with their toes and the ball of the foot as they go, or tapping the mud with a long digging stick, machete or metal bar held vertically. If the implement makes a dull resonant 'clak' the shells have been found. If the mud is drier, or if a layer of sand has been deposited over the mud on the edge of the mangroves, slight cracks might be seen, sometimes with the end of the shell just visible, and the shells are quickly dug out. They can be almost as big as the palm of the hand.

The mangrove colonies near Cairns offer a source of bush food to Thancoupie. She is digging out the delicious mud oysters she calls *acul.*

PHOTO: JENNIFER ISAACS

Some edible shellfish of the northern coast. Aboriginal names are those used at Weipa, north Queensland.

1 'Congol', *Conus figulinus*
2 'Acul', *Batissa violacea*
3 'Drangol', *Nerita lineata*
4 'Arrani', *Melo amphora*
5 'Fundul', *Trisidos yongei*
6 'Kumbuk', *Anadara aliena*
7 'Kaanthuc', *Hyotissa quirites*
8 'Evite', *Lioconcha sulcatina*
9 'Armeg', *Marcia liantina*
10 'Pipi', *Donax cuneatus*
11 'Tha'arr', *Terebralia palustris*
12 *Xanthomelon pachystylum,* jungle snail

PHOTO: MICHAEL COURTNEY

A quick hot fire is lit over the shells which burns itself out in minutes. The shellfish are removed immediately they begin to open so that no delicious juices will be lost.

PHOTOS: JENNIFER ISAACS

Large bivalves are cooked in similar ways across the entire northern coastline of Australia, with small local variations. After being washed to remove mud or sand, the shells are placed in rows abutting each other, with 'heels' up and 'lips' down. In some areas the shells are placed directly on the sand, but Thancoupie demonstrated the Weipa method in which they are first placed on a bed of dry leaves and small flat sticks. A quick and hot flaming fire is made over the top of the shells using, in Thancoupie's case, bamboo leaves and small dry casuarina branches. The fire is important—too long and slow a heat will make the shellfish tough. The fire must get very hot immediately and burn itself out in three to five minutes. The charred twigs and ash that cover the shells are then flicked off with a fresh green branch of casuarina and the shells can be opened and eaten hot. Inside are large, succulent shellfish swimming in their own juices, aptly named 'mud oysters' and deserving of as much culinary acclaim as mud crabs.

PIPIS *Marcia* spp.

Pipis are well known in the shellfish diet of the Australian community and are regularly served in a number of restaurants. They abound on Queensland beaches and I recall gathering them as a child at the water's edge on Stradbroke Island as each wave receded. We used them for bait, though some people ate them.

Aborigines are expert at 'catching' pipis. The hunter must be a fast digger and have very sharp eyesight. As the tide turns and each wave laps the sand, pipis bury themselves deeper in the wet sand. They go vertically, leaving only a small hole or bubble visible on the surface of the sand. They are very fast and can descend 30 centimetres in a couple of seconds.

Dhuwandjika watches for bubbles from pipis in the sand beneath the clear water of the Gulf of Carpentaria.

PHOTO: DAVID ISAACS

Shellfish are often roasted at the edge of the fire and served on a bed of leaves.

PHOTO: JENNIFER ISAACS

In eastern Arnhem Land, Dhuwandjika showed me a different technique of gathering pipis when the tide is in. Standing thigh deep in water behind the gently breaking waves, she watched for bubbles in the sand beneath the clear water. Then she reached down, bringing up the pipis together with handfuls of sand.

Pipis, like most seafood, are only plentiful seasonally. These small bivalves are usually boiled in billies until they open a little, or they may be roasted gently on the ashes at the edge of the fire.

OYSTERS   *Hyotissa* spp.

Oysters, part of international cuisine, are enjoyed by many people and are usually, though not exclusively, eaten raw. There are many Australian species. Aborigines prefer them all cooked, though most people eat at least half a dozen before bringing them back to the campfire. One favourite is the large black-lipped oyster, which can be found on the outer islands off the northern Australian coast. Others include *Saccostrea tuberculata* and *Lopha folium*.

Oysters are collected in three ways. Sometimes they are tapped or hit with a heavy instrument such as a rock or a file so that the upper shell is cracked and the juicy flesh can be removed and put into tin mugs or bowls. Sometimes clumps of oysters are smashed off the rocks and carried back to camp in buckets. The third technique is used for varieties fastened on to mangrove roots. Then the root itself is cut off and carried back to camp,

174

usually on the women's heads or cushioned in some way, as the shells are very sharp. Most women seem to sustain a few small cuts.

To cook oysters clumps of shells are turned frequently on the coals to expose all faces. The process is simple but delicate. It is important that when they are opened the oysters are still moist and juicy, and the cook is chided if they are 'dry'. When the clumps of oysters are cooked the flesh is removed by smashing the top with a rock or hard metal instrument.

MANGROVE WORMS, SHIPWORMS   *Terodo* spp.

Mangrove worms, or shipworms as they are known in other parts of the world, are the scourge of wooden-hulled boats, as they eat timber below the waterline. Although they look like worms, these evil-looking delicacies are actually bivalve molluscs. Their shell plates have been modified to a tiny pair of abrasive plates at the head end. The worms are found in the intertidal roots of mangroves, often in the wood that has collected between the branched elbow-like supports that spring out from the trees into the mud.

Moving through these mangrove areas is very difficult. On a trip with friends from Ramingining the women walked quickly ahead of me, their

The Malangai family collects mangrove worms from the roots at Dhabila, central Arnhem Land. These 'shipworms' are actually bivalves which eat their way through the mangrove roots. They are relished as delicacies, eaten raw or cooked.

feet hardly sinking into the mud and, when they reached the interlocking roots, they simply walked along them, stepping from one to another. This proved too difficult for me and I had to content myself with waiting within sight of the mangrove edge. The women gathered worms using a small tomahawk to prize open the timber.'

There are two types of mangrove worm: a small white one and a long grey-pink one. The small white worms must be cooked; if eaten raw this type makes the throat sore. They are usually boiled in a large shell in the coals. The juice formed in the cooking is then drunk. The longer pink worms are eaten raw. They can be up to 30 centimetres long and 2.5 centimetres wide and have a 'lid' and 'teeth' which must be removed, along with the tail. The insides are usually sucked out or 'milked' and discarded, then the whole worm is eaten. Although most Arnhem Land people regard these worms as delicacies, I must admit to finding them completely unpalatable, tasting largely of rotting wood.

GASTROPODS

MANGROVE SNAILS   *Telescopium telescopium; Terebralia palustris*

This cone shell, which lies in or on the mud of mangroves, is one of the most interesting Aboriginal shellfish foods. When cooked, the flesh is bright green and, unless watching Aboriginal friends devour it with gusto, the colour would probably put most people off. Known as *congol* in Cape York, the shells abound in the mangrove areas around Cairns and can be collected at low tide. After being washed, they can be roasted in the coals, steamed over the fire on a wire grill or boiled in the billy. When the shells are roasted or steamed they are placed with the open end upward to retain liquid. The flesh literally boils in its own juice, and frothy bubbles can be seen coming out of the mouth of the shells.

Opening the shells is not easy. They are picked up from the fire when very hot and brittle and hit sharply in a circular motion around the perimeter of the mouth, each blow cracking off particles of shell and exposing more of the spiralling green flesh. Sometimes the shell is cracked in the centre and the two halves pulled gently apart so the flesh can be eased out.

In some parts of Arnhem Land and Bathurst Island these shellfish are eaten without cleaning, though those gathered in the mangroves near Cairns needed to be 'stripped' before eating. When 'stripping' the shell flesh, Thancoupie held the cooked green flesh so that it hung down from finger and thumb and used the other thumb to separate the slimy green matter of the digestive tract from the cream gonads. The cream-coloured mass was eaten and the green discarded. This may be a matter of taste due to the environment in which the shellfish are found.

Congol, mangrove snails of the *Telescopium* species, sit on the mud between the mangrove roots near Cairns, Queensland. After cooking the turquoise flesh is extracted and 'stripped' before being eaten.

PHOTOS: JENNIFER ISAACS

Arkapenya of Aurukun with a mud crab. These delicacies are easily obtained seafood staples. They are hunted seasonally when signs in flowers or plants indicate they are 'fat'.

PHOTO: REG MORRISON/WELDON TRANNIES

Mud crabs are simply roasted in their shells on the coals of a fire until they turn orange.

PHOTO: REG MORRISON/WELDON TRANNIES

MUD CRABS *Scylla serrata*

Like oysters, mud crabs are part of international cuisine. Although well known in the general Australian diet they are, nevertheless, expensive delicacies. To coastal Aborigines they are a delicious, easily obtained seafood staple.

Mud crabs, as the name suggests, inhabit burrows in the intertidal mud on the edge of mangrove areas and are particularly plentiful in settled tropical areas. A crab hunt is rather like a goanna hunt in the desert. When the burrow, or hide, is located the women plunge sticks into the mud in an area some distance from the hole until the crab is located and dug out quickly. The crabs are always cooked immediately at the edge of the beach. They are placed on the fire until they turn orange and then removed. All the flesh and intestines are eaten, including the juices, fat and eggs.

Small black nerites, known as *drangol,* cling to the mangrove roots.

PHOTO: JENNIFER ISAACS

Jungle land snails are found in the leaf litter at the base of forest trees. They are occasionally eaten in Arnhem Land and Cape York after being lightly roasted at the side of the coals.

PHOTOS: LEO MEIER/WELDON TRANNIES

BLACK NERITES *Nerita lineata*

These shellfish, called *drangol* in Cape York, live on the lower branching above-ground roots of mangrove trees. Although small, they are quite delicious, rather like periwinkles. The shells are simply picked off the wood, though force is sometimes needed to prize off clinging individuals.

These shells are usually boiled. To remove the flesh a pin or strong, sharp fishbone is hooked into the flesh at the opening and the pin and shell are rotated in opposite directions so that the flesh comes out (one hopes) in a complete spiral. Black nerites are never a staple food but add variety to the diet.

JUNGLE LAND SNAILS *Xanthomelon pachystylum*

These snails, found under leaf litter at the base of trees in Cape York and Arnhem Land, are gathered, cooked and eaten. They are simply and quickly roasted on the coals and the snail flesh extracted as for nerites or periwinkles. In western Arnhem Land the shells are kept and decorated with dotted designs. They are tied in groups and clanked together to serve as musical instruments during ceremonies.

CRUSTACEANS

YABBIES   *Cherax* spp.

In mainland estuaries or freshwater streams, yabbies or crayfish were a favourite Aboriginal food. Large species grow to 25 centimetres and are still hunted enthusiastically by country children. Pollution, over-clearing of agricultural land and introduced predators, such as carp and trout, have reduced their numbers but they are now commercially farmed and are offered on restaurant menus as a gourmet delicacy.

In Tasmania, very limited evidence suggests that fish were not eaten but that Aboriginal women dived for marine crayfish, which were a staple form of protein in coastal areas.

On the Arnhem Land coast Elsie Ganbada and the women from Yathalamara cross the salt pan to the sea with buckets, axes, dilly bags and knives to gather food from the beaches and mangroves.

PHOTO: REG MORRISON/WELDON TRANNIES

FOURTEEN

BILLABONG AND SWAMP ANIMALS

At the close of the dry season and beginning of the Wet the waterholes of the tropical north slowly fill to become enticingly cool, peaceful places offering good supplies of bush tucker. Whistling ducks build their nests at the beginning of the wet season and geese, brolgas and jabirus can also be seen. Long-necked turtles are found beneath the water as the billabongs fill, or beneath the mud during the dry season when they go into hibernation. The billabongs are distinctive in that they are frequently surrounded by the pale trunks of stringybark trees. The air is heavy with the dank smell of rotting debris though the water is sweet, frequently covered with white, pink or blue waterlilies. Women and children dive into the water and seek the corms of waterlilies as they look for turtle meat or file snakes.

GEESE, DUCKS, IBIS AND WATER BIRDS

Although guns are generally used when hunting birds near billabongs or swamps, many ingenious traditional techniques were once employed. In the southeast of the continent large nets were strung close to billabongs and flocks of water birds were frightened so that they flew off and were

Above: Jabiru, Northern Territory.

Billabongs and swamps, surrounded by the pale trunks of paperbark trees, are enticingly cool places offering plenty of bush tucker.

181

Paperbark swamp, northeast Arnhem Land.

PHOTO: JENNIFER ISAACS

trapped in the nets. Another rather humorous practice, also from the southeast, was for a hunter to swim undetected underwater until directly underneath the ducks on the surface. Then, with a sharp tug, he would pull the ducks beneath the water by their feet and render them helpless. Geese could be tricked by imitating the cries of other geese. As they came down from the high branches, they were quickly beaten with sticks or, in some areas, with boomerangs.

Boomerangs, one of the most ingenious weapons used by Aboriginal hunters, came into their own in the hunting of birds. They were thrown into flocks as they were landing on water or taking off. The returning boomerang was thrown in a downward motion toward the ground. It then kicked up into the flock of birds, stunning or killing one so that it fell to the ground.

The goose egg season in Arnhem Land was described vividly by ethnographer Donald Thomson. The hunters and their families moved to the swamps where they built houses to await the coming of the geese and their nesting. Elegant flotillas of bark canoes headed out into the wide waters to catch geese and gather eggs, returning at night to special platforms built over the water, where the men feasted and slept.

Other birds caught near billabongs and swamps include pelicans, ibis and ducks. They are usually shot and carried back to camp for plucking and cooking. Large birds such as pelicans, ibis, and brolgas were once cooked in ground ovens. Today it is quite common to see fresh birds boiling in large billies.

Waterlilies *(Nymphaea* sp.) grow freely on billabongs and swamps and offer several foods.

PHOTO: LEO MEIER/WELDON TRANNIES

Bark painting of magpie geese and their nest from Ramingining, central Arnhem Land.

PHOTO: REG MORRISON/WELDON TRANNIES

PHOTOS: LEO MEIER/WELDON TRANNIES

LONG-NECKED TURTLES   *Chelodina* spp.

The meat of long-necked turtles is a delicacy throughout northern Australia. Most freshwater turtles are snake-necked turtles, which hide their head or neck under the front part of the carapace, retracting them in an S-shaped curve.

When the waterholes are low at the close of the dry season women tread around the edge in the soft wet mud, raising their toes one after another in a pushing, dancing motion. If they reach a patch of mud that they cannot push down with their foot, they are sure there is a hibernating turtle below. Of all the hunted creatures turtles are the most easily caught, offering little resistance. In the wet season, when the waterholes are high, women must swim beneath the water to look for turtles among the reeds or watch quietly until the still waters reveal their small round heads bobbing to the surface for air.

Because the billabongs are often some distance from camp, turtles are usually cooked while the women are out on the hunt, though some are always taken back home. A fire is lit and the turtle placed on the open flame. It is usually killed beforehand with a quick twist of the neck, but

Elsie Ganbada and other women in the family from Yathalamara hunt long-necked turtles hibernating in the mud. When they are located with feet or crowbar they are pulled out by the neck and carried back to camp in woven pandanus bags.

large and obstinate animals are put on the fire while still moving. After about ten minutes on its back on the open fire, the carcass is taken off. A slit is made under the neck and the intestine removed. The large intestine is cleaned out and thrown on top of the coals. It cooks quickly into a crisp, delicious meal, somewhat like roast chicken skin. The turtle itself is placed back in the coals. After cooking for twenty minutes on one side it is turned over and cooked on the other side for an equal length of time. To serve the meat the turtle is turned on its back and a slit is made around the plastron at the point where it joins the back, or carapace. The plastron is removed in one action, leaving the meat in one whole piece in the carapace, which acts as a bowl. It can easily be cut loose from the shell and divided into portions. The juices remaining in the carapace are drunk and it then used as a dish in which to divide the meat for members of the family.

Turtle meat is extremely oily but delicious, and the entire animal is eaten except for the head. Cooked turtles can be transported and stored for a day or so. Recently on a hunt in Arnhem Land we were unsuccessful and hungry. One woman produced 'packed lunch' from her grass dillybag: a whole cooked turtle, caught the day before, which she had brought 'just in case'.

FILE SNAKES

Several snakes are caught and eaten by Aboriginal people but the file snake is one of the most favoured. This large, harmless, wide-bellied reptile inhabits lagoons and swamps, and is generally caught in the water by women on turtle-hunting expeditions. Small file snakes can often be seen in billies in the camps, either kept as children's pets or waiting to be cooked on the fire. Their skin is very rough, like sandpaper.

When caught, the file snake is killed by holding the head in the mouth and giving the body a sharp yank downwards to break the backbone. The snakes are cooked whole on the coals.

Hunting snakes and turtles, Fogg Dam, Northern Territory. File snakes are often found while on turtle-hunting expeditions. The snake is enthusiastically wrenched from the water and the back broken with a quick downward pull while holding the head between the teeth.

PHOTOS: GUNTHER DEICHMANN

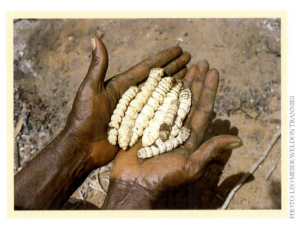

FIFTEEN

INSECTS AND GRUBS

Many insects and their larvae are devoured with relish by Aborigines. Edible grubs can be found in both live and dead trees, in branches and in roots. Some writers, because of their own aversions, regard eating insects as the last straw and pass judgments such as 'in arid lands when food supplies were scarce even the humblest insects were captured and devoured to enable people to survive'. This view denies the truth of the matter. Some species of insects and larvae are not 'last resort foods' but are relished. Such delicacies include finger-sized witchetty grubs and nectar-laden honey ants.

Any account of Aboriginal harvesting of edible grubs and insects would not be complete without mentioning the extraordinary moth feasts that once occurred in the Bogong mountains of southern New South Wales. The Omeo-Monaro tribes of the Bogong country are now fewer in number and the moths remain unmolested, aestivating in millions every year in the same rock shelters of the mountains where hundreds of people once gathered and grew fat on their nutritious bodies.

From November to January up to seven hundred people from different tribes would assemble for huge feasts on the moths, *Agrotis infusa*, which could be found sheltering in the recesses of rocks and in caves. The stone

Above: Cooked witchetty grubs, a delicious desert staple.

Honey ants *(Melophorus bagoti)*.

Bogong moths aestivate in great numbers in the colder mountainous areas of Canberra and southern New South Wales.

PHOTO: VIC CHERIKOFF

surface of every crevice was covered with a layer of tightly packed moths. Aborigines collected moths by dislodging the bottom row with a stick and catching them as they fell on a kangaroo skin or a specially woven fibre cloth placed on the floor of the cave or on the ground below the rock. They cooked the moths by rolling them lightly in hot ashes and sifting the bodies gently in a string bag to separate the wings and heads from the bodies. The resulting mass of flesh was very small; one writer described it as the size of a grain of wheat after cooking. Occasionally the moths were pounded up and made into a form of cake that apparently could be kept for a few days. The early literature described the moths as being extremely 'nice and sweet, with the flavour of walnut'.

Bogong moths are highly nutritious. Observers reported that when the Aborigines returned from the mountains after the feasts their skin was glossy and they were quite fat. Old accounts of Bogong moth feasts were drawn together by Josephine Flood in her book *The Moth Hunters,* which gives a fascinating account of the harvesting of insects *en masse*, a practice apparently unique in Australia.[1]

UNIDENTIFIED GRUBS

It would seem that almost all grubs that look fat, white and edible, and that are found inside live trees and bushes, *are* edible, though they are palatable to differing degrees. In Tasmania long wood grubs, found in old timber and *Banksia* species, were eaten as delicacies, tasting to Europeans who tried them, 'like nuts or almonds'[2], and in Victoria pupae found at the foot of gum trees were gathered and cooked in the ashes. These were apparently the pupae of processional caterpillars. Also in Victoria grubs were cut out of trees and eaten live 'with as much pleasure as a white man eats an oyster'.[3] The hunters carried special small hooked wooden implements to insert into the trees and haul the grubs out. Another large, fat grub was found on the banks of marshes. These could be drowned out of their holes, cooked and eaten.

In Queensland, historical accounts speak of edible grubs found in 'dead' hickory trees, in bluegum saplings and at the base of the grass-tree *Xanthorrhoea* species.[4] Hunters looked for borer dust on the ground beneath the trees and scaled them until they found the hole, or they noticed dead leaves in the centre of grass-trees and knew the larvae were doing their destructive work.

WITCHETTY GRUBS   *Cossidae* spp.

Witchetty grubs are the most important insect food of the desert and a much valued staple in the diet of women and children. Men also love witchetties but seldom dig them. By the time the women have returned to camp, there are small pickings left, the women and children having already eaten well of the grubs in their raw state.

Marinka Nungala from Papunya feasts on freshly dug witchetty grubs.

PHOTO: LEO MEIER/WELDON TRANNIES

Linda Sideek and Rebecca Kamilyna search for grubs in
the roots of witchetty bushes (*Acacia kempeana*).

PHOTO: HAROLD WELDON/WELDON TRANNIES

The grubs are eaten raw or lightly cooked in the ashes.

PHOTOS: HAROLD WELDON/WELDON TRANNIES

Witchetty grubs are found in the superficial roots of *Acacia kempeana* bushes, commonly known as 'witchetty bush' around Alice Springs and central Australia. A group of women, usually with older children, will always stop for witchetties if they come to a likely stand of bushes. These days flattened crowbars are highly regarded as tools as they require less physical effort than the older sharpened mulga digging sticks. Low to the ground, bending beneath the spreading branches, the women jab the ground into the roots with the point of the bar or stick. It takes skill and practice to determine the direction of the roots by close examination of the hardened earth surface. The women move around the bush jabbing at roots until they feel them give. This indicates that they have located the grubs. Sections of root are then levered out of the ground or chopped off with tomahawks. The huge fat grubs may be 10 centimetres long and 2 centimetres in diameter, though many are much smaller.

After a good haul and a snack of a few here and there, the women carry some home either in traditional wooden coolamons, jam tins or other containers (pockets come in handy, too!). Children are usually indulged during a witchetty harvest and eat their fill. The grubs leak a brown watery juice all over the fingers when held. After collecting several, my hands had brown dribble marks all over them as though I had been painting with furniture stain, but my companions stopped my attempts to wipe them, commending me for 'looking like a proper *kunga* (woman) who could find bush tucker'. At Mt Liebig, the women collecting witchetties told me 'They are fat in summer time. When you're perishing you take one of these, feel good.'

The grubs are cooked quickly in the ashes, care being take to push away all coals. With a long stick they are very gently rolled in the hot ash several times and checked from time to time. They swell and the skins stiffen. I have eaten these delicacies on many occasions and consider them a luxury food of world class, unique to Australia. The skin is crisp, like roast chicken, and the insides become solid and bright yellow, like fried egg. They have frequently been likened to almonds in taste.

HONEY ANTS *Melophorus bagoti*

Honey ants are among nature's more extraordinary creations. As a means of drought endurance, the working ants gather honeydew and nectar from scale insects and psyllids and feed it to other workers who become mere nectar-storage vessels, or 'honey-pots', with tergum and sternum appearing as dark patches in the greatly distended abdomen. These helpless bloated ants are kept safe from the effects of drought in underground galleries and regurgitate some of their nectar to feed the other workers when solicited.

Women of central Australia, particularly in the desert areas of the MacDonnell Ranges, gather these ants from nests under mulga trees to rob

Graffiti on the store wall at Papunya.

PHOTO: LEO MEIER/WELDON TRANNIES

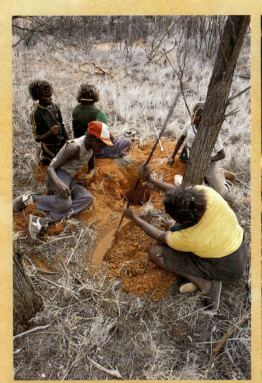

The desert near Papunya is honey ant country.
Groups of women, watched by their children, search for
the small hole in the red earth, and must then dig up to
a metre deep to search the side chambers of the nest
for the sweet nectar-storing morsels.

PHOTOS: LEO MEIER/WELDON TRANNIES

Tjupi Tjukurrpa, Honey Ant Dreaming, a contemporary painting by Entalura Nangala depicting the journey of the honey ants ancestors to Warumpi rockhole.

PHOTO: REG MORRISON/WELDON TRANNIES

them of the honey stored in their distended abdomens, swollen to the size of grapes. The nest consists of a vertical shaft, which may descend from 1.8 metres to 2.4 metres, along which horizontal shafts house honey ants in every chamber. The women must dig deeply to gather a small handful of prized ants.

Honey ants are particularly plentiful around Papunya, named for the ant itself—literally 'Honey Ant Dreaming', and many contemporary Aboriginal paintings from Papunya are symbolic stories recounting the travels of the ancestral honey ant people to Papunya.

INSECT ACTIVITY ON PLANTS

Sugar bread. These sweet-tasting crusty patches on gum leaves are the results of insect activity.

PHOTO: HAROLD WELDON/WELDON TRANNIES

The activities of insects on plants result in a number of edible substances including the galls on acacias and lerp, crusty exudations on gum leaves. This sweet-tasting lerp or manna (to give it the biblical title) was once prized by Aborigines all over the continent, particularly in the southeast where it was enjoyed for its sugary taste and also made into drinks (see Chapter 10). Arrente (Aranda) people of central Australia still gather this substance. Children from Yipirinya Aboriginal primary school in Alice Springs are taken on bush food-gathering trips as part of general school activities and continue to learn about Arrente foods from the older experts. In this area it is commonly called 'sugar bread', or in Arrente *merne peralke.*

Galls on bloodwood trees are formed by an insect. On hunting trips the galls are gathered and split to reveal a small, but refreshing amount of liquid and the edible grub.

PHOTOS: LEO MEIER/WELDON TRANNIES

Bloodwood (*Eucalyptus terminalis*) galls are the result of the activities of an insect, *Apiomorpha pomiformis,* which feeds on the bloodwood's juices. The female insect burrows under the bark, irritating the tree so that it forms a gall around her. The grub or 'bug' has sucking but no biting mouthparts and lives inside the gall for its entire life.

Old galls can be seen on almost every large *Eucalyptus terminalis* tree in the MacDonnell Ranges. The juicy caterpillar and its watery surround are only found in fresh but 'mature' galls of light tan colour. The old dark brown ones are dry and inedible. On long hunting trips these galls offer people a small refreshing drink as there is sometimes a dessertspoon of liquid inside, as well as a juicy grub in its edible inner gall case. Among the Pitjantjatjara they are known as desert apples; in Alice Springs they are called wild coconut.

Smaller insect galls on mulga trees (*Acacia aneura*) are also eaten whole in desert areas.

GREEN ANTS

In the Kimberley region of northwest Australia during the growing time of the wet season, root crops become sour. To make them palatable people collect green ants' nests and squash the ants into pounded edible bulbs of the *Microstemma* species. This gives the food a lemony taste.[5]

SIXTEEN

HERBAL MEDICINE

Aborigines who have been brought up to live at least partially off their own lands are familiar from childhood with the multiple properties of many plants. The fruits of a particular bush may be eaten, the roots made into dye and the sap or bark used as medicine. As Banduk said, 'All my foods have so many other uses.'

Aboriginal herbal medicinal knowledge has been gleaned by the best scientific technique of all – extensive trial, and presumably error, and observation of the results, not on animals in test laboratories but on human patients over thousands of years. Potent cures were recognised and the intricacies of their preparation and uses passed on through generations.

Most bush medicines are used simply, as inhalants, antiseptics and 'rubs' or liniments. Only a few are drunk or eaten. A bilingual booklet explaining bush medicine produced by the Warlpiri Literature Centre gives a strong warning to Aboriginal health workers and other readers: 'You must be very careful so as not to poison anyone. Make sure you have the right plant. Ask an old person and wait until you are really sure because some plants are very poisonous.'[1]

Above: Dry and fresh leaves of aromatic native lemon grass
(*Cymbopogan ambiguus*) can be sniffed for headaches or colds.

Musty Sideek boils the dark inner bark of central
Australian river red gums to make an antiseptic liquid.

Maude Nungarai collects small branches of *Prostanthera striati-flora,* a poison used in waterholes to stun emus so that they can be easily caught.

PHOTO: LEO MEIER/WELDON TRANNIES

In traditional communities a person became sick for one of three reasons: a natural physical cause was responsible, a spirit was causing harm, or the sickness was due to sorcery. Natural illnesses included all types of injury, eating excesses or imbalances and minor sores, boils and bites. Spirits were angered when a person disobeyed tribal laws by entering forbidden territory, looking at sacred objects or eating taboo foods. In Cape York, for example, Joyce Hall explained that pregnant women and women with young babies must not eat brolga or emu flesh because 'the bird spirit might peck that baby on the head and make him sick or die'. Sorcery or malevolent magic perpetrated by other people was believed to cause some illness and death. In this case the victim was attacked secretly by agents with malevolent powers and at some later time would mysteriously become very sick and die.

Whatever the cause, herbal medicines are initially used to treat the patient and alleviate symptoms. In serious illnesses believed to have 'deeper' causes, where herbal remedies fail, the healer can use medicinal charms and magic or even sorcery. Certain individuals in the community are doctors or spiritual healers close to the spirit world and have magic bags of medicines. A young girl of twelve from Yirrkala on a holiday with me in Sydney told me of an old man who camped alone near her family on the beach: 'He can do magic, he talks to *mokoys* [spirits]... [then whispering] I've seen his bag, it has *mokoy* blood in it and he *eats* it!'. Such a person is known as *marrnggitj* at Yirrkala, and is summoned to help in cases of illness where no known physical cause is to blame, or where herbal remedies and European medicine are failing and sorcery is suspected.

Other people in each community, usually women, are accepted as the herbal medicine authorities, though everyone knows the plants commonly used for complaints such as headaches, diarrhoea and vomiting, small sores and aching muscles. Nevertheless, if the assistance of the herbal medicine healers is sought, the healers can expect favours in return from those who are cured.

The need to keep wounds and treatments for eyes and ears sterile is apparently well known. Wounds are frequently cleansed with sterile urine rather than water, and ears (and sometimes eyes) are treated with herbal infusions made with breast milk, another sterile body liquid with a much more gentle non-astringent action on sensitive membranes than urine.

White clay is ground, mixed with water and eaten as a medicine, a practice similar to the Western medicinal use of kaolin.

PHOTO: JENNIFER ISAACS

Clay is eaten, both as a food and as a medicine. On Groote Eylandt pregnant women eat it 'to make their stomachs cool', or if they are hungry as, they report, it tastes like fish. In Cape York, Joyce Hall told me that old people always ate white clay taken from the beach, but first they would wash, strain and settle it. She said it was good for coughing or tuberculosis. In other areas clay is eaten for diarrhoea just as kaolin is administered in Western medicine.

Bites and stings of sea creatures and insects are treated by a mixture of remedies, the pharmacological basis of which has never been tested but which would certainly prove interesting. Scorpion bites are instantly treated by crushing the insect itself and rubbing it on the sting. Hot sand and bush cockroaches are utilised as an anaesthetic for stingray stings. Redback spider bites near a beach are treated with heated leaves of the purple beach convolvulus (*Ipomoea brasiliensis*) and a piece of string is tied above the bite.

Crushed green ants are added to other medicines for chest complaints. On Elcho Island nursing mothers rub their breasts with a paste made from crushed ants and pupae so that babies with a cold will 'smell the rubbing medicine and feel better'.[2]

Unusual desert medicines of non-botanical origin include the cooked brains of the desert rat, which are rubbed on the chest of babies with colds, and the yellow uncooked matter from witchetty grubs, which is rubbed on the forehead for headaches. Dry finch droppings are also collected and used as a medium to mix with eucalyptus gum for treatment of sores.[3]

Literally thousands of herbal remedies have been adopted by Aboriginal people throughout the Australian continent. Sometimes twenty or so plants could be used for the one complaint. Aromatic leaves are called 'sniffing medicine' for sinusitis or head colds and the one selected depends on where people are at the time—the remedies close at hand being tried first. However, for the cure of specific ailments, young relatives are sent off to find the potent and essential leaves, bark or bulbs.

It has long been known that Australian plants contain important substances useful to medicine. What is recent, however, is an understanding and acceptance of Aboriginal expertise in medicinal botany. Researchers following Aboriginal footsteps and the information recorded by early settlers, have analysed some Australian herbal medicines. Barks of wattles and eucalypts frequently used in decoctions for dysentery contain high proportions of astringent tannin. Kino, or eucalyptus gum, may contain up to 50 per cent tannin and was used in pellets by the early European settlers to control dysentery. The medicinal use of aromatic eucalyptus oils is also known throughout the world, but the most significant components in Australian plants are perhaps the alkaloids. Bitter bark (*Alstonia constricta*) was exported during the Second World War to treat malaria and typhoid fever, probably because the taste resembles quinine. The bark, however, has been shown to contain reserpine—useful in treating high blood pressure. Species of *Duboisia* used by Aborigines as chewing narcotics and as emu poisons contain useful alkaloids such as scopolamine and tigloidine, similar in action to atropine. These were first used by Australian doctor Joseph Bancroft as a mydriatic, to dilate the pupil.

One of the most interesting facts to emerge from research into Aboriginal medicines in recent years is the correlation of medicinal plant uses in Arnhem Land and the Indo-Malaysian region.[4] Of thirty six species found in both areas, 89 per cent are put to similar medicinal use. This

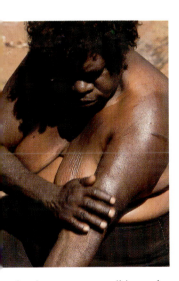

In the desert, goanna oil is used as a cosmetic and to prevent the skin from drying.

PHOTO: JENNIFER ISAACS

Maude Nungarai and women relatives return with quantities of bush medicines to treat the community at Mt Liebig

suggests that Malaysian-Indonesian medicinal knowledge was brought to Australia with successive migrations of Aboriginal ancestors, or that it was gradually built up with help from Macassan fishermen who visited the northern shores for centuries before white settlement and who traded with Aborigines for medicinal plants as well as harvesting trepang from the waters. No doubt the truth is many-faceted, but the evidence is clear that regardless of the origin of botanical knowledge, the specific remedies common to both areas are likely, if analysed chemically, to contain significant therapeutic properties.

The information that follows is not an exhaustive survey of Aboriginal medicines. The Aboriginal people who found and prepared the foods photographed in this volume also explained the multiple uses of plants as we came across them in the desert, Arnhem Land and Cape York.

Infected Sores, Burns, Boils and Wounds

Small sores developing from scratched insect bites are treated in the same way as small burns. Deep wounds, however, require different treatment.

Cocky apple trees grow along the coast of Arnhem Land and Cape York. The fruits are edible and a wound-cleansing decoction is also made from the crushed inner bark.

PHOTO: JENNIFER ISAACS

COCKY APPLE   *Planchonia careya*

Sores and burst boils are treated with a warm decoction from the crushed inner bark. When the water turns red from the bark, it is poured over sores and boils. The roots are also used for burns. When smashed, the roots are quite moist and this liquid is rubbed gently over burns. Solutions made with the bark contain saponins that foam like soap and the practice is similar to the modern use of pure soap flakes to clean infected ulcers.

PAPERBERRY   *Grewia retusifolia*

The leaves of this widespread herbaceous plant, known as *muta muta* at Yirrkala, can be used as an antiseptic. The leaves are pounded and soaked in water and the liquid is poured over small sores or wounds. Boils are 'opened' with an infusion made from the crushed roots.

SALTWATER RUSH   *Eleocharis dulcis*

On Groote Eylandt only the reeds growing in saltwater swamps are used as medicine, though they are the same as those growing in fresh water. The rushes are soaked thoroughly in sea water and the liquid poured into the wound, then the soft hollow stems are packed over the injury. They adhere and seal the wound. These stems are treated as for sores but no extraneous fibre or plant matter is allowed to enter the wound. Smoke or urine is often used as a cleanser. Wounds are sometimes packed with clay or bound with roots and bark of the same medicinal plants used as antiseptics.

Many *Eucalyptus* species can be used medicinally. Arnhem Land people infuse the red tips of ringybark *(Eucalyptus tetrodonta)* to make an antiseptic.

STRINGYBARK   *Eucalyptus tetrodonta*

The very young red leaves of the common stringybark tree, or *gardayga* in Yirrkala, are crushed and mixed with water. Infected skin sores are treated by washing the skin with the infusion. The inner bark is also of medicinal use when shredded and soaked in water. It heals small mouth sores when used as a mouthwash. Wounds can also be packed with this pounded inner bark and covered with a paperbark bandage tied with bush string. A gaping wound can be closed a little with the sticky juice from the stems of wild orchids (also used as fixatives for bark paintings).

BUSH GRAPE   *Cissus* sp.

This low vine or *lingarr* twines through the lower storey of the open stringybark forests of northeast Arnhem Land and is also widespread in other states. The blue-black grape-like edible fruits are crushed and rubbed on the skin for rashes and irritations. It is also used as a bush remedy for ringworm.

Leaves of a bush grapevine *(Cissus* sp).

MAANYARR   *Avicennia marina; Alphitonia petriei*

Scabies is endemic in many Aboriginal communities and in its advanced form the body can be covered in sores from infected scratches. Herbal healers have applied one of the strongest traditional 'sore' medicines to the treatment of scabies, apparently with some success, though reinfection usually occurs. Dead branches of *maanyarr* are gathered from mangrove areas behind a beach. These are burned in a well in the centre of a fire to produce a pure white ash. When mixed with water and applied to the skin

Banduk Marika gathers dry branches of *maanyarr (Avicennia marina)*. Burnt to a white ash, this is an excellent treatment for skin infections. It is mixed with water and applied to the skin.

PHOTO: JENNIFER ISAACS

Bulb and leaves of the sand lily, dug from the swamp at Yirrkala. This is used as a dressing and to heal large wounds.

PHOTO: JENNIFER ISAACS

all over the body it produces an intense burning sensation, somewhat similar to western treatments such as Ascabiol (benzyl benzoate). The ash and water paste is also used to treat sores, cuts, boils, burns and ringworm.

WHITE SAND LILY   BUSH LILY   *Crinum asiaticum; C. uniflorum*

This, according to Dhuwandjika, is a 'strong medicine'. The large onion-like bulbs are crushed and soaked in water and the crushed bulb and liquid are applied to large infected sores and wounds as healing dressing. On Groote Eylandt it is particularly used for abscesses in the rectum. The plant has large strap-like leaves and an onion bulb the size of a grapefruit. It is found near waterholes and in damp forest areas of Arnhem Land. The crushed bulb is not inserted into deep wounds; only the liquid is poured in.

JIRRPIRINYPA   *Stemotia viscosa*

This very aromatic herb grows to a height of around 50-65 centimetres in well-watered areas of the central desert. It has purple flowers. Maude Peterson harvested this shrub near Mt Liebig to make a disinfectant liquid by crushing and boiling the leaves and stems. This is used in the desert for sores and as an eyebath. Termed a 'sniffing and rubbing medicine' only, it must not be drunk.

RIVER RED GUM   *Eucalyptus camaldulensis*

The beautiful spreading trunks of the central Australian river red gums offer a powerful antiseptic called *purra undapa* by the Pintubi. The dark inner bark is boiled 'until the red gum is coming out'. When it is cool it is used as a rubbing medicine for sores such as those from scabies. Charlie

The red liquid made by boiling the dark inner bark of desert river red gums is rubbed on the skin for a range of skin irritations and small abrasions. It is a powerful traditional antiseptic used by desert communities.

PHOTOS: LEO MEIER/WELDON TRANNIES

Tjungarrayi from Papunya who demonstrated its use to me reminisced: 'When I was small my mother put this medicine on sores. We can shower with this one, rub it on with soft grasses or our hands.'

CHEESE FRUIT; Great morinda   *Morinda citrifolia*

These fruit are called *guniniyi* at Ramingining and *burukpili* at Yirrkala. The egg-sized soft pulpy fruits of the morinda are eaten when ripe, but can be used as medicine when still green. On Groote Eylandt they are crushed and placed directly on sores.

NATIVE PINE   *Callitris columellaris*

In the Centre, these Australian aromatic pine trees are occasionally found on the sides of rocky hills. Maude Peterson and her family from Mt Liebig collected some of these pine branches from Wangardi country, between Mt Liebig and Papunya. The leaves are ground quite finely and boiled in water. This is a 'washing' medicine for the treatment of sores and scabies, and can be rubbed on the chest to relieve coughing, rather like Vicks Vaporub.

Desert pines *(Callitris columellaris)* grow on rocky outcrops in the western desert. The fresh green needles are chopped up and boiled to make a 'washing medicine'.

PHOTOS: LEO MEIER/WELDON TRANNIES

In northern Australia the tips of young paperbark trees are crushed and the scent breathed deeply to clear sinus congestion.

PHOTO: LEO MEIER/WELDON TRANNIES

Green ants' nest.

PHOTO: JENNIFER ISAACS

HEADACHE, COUGHS AND COLDS, ACHES AND PAINS

PAPERBARK LEAVES   *Melaleuca* spp.

For headaches, coughs and runny nose, the tips of very young paperbark trees growing around swamps are crushed in the hands and sniffed deeply. The leaves are also soaked in hot water on the fire and the steam inhaled, after which the leaves and liquid are rubbed on the forehead. Broad-leaved paperbark leaves are also made into an infusion and drunk in small quantities for coughs. This infusion can be poured over the body for generalised aches and pains. This medicine was once used throughout Australia.

GREEN ANTS   *Oecophylla smaragdina*

To cure headache the nests of green ants are squashed into a dish with water. A little can be drunk, or the wet mass can be placed on the forehead. This treatment has mainly been observed in northeast Arnhem Land and offshore islands.

The distinctive white-trunked ghost gum of the central desert. The sap is a strong disinfectant.

PHOTO: HAROLD WELDON/WELDON TRANNIES

GHOST GUM   *Eucalyptus papuana*

The sap, in both liquid and crystallised form, is collected and soaked in water or boiled to make a strong disinfectant. This, and similar disinfectants from eucalyptus sap, are used throughout the continent. It is also used as a liniment to ease cramps or pains.

SHELF OR PLATE FUNGI   *Phellinus rimosus*

The common plate fungus found on trees and upright dead trunks in Arnhem Land is used for headache, coughs and sinus congestion. At Yirrkala, Dhuwandjika and Mararu gathered only dry fungi, but selected large ones for preference. They made a fire of the fungi and inhaled the smoke.

Plate fungi collected from the dry forest in eastern Arnhem Land.

PHOTO: JENNIFER ISAACS

LEMON GRASS   *Cymbopogon ambiguus*

The wild and strongly scented desert lemon grass is used as a 'drinking and rubbing medicine' by northern desert tribes. Among the Warlpiri it is called *kalpalpi;* to the Pintubi it is *tjanpi.* The grass is found along watercourses and at the base of rock outcrops where water run-off has made the soil suitable for herbs and grasses. The plant is uprooted and dried in the sun, then chopped or ground between stones and boiled. The resulting yellow green tea is used as a liniment for sore muscles or headaches and as an antiseptic to treat sores. Very small quantities can be drunk for bad coughs.

In the central desert, the beautifully scented
wild lemon grass grows near water sources at the base of
rock outcrops. The 'tea' made by boiling the pulverised
grass *(Cymbopogon ambiguus)* is rubbed on tired
muscles to act as a liniment and bathed on the
forehead for headache.

PHOTOS: LEO MEIER

TAMARIND   *Tamarindus indica*

Tall tamarind trees can be found around waterholes along the coast of Arnhem Land and offshore islands, often near sites where Indonesian fishermen set their camps during the trepang season. Tamarind fruits feature in much Malaysian and Indonesian cooking. To use as a medicine, Aborigines soak the fruit from inside the pods in water overnight and easily separate the pulp from seeds and fibre. The liquid and pulp, high in vitamin C, are drunk for colds.

SNAKE VINE   *Tinospora smilacina*

In all areas, headaches are sometimes cured by tightly binding the head with fibre. In the northern coastal areas pounded snake vine is sometimes used in this way.

BUSH CUCUMBER   *Melothria micrantha*

Around Papunya and Mt Liebig the women gather these green fruits about the size of cherries. They are called 'kangaroo food' but are considered 'good medicine for headaches'. The berries are simply squashed and rubbed all over the top of the head and forehead.

Bush cucumbers
(*Melothria micrantha*).

PHOTO: LEO MEIER/WELDON TRANNIES

WOMEN'S MEDICINE

Women have their own extensive herbal medicines for gynaecological use. Usually older women relatives officiate at a young girl's first menstruation and offer remedies for unduly painful menses later. Ritual cleansing, using steam produced from leaves and grasses, is common all over Australia and steam is also used to bring on breast milk.

Particular plants were used to effect abortions and others were championed as contraceptives, the latter often accompanied by magico-religious practices. Usually one or two highly skilled and experienced Aboriginal women in a community were called on to deliver babies with the help of female relatives. Men were kept fully isolated from the women during the birth of the baby.

AFTER CHILDBIRTH

There is a remarkable similarity of postnatal technique in areas ranging from Cape York and Arnhem Land to the MacDonnell Ranges in central Australia. The leaves and plants may vary but the procedure does not alter very much. A pit is dug and the medicinal steam-producing leaves are placed over a small fire inside. When the fire subsides, the green plants give off a great deal of steam. The woman who has just given birth is hoisted over the steam by her relatives and squats or sits over the pit so that

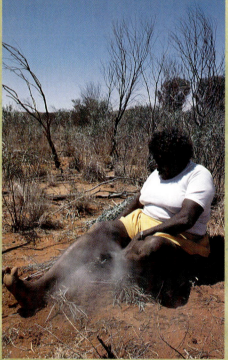

The desert shrub *Eremophila longifolia* is important
in women's medicine. A pit is dug and the leaves are placed
over a small fire within so that a great deal of steam is
given off. Maude Nungarai and the women from Mt Liebig
demonstrate how this purifying steam is used after
childbirth and to bring on breast milk.

PHOTOS: JENNIFER ISAACS

211

the steam goes right into her body. In northeast Arnhem Land the steam bath is produced by placing *rakay* rushes (*Eleocharis dulcis*) or the bark of stringybark trees over the fire. The bark from *Erythrophleum chlorostachys*, when used similarly after childbirth, is thought to sterilise the woman.

In the centre, branches of the common plains plant *Eremophila longifolia* are placed over a fire to make a cleansing steam medicine used after childbirth. Similarly, to bring on breast milk, the woman lies down on her stomach with breasts suspended over the steam-filled pit.

In Cape York leaves known as 'milkwood leaves' are placed directly on the breasts to bring on milk. Three strokes are made on each breast after the baby is born and the new mother is urged to drink nonda plum milk and eat lots of shellfish. She must not have sex for three months. Traditionally, on western Cape York, the babies are not brought to their father 'until they have their second skin'.

DIARRHOEA AND CONSTIPATION

Constipation is easily cured with an overdose of tamarind juice or wild honey, but diarrhoea requires prepared herbal remedies.

PAPER BERRY, Emu Berry   *Grewia retusifolia*

The juice prepared from pounded roots for eye problems can also be drunk for diarrhoea. This species is widely used by Aborigines and Queensland bushmen are reported to drink a decoction of the leaves to alleviate diarrhoea and dysentery.[5] Its success is probably due to the high mucilage content of the plant.

PANDANUS   *Pandanus* spp.

On Groote Eylandt the bitter inner core of the growing tip of young pandanus trees around 2 metres high is eaten raw to cure diarrhoea and stomach cramps.

FIG   *Ficus opposita*

At Yirrkala an infusion is made from the scrapings of the inner bark of the young wild fig tree mixed with water. This infusion is drunk to treat diarrhoea.

CAUSTIC WEED   *Chamaesyce* spp; formerly *Euphorbia* spp.

Various species of *Chamaesyce* are known throughout Australia to be useful bush remedies, though most are toxic. In some areas the fresh milky sap is used to heal sores. The smaller euphorbias, known as *wartworts*, are used by Cape York people for diarrhoea. At Mayngom near Weipa, Joyce

A sapling of a northern Australian fig tree. The inner bark is scraped, mixed with water and drunk for diarrhoea.

PHOTO: JENNIFER ISAACS

Janita Motton holds a small caustic weed from the bush at Weipa. Known as 'irimalong No 2 medicine', it is used externally for diarrhoea.

PHOTO: JENNIFER ISAACS

Hall collected a small specimen growing behind the sand dunes at the edge of the sea. She described how it could be prepared to treat babies with diarrhoea:

> We pulverise this plant that we call *irimalong* No.2 medicine in a nice clean place. Then we put it in an *acul* [mangrove oyster shell] with water and squeeze it to get the milky water. Then we lay the baby down, rub it on the belly, put the 'mucus' in the navel and then turn the baby over and put it on the two bottom dimples. Then put on a nice clean nappy.

Taken internally, however, the various species of euphorbia are usually violent purgatives.

EARS AND EYES

WILD PLUM   *Buchanania obovata*

At Yirrkala the outer bark of young saplings is removed and the inner bark and wet sap wood scraped, pounded and soaked in water for a few hours. All the rubbish and fibre are removed and the clear water used as an eyewash.

PEANUT TREE   *Sterculia quadrifida*

This northern tree is famous for its delicious nuts but, like many other native plants, has multiple uses to Aborigines. The soft inner bark of the stem of a young sapling is scraped and mixed with breast milk, then the liquid is squeezed into sore eyes or ears.

The inner stem of the peanut tree is scraped, mixed with breast milk and used for ear infections.

PHOTO: JENNIFER ISAACS

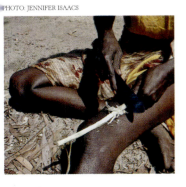

EMU BERRY   *Grewia retusifolia*

This common herb of the forests of northern Australia is both a food and medicine. The roots are cooked in ashes, pounded and soaked in water. The resulting liquid is strained and used as an eyebath for sore eyes.

GEEBUNG   *Persoonia falcata*

In eastern Arnhem Land the inner wood of the stem of a very young tree is picked and scraped. The shavings are mixed with breast milk and put in sore eyes.

TOOTHACHE

WILD PLUM   *Buchanania obovata*

In Arnhem Land the inner bark of the wild plum tree or *munydjutj* is scraped or grated finely, then pounded and packed into the tooth cavity to ease pain.

PANDANUS   *Pandanus* spp.

The inner core of the growing tip of the tree and branches is pounded and the juice mixed with water. This is gargled for sores in the mouth, including toothache.

Pandanus pulp is gargled for mouth sores and toothache.

PHOTO: JENNIFER ISAACS

COSMETICS

Good health depends on a person's complete social integration and sense of well-being. To enhance beauty and keep skin smooth and glossy, various animal oils are used as rubs. In Arnhem Land dugong oil and turtle oils are favourites. The men, but more often the women, rub the fatty oil from the meat all over the face and body and put it through the hair. Then they submerge in the salt water. This they say, makes them 'fresh and clean'. These oils are also used in Cape York as well as coconut oil, extracted by boiling up scrapings of coconut flesh. In the desert, goanna oil serves the same purpose. The oils are not merely cosmetic but protect the skin from drying and cracking in the harsh outdoor climate.

'Soaps' are made from leaves. In eastern Arnhem Land young girls wash themselves with the crushed leaves of a bush passionfruit vine, which make a bubbly lather. A similarly used plant is called 'shampoo tree' by Weipa people. This is the common *Alphitonia excelsa*, a small, slender tree of the open woodland. The distinctive soft leaves are green on the upper surface and white beneath. Thancoupie makes her own 'soap' by gathering these leaves from her Cairns garden and roughly and vigorously 'washing' them in a bucket of water until soapy bubbles rise to the surface.

Cora Yunkaporta, from Auru-kun, lathers up 'soapy-leaves' (*Alphitonia excelsa*).

PHOTO: VIC CHERIKOFF

CHEWING TOBACCO

A number of plants are still used as indigenous 'tobaccos', including the *pituri* of northern desert tribes and *mingulpa* of the Pitjantjatjara and southern people.

Below right: Maudie Nungarai enjoys her wad of *pituri (Duboisia hopwoodii)*.

PHOTO: JENNIFER ISAACS

NATIVE TOBACCO; Pituri   *Duboisia hopwoodii*

It is remarkable that Aborigines should have discovered a plant containing a potent nicotine, one of the most widely used habitual drugs. Pituri contains d-nor-nicotine, an alkaloid four times more potent than nicotine, and was once an important item of trade. When ground and combined with ashes into balls, it has a marked intoxicating effect. The ashes may be acacia or eucalyptus. This plant must not be confused with *Duboisia myoporoides*, used in waterholes to stun emus, but not chewed.

TOBACCO; Mingulpa   *Nicotiana* spp.

These wide-leaved plants are found infrequently but are the source of much satisfaction and pleasure to the Pitjantjatjara. The leaves are ground up fresh or dry and mixed with the ash of mulga. Like *pituri*, they are chewed. When not in use, both *pituri* and *mingulpa* are kept in balls behind the ear.

Pitjantjatjara women eagerly seek out stands of the chewing 'tobacco', *mingulpa*, which is ground and mixed with ash.

PHOTOS: REG MORRISON/WELDON TRANNIES

215

Appendix

TABLE OF PLANT FOODS

This listing includes many foods no longer gathered, as well as those eaten today. It has been compiled from a number of previously published sources, complemented by Aboriginal comments and observations of current practice. The region listed refers to Aboriginal usage; the actual occurrence of the plants may be wider. Food values have been provided by researcher Vic Cherikoff of the Department of Nutrition, University of Sydney.

Edible seeds of the witchetty bush (*Acacia* species).
PHOTO : LEO MEIER/WELDON TRANNIES

BOTANICAL NAME	COMMON NAME	REGION	USE
Abelmoschus moschatus	Creeping hibiscus	WA	Important root crop in Kimberleys.
Acacia spp.	Wattle	All states	Gum is collected from notches cut in the bark of trees and soaked with honey or manna to make a sweet liquid. FOOD VALUE: Acacia seeds are exceptionally nutritious, with higher protein and fat contents than wheat, rice or even some meats. Gums are good sources of dietary fibre.
Acacia aneura	Mulga	Central desert	Seeds roasted and ground for damper. FOOD VALUE: High in energy, protein and carbohydrate.
Acacia coriacea	Wiry wattle	Central desert	Large black dry seed ground for flour or eaten whole when green. Has a delicious sweet flavour. Beverage produced by steeping seed with cap in water. FOOD VALUE: High in energy, protein, fat, carbohydrate and water; good trace elements.
Acacia cowleana	Hall's Creek wattle	Central desert	Seeds cooked and ground with water to make fine, sweet paste. FOOD VALUE: High in energy, protein and carbohydrates.
Acacia difficilis	River wattle	Arnhem Land, Groote Is.	Brown fibrous bark gives off large quantities of a clear brown edible gum if injured. FOOD VALUE: A good source of carbohydrate and fibre.
Acacia dunnii	Elephant-ear wattle	WA	Large leaves used to wrap food for cooking in bush oven or hot ashes; lily seeds are wrapped in these leaves.
Acacia estrophiolata	Ironweed	Central desert	Seeds parched and ground. Gum also eaten. FOOD VALUE: High in energy, carbohydrates and fibre.
Acacia kempeana	Witchetty bush	Central desert	Seeds roasted and ground: witchetty grubs living in roots also eaten. FOOD VALUE: High in energy, protein and carbohydrates.
Acacia ligulata	Umbrella bush	Central desert	Seeds ground and roasted for damper. Grubs in roots eaten.
Acacia murrayana	Murray's wattle	Central desert	Seeds ground and roasted for damper. FOOD VALUE: High in energy, protein and carbohydrates.
Acacia notabilis	Black wattle	Central desert	Gum eaten and seeds ground and roasted for damper.
Acacia pyrifolia	Kanji bush	Central desert	Seeds ground and roasted for damper.
Acacia sophorae	Coastal wattle	Tasmania	Green seeds lightly roasted in pods and eaten.
Acacia stenophylla	River cooba	Vic, NSW, SA	Found along Murray River. Seed pods roasted and seeds eaten.
Acacia tetragonophylla	Dead finish	Central desert	Seeds ground and roasted for damper.
Acacia tumida	Pindon wattle	WA	Seed pods can be eaten raw or the pods can be cooked in ashes after seed eaten.
Atacia victoriae	Bramble wattle	Central desert	Seeds ground and roasted for damper. FOOD VALUE: High in energy, protein and carbohydrates.
Acmena smithii	Lillypilly	Vic, NSW, Qld, northern Australia	Medium tree with white flowers, followed by white, pink or purple fruits. Widely eaten and also popular with early settlers for making jam. FOOD VALUE: Good source of water; some minerals.
Adansonia gregorii	Boab	Northern Australia	Large round fruit (10 cm in diameter) eaten. Trunk and roots can also be tapped for water.
Aleurites moluccana	Candlenut	Qld, NT	Nuts must be roasted before eating. FOOD VALUE: High in energy, fat and protein.
Allocasuarina verticillata	Mountain she-oak	Vic, NSW, Tas, SA	Leaves and young cones chewed raw when thirsty.
Alocasia macrorrhiza	Cunjevoi	Cape York, Qld, NSW	Rainforest plant. Roots soaked to remove toxins, then pounded and made into cakes.
Alpinia spp.	Wild ginger	Cape York, Qld, NSW	Buds, stem and root eaten raw, leaves used for flavouring.

BOTANICAL NAME	COMMON NAME	REGION	USE
Amaranthus mitchellii *A. grandiflorus*		Central desert	Seeds made into damper.
Amorphophallus variabilis	Pink lily	Arnhem Land, Melville Is.	Found in 'jungle'. Tubers up to 15 cm in diameter are used and must be cooked for 24 hours.
Ampelocissus acetosa	Native grape	Northern Australia	Vine grows in jungle or near beaches. Fruit eaten and thick root cooked: important food in Kimberleys, WA.
Amyema linophyllum *A. maidenii* *A. pendulum*	Mistletoe	All states	Berries eaten FOOD VALUE: Moderate energy, water; small amount of protein and fat. Good source of vitamin C.
Amyema sanguineum	Mistletoe	Central desert, northern Australia	Sweet, sticky berries eaten, flowers eaten for nectar from desert to Kimberley area.
Anguillaria dioica	Lily	Vic, NSW	Edible tubers.
Antidesma bunis		Cape York, Qld	Small, sour cherry-like fruit found on beaches in the Cairns area.
Antidesma dallachyanum	Herbert River cherry	Cape York, Qld	Small, sour cherry-like fruit that makes good jam and jelly. Once common around Cairns but disappearing as swamps are cleared.
Antidesma ghaesembilla	Black currant tree	Northern Australia	Small tree with small, deep red cherry-like fruit in bunches. Tastes very sweet raw. Widespread from Qld to Kimberleys.
Aponogeton elongatus	Waterlily	WA	Yellow-flowered waterlily with edible tuber that is cooked in ashes and peeled to eat.
Araucaria bidwillii	Bunya pine	Qld, northern NSW	Bunya nuts were formerly eaten at large-scale gatherings. FOOD VALUE: Very high energy; some water; very good protein, carbo-hydrate and fat; many trace elements.
Arthropodium milleflorum	Vanilla lily	Vic, NSW	Edible tuberous roots.
Arthropodium strictus	Chocolate lily	Victoria	Flower has strong chocolate/caramel perfume in spring: roots roasted or eaten raw. Older roots hammered before eating.
Astroloma humifusum	Ground berry, native gooseberry	All states except Qld and NT	Edible fruit has a sweetish pulp and a large seed.
Atriplex nummularia	Old man saltbush	Central desert	Large quantities of seeds produced after flowering in spring and autumn. Seeds ground into flour mixed with water to make dough and cooked in coals.
Avicennia marina	White mangrove	Cape York	Seed or cotyledon cooked. Baked in ground oven for two hours then leached in water and mashed.
Banksia spp.		All states	Flowers sucked for nectar.
Banksia dentata	Swamp banksia	Arnhem Land	Copious flow of nectar is collected from flowers early in the morning.
Banksia marginata	Silver banksia	Vic, NSW	Nectar sucked from flowers or flowers soaked in water to produce a sweet liquid.
Beilschmiedia bancroftii	Yellow walnut	Cape York, Qld	A rainforest tree that bears great quantities of nuts.
Billardiera scandens	Apple berry	Vic, NSW	Pleasant-tasting berries were eaten raw.
Blechnum indicum	Swamp fern	Arnhem Land, Qld	Underground stems are hammered to break fibres, then roasted in ashes. Can be eaten any time but best during the Dry.
Boerhavia diffusa	Tar vine	Central desert, northern Australia	Ground creeper with edible root that is roasted in fire — considered a good food from desert to Kimberleys, where several varieties are used. FOOD VALUE: Moderate energy; high water and carbohydrate content.
Brachiaria piligera *B. miliiformis*	Hairy armgrass; Green summergrass	Central desert	Seeds milled with water and baked.
Brachychiton spp.	Kurrajong	Central desert, northern Australia, NSW, Vic	Water-bearing trees whose roots can be tapped for water in times of drought.
Brachychiton diversifolium	Northern kurrajong	Arnhem Land	Large seeds roasted to burn off irritant hairs, then pounded and eaten. FOOD VALUE: Very high water content; some energy.

BOTANICAL NAME	COMMON NAME	REGION	USE
Brachychiton gregorii	Desert kurrajong	Central desert	Seeds and roots used: seeds collected from crow droppings at waterholes. FOOD VALUE: Very high water content; moderate carbohydrate.
Brachychiton paradoxum	Red flowering kurrajong	Central desert	Large seeds roasted to burn off irritant hairs then pounded and eaten. Sometimes mixed with honey or nectar. Pleasant nutty flavour. FOOD VALUE: High energy content.
Brachychiton populneum	Black kurrajong	Vic, NSW, central desert	Young roots, gum and seeds eaten: seeds are hard, but can be crushed. FOOD VALUE: High energy, protein, fat and carbohydrates.
Bruguiera gymnorrhiza	Orange mangrove	Cape York	Fruit pulped, soaked and mashed through a basket before being eaten. FOOD VALUE: High in protein.
Bruguiera rheedii	Mangrove	Cape York	Fruit and germinating seed eaten after involved process of cooking, pounding and washing. An important staple food, resembling the yam, *Dioscorea bulbifera,* when prepared.
Buchanania spp.		WA	Tree with edible fruit and root. Fruit eaten raw; root cooked, hammered to make soft and mixed with gum if available.
Buchanania arborescens	Gooseberry	Cape York, Arnhem Land	Found in monsoon forests; fruit eaten in Wet season.
Buchanania muelleri	Wild plum	Arnhem Land, Qld	Fruit may be harvested in wet season and dried like prunes, rubbed with red ochre and stored for months before being reconstituted with water.
Buchanania obovata	Wild plum	Northern Australia	Fruit (1 cm in diameter) grows in clusters and is eaten raw. Important and popular food from Qld to Kimberleys. FOOD VALUE: A good source of vitamin C.
Bulbine bulbosa	Native leek	Vic, NSW	Edible tubers, common in grassy woodland areas.
Bursaria spinosa	Australian blackthorn	Vic, NSW	Nectar is sucked out of flowers.
Calamus caryotoides	Lawyer cane, fishtail	Qld	Young shoots eaten raw as 'salad'; berries also eaten.
Calandrinia balonensis	Parakeelya	Central desert	An important food: Leaves eaten as greens and as a thirst quencher. Seeds also ground to a paste with water and eaten raw or cooked. FOOD VALUE: High energy, fat, carbohydrate; moderate protein. Leaves very high in water.
Callistemon spp.	Bottlebrush	All states	Flowers sucked for nectar.
Canarium australianum	White beech	WA	Edible seed roasted in the Kimberleys.
Canavalia maritima	Large bean vine	Cape York, Qld	Beans soaked in water to remove toxins, then pounded, made into cakes, and roasted.
Canthium latifolium	Native currant	Central desert	Edible fruit plentiful on sandhills and ranges.
Capparis lasiantha C. mitchellii C. spinosa var nummularia	Wild orange, wild caper	Central desert	Edible fruit providing moderate energy, water, carbohydrates. In summer, a good source of vitamin C and thiamine.
Capparis umbonata	Native pomegranate	WA, northern Australia	Tree with large round edible fruit resembling a mango.
Carissa lanceolata	Konkleberry	Central desert	Fruit, eaten during short harvest, is a valuable addition to diet. FOOD VALUE: Moderate energy, water, carbohydrates; some protein and fat.
Cartonema parviflorum		WA	Small prickly plant with white flowers and small edible tubers that are cooked in hot ashes; an important root food in the Kimberleys.
Cassytha melantha	Dodder laurel	Vic, NSW	Parasitic vine with small edible fruits.
Castanospermum australe	Moreton Bay chestnut, black bean	Cape York, Qld, NSW	Nuts soaked and pounded to remove toxins, then made into cakes and roasted. FOOD VALUE: High water content; some protein, fat and fibre.
Chenopodium rhadinostachyum	Green crumbweed, crumbweed	Central desert	Seed soaked in water, rubbed between stones to make damper. FOOD VALUE: High protein; a little fat.

BOTANICAL NAME	COMMON NAME	REGION	USE
Cissus hypoglauca	Wild grapes	Vic, NSW, Qld	Fruit eaten. Vines, found in rainforest, used as a water source.
Colocasia esculenta	Taro	WA, NT, Qld	Large edible rhizome is cooked overnight in a bush oven. Some may need repeated pounding and roasting.
Convolvulus erubescens	Blushing bindweed	NSW, Vic	Evergreen ground creeper, ranging from mallee to coastal heath and drier forest lands. Roots eaten: one of principal foods in winter when yam daisy is out of season. Roots cooked, then kneaded on bark to form dough.
Cucumis melo ssp. *agrestis*	Native cucumber	WA	Small round fruit, now cooked by boiling, previously wrapped in paperbark in hot sand — Kimberleys.
Curculigo ensifolia	Grass potato	Northern Australia	Thick root roasted in hot sand and ashes, hammered between two stones to break fibres and eaten. Popular from Qld to Kimberleys.
Curcuma australasica	Cape York lily	Qld	Roots roasted; this plant is related to Asian Curcuma, the source of turmeric spice.
Cyathea sp.	Tree fern	Qld, Vic, NSW	Trunk split open and starchy pith eaten raw or roasted.
Cycas armstrongii *C. media*	Zamia palm, cycad	Northern Australia, NSW	Nuts cracked, dried, soaked, fermented, then roasted.
Cymbidium canaliculatum	Orchid, native arrowroot	Qld	Fruits and pseudobulbs eaten raw.
Cyperus bulbosus	Onion grass, nut grass	Central desert, northern Australia	Bulbs eaten throughout year. Important food from desert to Kimberleys. FOOD VALUE: High energy, water; some protein, fat and carbohydrates.
Dactyloctenium radulans	Button grass	Central desert	Seeds collected by ants, removed from ant's nest by women then husked by 'working with feet', winnowed and ground.
Davidsonia pruriens	Davidson's plum	Qld, northern NSW	Large rainforest tree. Leaves have irritant hairs, as do the large, dark plums; flesh is scarlet. Fruit makes good jam.
Dianella spp.	Flax lilies	Qld, NSW	Blue berries and roots are edible.
Dicksonia antarctica	Soft tree fern	Tas, Vic, NSW	Soft pithy tissue near top of trunk contains considerable quantities of starch, eaten raw or cooked.
Dioscorea bulbifera	Round yam, cheeky yam	Northern Australia	Hairy tuber on vine grows in jungles. Important food. Grated roasted tubers soaked for 6 hours before eating. FOOD VALUE: High water content; some energy fat and carbohydrates; a little protein. Very high vitamin C, even after cooking.
Dioscorea hastifolia	Native yam	Southwestern WA	Yam so prolific that it once supported a sedentary population.
Dioscorea transversa	Long yam, parsnip yam	Northern Australia, NSW	Large underground tubers growing at edge of jungle; dug from end of March to end of August. FOOD VALUE: High energy, water, carbohydrates; some protein and fat; trace elements.
Diospyros australis	Black plum	Qld, NSW, Vic	Soft purple fruit found in rainforest brush and much relished.
Diploglottis campbellii	Small-leaved tamarind	Qld	Delicious acid red fruit on medium sized rainforest tree.
Disphyma clavellatum	Rounded noon-flower	Vic, NSW	Abundant along temperate coasts and tidal marshes as well as inland saline tracts. Fleshy leaves eaten raw as a type of salad or baked. Leaves have pleasant, mildly salty flavour.
Elaeocarpus bancroftii	Queensland almond	Cape York, Qld	High yielding nut-bearing tree, intensively exploited. FOOD VALUE: Nut rich in carbohydrate, protein and fat.
Eleocharis dulcis	Spike rush, water chestnut	Northern Australia	Small tubers to around 1 cm in diameter are dug with digging sticks. Eaten raw or cooked. FOOD VALUE: High energy, water, some protein and fat; high carbohydrates; fibre; some trace elements and vitamins.
Eleocharis sp.	Tall spike rush	NSW, northern Australia	Small tubers usually eaten raw; cooked in ashes or hot sand in Kimberleys.
Endiandra palmerstonii	Black walnut	Cape York	High yielding, nut-bearing rainforest tree.

Dioscorea bulbifera, the round yam.

PHOTO: VIC CHERIKOFF

Bush potatoes (*Microstemma tuberosum*).

PHOTO: JENNIFER ISAACS

Sweet starch is extracted from the fibrous cooked roots of young trees (*Erythrina vespertilio*).

PHOTO: LEO MEIER/WELDON TRANNIES

Edible grass seeds (*Eragrostis* species) for damper or seed paste.

PHOTO: REG MORRISON/WELDON TRANNIES

Emu berries (*Grewia retusifolia*).

PHOTO: JENNIFER ISAACS

BOTANICAL NAME	COMMON NAME	REGION	USE
Entada phaseoloides	Matchbox bean	Cape York	Beans (available all seasons) are roasted, pulverised after prolonged soaking and cooked again.
Eragrostis dielsii *E. leptocarpa*	Love grasses	Central desert	A staple seed milled with water for damper.
Eragrostis eriopoda	Woollybutt grass	Central desert	Seeds (so abundant they could support several families at one well for several weeks) collected by ants after falling from seed heads. Gathered by women at ant hill entrances and milled with water. FOOD VALUE: Very high energy, protein, carbohydrates; some fat and fibre; good trace elements.
Eremophila spp.	Native fuchsia	Central desert	Flowers eaten, nectar sucked from flowers.
Eremophila latrobei	Crimson turkey bush	Central desert	Flowers eaten. FOOD VALUE: High water content; some energy; a little protein and fat.
Eriosema chinense	Bush potato	Northern Australia	Important staple food from Qld to Kimberleys. Root eaten after cooking in fire; epidermis peeled off, and eaten without further treatment. FOOD VALUE: High energy and carbohydrates; good water; some protein, fat and ash.
Erythrina vespertilio	Bean tree, coral tree	Central desert	Young shoots steamed and eaten: roots of young trees pounded and cooked.
Eucalyptus dumosa *E. gracilis* *E. oleosa* *E. paniculata* *E. populnea* *E. transcontinentalis* *E. uncinata*	Gum tree		Water trees whose roots are sometimes tapped for water.
Eucalyptus gamophylla	Blue mallee	Central desert	Seeds ground for damper: nectar drunk.
Eucalyptus gunnii	Cider tree	Tas	Holes were bored in tree to release the sweet sap which, if left for any length of time, fermented and became intoxicating.
Eucalyptus incrassata	Yellow mallee	Vic, central desert	Lateral roots cut into lengths of 20-25 cm and placed on end to yield water: up to a litre can be obtained from eight or nine metres of roots using this method.
Eucalyptus leptopoda	Tammin mallee	Central desert	Seeds and galls eaten.
Eucalyptus microtheca	Coolabah	Central desert	Branches broken off, laid on claypan. Seed capsules open after five days, and debris collected and winnowed. Seeds soaked, cleaned, dried and ground and resulting paste eaten. Roots may also be tapped for water.
Eucalyptus pachyphylla	Gum	Central desert	Nectar drunk.
Eucalyptus terminalis	Bloodwood	Central desert	Nectar drunk: large galls (known as 'bush coconuts') with tasty grub eaten. Roots may be tapped for water and trunk often harbours wild bees.
Eucalyptus viminalis	Manna gum, ribbon gum	Vic	Manna and lerp are insect exudations found mostly on leaves of eucalypts: Aborigines collected these exudations during summer to early autumn. The sugary substance was eaten raw or mixed in a wooden vessel with gum from *Acacia* trees dissolved in water. Up to nine kilograms of manna could be collected from a single tree; *E. viminalis* is the best source of manna.
Eugenia grandis	Cherry	WA	An important fruit in the Kimberleys.
Eugenia reinwardtiana	Sweet cherry	Cape York, Qld, Arnhem Land	Popular fruit on the coast.
Exocarpus cupressiformis	Cherry ballart, native cherry	Vic, NSW	Small green fruit supported on larger swollen fleshy stalk is eaten in winter when deep red; sweet and palatable.
Exocarpus latifolius	Broad-leaved native cherry	Cape York	A popular fruit that grows from rainforest to inland locations.

BOTANICAL NAME	COMMON NAME	REGION	USE
Ficus spp.	Fig	Northern Australia, Qld, NSW	Fruit from all these species is eaten raw: *F. albipila*; *F. benjamina*; *F. congesta*; *F. drupacea*; *F. fraseri*; *F. superba var henneana*; *F. hispida*; *F. microcarpa*; *F. obliqua*; *F. scobina*; *F. variegata*; *F. virgata*.
Ficus opposita	Sandpaper fig	Northern Australia	Edible fruit eaten raw — widespread food from Cape York to Kimberleys.
Ficus platypoda	Rock fig	Central desert, northern Australia	Yellow fruit, eaten raw, from desert to Kimberleys. FOOD VALUE: Some protein and fat.
Ficus racemosa	Cluster fig	Northern Australia.	Eaten from Qld to Kimberleys. FOOD VALUE: High water content; some energy; a little protein and fat.
Ficus superba var *henneana*	Sand fig, cedar fig	Arnhem Land	Fruit, around 2 cm diameter and black when fully ripe, is eaten raw. Ripens from May to December.
Ficus virens	Banyan, white fig	Northern Australia, NSW	Small fig around 1 cm in diameter is ripe in October.
Flemingia involucrata		WA	Long, thin root scraped and roasted in hot sand, hammered flat and eaten — Kimberleys.
Flueggea microcarpa		Cape York	Small, sweet fruit resembling a currant is available in great abundance from December to March.
Flueggea virosa var *melanthesioides*		WA	Bush with yellow flowers and small white fruit tasting like lillypilly fruit eaten raw — Kimberleys.
Ganophyllum falcatum	Termite tree, scaly ash	Arnhem Land	Red berries, 1 cm long, ripen in January and are eaten raw.
Gastrodia sesamoides	Native potato, potato orchid	NSW, Vic, Tas	Tubers, found in leaf litter under snow gums, were roasted. Taste reported as similar to potatoes.
Geodorum neocaledonicum	Orchid	Northern Qld	Tubers used as food — many early references to small 'yams' actually refer to orchid tubers.
Geranium solanderi	Native carrot	NSW, Vic, Tas	Large, fleshy roots roasted; available summer and autumn, common in damp habitats.
Grevillea spp.		All states	Nectar sucked from flowers or made into drinks.
Grevillea eriostachya	Inland flame	Central desert	Sweet yellow flowers eaten.
Grewia polygama G. breviflora G. orientalis G. retusifolia	Wild currant, emu berries	Northern Australia	Fruits eaten; a good drink when boiled in water.
Hakea ivoryi H. lorea		Central desert	Nectar sucked from flowers or gathered and mixed with water to make a sweet drink.
Hakea leucoptera	Needlebush	Central desert	Water-bearing root broken into pieces and stripped of bark. Blown at one end to expel water. Nectar also eaten from flowers.
Hakea suberea	Corkwood	Central desert	Nectar sucked from flowers.
Hibiscus heterophyllus	Native rosella	Qld, NSW	Leaves and buds of this plant eaten.
Hicksbeachia pinnatifolia	Monkey nut	Qld, NSW	Relative of commercial macadamia nut — very palatable. Kernel, surrounded by woody flesh with shiny red skin, can be cut out with knife. FOOD VALUE: Good energy, water, carbohydrates and trace elements; some protein and fat.
Hornstedtia scottiana	Native ginger, native cardamon	Cape York	Sweet plant with small fruiting heart shaped body with seeds inside, wrapped in small fleshy packets. The sweetest thing apart from honey. Found in swamps.
Hovea spp.		Vic, NSW, Qld	Young pods eaten; common in open and wet sclerophyll forest.
Hydriastele wendlandiana	Cut-leaved palm	Northern Australia	Top of trunk near fronds and growing shoot is cut and eaten raw after outer layer peeled off. Grows in swamps, eaten in dry season; a popular food with a pleasant nutty flavour.
Hypoxis hygrometrica	Golden star	Vic, NSW	Small fleshy tubers eaten.
Hypoxis marginata		WA	Small plant (15 cm high) with yellow flower and edible bulb eaten raw — Kimberleys.

BOTANICAL NAME	COMMON NAME	REGION	USE
Ipomoea costata	Desert yam	Central desert	Staple food in pre-European times and still eaten. Distinguished by runners when growing and by dead or dormant stems. One of the most valuable desert foods, available in all seasons. Leaves eaten like spinach. FOOD VALUE: Moderate energy; high water; some protein and fat; thiamine and vitamin C.
Ipomoea graminea I. abrupta I. brasiliensis I. gracilis	Grass leaved, hairy-leaved, mauve and purple beach convolvulus	Northern Australia	Purple, mauve and pink flowered vines; thick roots and taproots roasted in hot sand and ashes. FOOD VALUE (I. graminea): High energy and water; high carbohydrate and protein; some fat and trace elements.
Ipomoea velutina		Northern Australia	Tuberous root 4 cm in diameter and up to 38 cm long, cooked and pounded, then eaten.
Lambertia formosa	Honey flower, honeysuckle	NSW, WA	Flowers contain large amounts of honey-like fluid, sometimes covering twigs. Drunk in quantity, the fluid produces nausea and headaches.
Leichhardtia australis	Wild pear, bush banana, wild cucumber	Northern Australia	Egg-shaped fruit 8 cm long, tastes like young peas. Fruit may be roasted. Honey from flower is also eaten and leaves are steamed and eaten. FOOD VALUE: Moderate energy; high water; some protein, fat, thiamine and carbohydrates. More protein than usual in a fruit.
Leichhardtia sp.	Bush banana	Central desert	Fruit eaten. FOOD VALUE: High energy, protein, water and carbohydrates; and some fat.
Lepidium muelleri L. phlebopetalum L. oxytrichum	Peppercress	Central desert	Drought-evading plant; leaves and stems steamed on hot stones and eaten.
Leptomeria aphylla L. acida	Leafless currant bush	Vic	Small green succulent fruit eaten raw in spring. FOOD VALUE: Good source of vitamin C.
Linum marginale	Native flax	Vic, NSW	Numerous small seeds eaten. Common in grassy mountain gullies.
Livistona australis L. eastonii	Cabbage tree palm	Northern Australia, Qld, NSW	Important vegetable food: Young shoots and leaves eaten raw.
Livistona humilis	Palm	Northern Australia	Open canopy palm — stem and pith eaten. Important food.
Lomandra longifolia	Mat rush	Vic, NSW	Found in high altitude forests: bases of leaves and seeds eaten.
Lysiana exocarpi L. murrayi	Mistletoe	Central desert	Berries collected and eaten.
Macadamia integrifolia M. tetraphylla	Macadamia	Cape York, Qld	Nuts eaten after leaching and cooking. FOOD VALUE: Very high energy and fat.
Macrozamia communis	Burrawang	Northern Australia	Nuts eaten after leaching and cooking. FOOD VALUE: High water; good energy and carbohydrates; some protein, fat, fibre and trace elements.
Macrozamia miquelii M. spiralis	Burrawang	Qld, NSW, Vic	Found in rainforest; seed and heart of palm eaten after treatment.
Malaisia scandens	Burney vine, fire vine	Arnhem Land	Small red berry ripens in February; eaten raw or cooked.
Mallotus nesophilus	Yellow ball flower	Arnhem Land	White fruit covered with yellow powder. Peppery tasting kernel eaten.
Marsdenia viridiflora	Green berry creeper, native potato	Arnhem Land	Green fruit 5–6 cm long, yellow when ripe. Peeled before eating, sometimes eaten raw and sometimes cooked.
Marsilea drummondii	Nardoo	Qld, Cape York, NT, Vic	A water fern with quatrefoil leaves. Roots are pounded between stones, meal mixed with water, kneaded to a dough and baked in ashes.
Microseris scapigera	Yam daisy	Vic, NSW	Tubers a staple food of Victorian Aborigines. Roasted or eaten raw — a similar taste to sweet potato. FOOD VALUE: Moderate energy, carbohydrate, fibre; some fat and protein.

BOTANICAL NAME	COMMON NAME	REGION	USE
Microstemma tuberosum	Bush potato	Northern Australia	Bulbs eaten both raw and roasted from Qld to Kimberleys.
Morinda citrifolia	Cheese fruit	Arnhem Land	Oval fruit 5 cm long, white when ripe, collected after dropping from bush in January–February. Fruit eaten raw.
Murdannia graminea	Spiderwort	WA	Small plant with white flowers and swollen edible roots, which are cooked in hot ashes — Kimberleys.
Musa acuminata	Native banana	Qld	Narrow edible fruit have black seeds, little flesh.
Nelumbo nucifera	Sacred lotus or pink water lily	Arnhem Land	Seeds and rhizomes used as food; sweet and palatable. FOOD VALUE: Good energy; high water; good carbohydrates and fibre; some fat and protein and good trace elements.
Nymphaea sp.	Waterlily	Northern Australia	Seeds, bulbs and stems eaten. FOOD VALUE: Seeds: high energy, water and carbohydrate content; some protein, ash, fibre, fat and trace elements. Cooked bulb: high energy, carbohydrate fibre and protein; some water and fat; good trace elements.
Nymphaea gigantea	Blue waterlily	Northern Australia	Seeds, bulbs and stems eaten. Bulbs roasted in hot sand and ashes, stems eaten raw by women as gathered. Seeds sometimes ground and damper made from flour. Important staple from Qld to Kimberleys. FOOD VALUE: Stalk: high water content, a little protein, carbohydrate, fat, fibre, ash and trace elements. Seeds: moderate energy; high water and carbohydrate; some protein, fat and trace elements.
Operculina brownii	Bush potato	WA, northern Australia	Creeper with edible tuber roasted on fire — Kimberleys.
Orchidaceae Family	Orchids	Vic, NSW	Small tubers roasted. Family abundant; tubers largest in autumn and winter, but orchids easiest to find when flowering in spring.
Oryza sp.	Wild rice	Western Arnhem Land	Important seed food.
Oxalis corniculata	Yellow wood sorrel, sour grass	Vic, NSW	Small leaves eaten raw.
Pandanus spiralis	Screw palm	Northern Australia	Fruit segments chewed, seeds eaten raw. Hot to taste, stains teeth and mouth red. Fruiting September/October. Important and popular food nutritionally and socially. FOOD VALUE: Nuts extremely high in energy; very high protein and fat; high fibre; some trace elements.
Panicum australiense	Australian panic	Central desert, northern Australia	Seeds milled with water and baked for damper. FOOD VALUE: Seeds high in energy and protein; some water and fat.
Panicum decompositum	Australian millet, Mitchell grass	Central desert, northern Australia, Vic, NSW	Widely used grass seed, milled with water and baked for damper. A staple of the Bagundji seed milling economy of the Bogan and Darling rivers of NSW
Panicum effusum	Hairy panic grass	Vic, NSW	Plentiful seed ground and baked.
Parinari nonda	Nonda plum	Cape York	Important food on coast. Dry fruit, the size of a date, has a dry, mealy, nutty flavour. Can be dried, stored for later use and soaked in water to reconstitute.
Persoonia falcata	Geebung	Northern Australia, Vic, NSW	Small green fruit eaten raw. A popular food; important from Qld to Kimberleys.
Pittosporum phillyreoides	Weeping pittosporum	Vic	During autumn gum from branches was eaten. Gums high in carbohydrates; reported to have little flavour unless they contain tannin.
Planchonia careya	Cocky apple, bush mango, wild quince	Northern Australia	Ripe fruit size of a small apple, with soft pulp that must be yellow to eaten. Pulp and seeds sucked out.
Planchonella pohlmaniana *P. arnhemica*	Big green plum	Northern Australia	Fruit gathered after dropping from tree and roasted. Raked out with stick, folded in paperbark, placed on stone and hammered until squashed, then eaten. Large seeds discarded. An important and still popular food. Ripe from August to October — Kimberleys. FOOD VALUE: High energy, water, carbohydrates; some protein, fat and fibre; a few trace elements.

Fresh and dry nonda plums (*Parinari nonda*).

PHOTO: JENNIFER ISAACS

Seedpods of the northern Australian
waterlily (*Nymphaea* species).

PHOTO: JENNIFER ISAACS

BOTANICAL NAME	COMMON NAME	REGION	USE
Pleiogynium timorense	Burdekin plum	Cape York, northern Qld	Fruit looks like a plum-coloured miniature pumpkin. Fruit can be white or red inside, pulp scanty. After picking, left for a week or two until soft, then eaten.
Podocarpus lawrencei	Mountain plum, pine	Vic, NSW	Fleshy stalk of fruit edible, locally abundant in summer and autumn.
Polyporus mylittae	Native bread	Tas, Vic, NSW	A fungus that tastes like boiled rice; found near rotten trees. Widely distributed from arid country to mountain forests, but underground fungus rarely seen. Fruiting body (whitish, coarsely granular, with a rubbery, gristly texture which becomes extremely hard on drying) is eaten raw.
Portulaca oleracea	Pigweed	Central desert, Vic, NSW	Succulent plant: leaves eaten raw, roots cooked. Seeds collected in coolamon, ground, mixed with water and baked in hot ashes after being shaped into small cakes. Flavour resembles linseed. FOOD VALUE: Seed, stems, leaves, root; valuable food with good protein and water, dietary fibre and trace elements. A very rich source of minerals.
Portulaca pilosa		WA	A very small plant, growing at the base of boab trees, which has an edible tuber, cooked in hot ashes and then skinned before being eaten — Kimberleys.
Pteridum esculentum	Common bracken	Tas, Vic, NSW	Rhizomes eaten; beaten into paste with a stone and roasted in hot ashes. Black skin peeled off and eaten with meat.
Pterostylis barbata	Bearded greenhood	Vic	Tuber eaten raw or roasted; during autumn and winter, many species of orchid provided an abundance of edible tubers.
Ptychosperma macarthurii	Palm	Cape York	Rainforest palm: stem pith eaten.
Pygeum turneranum	Nut tree	Qld	In season from January to March. Nut is pounded, sifted through a dilly-bag then damped, kneaded into cakes, wrapped in wild ginger leaves and baked in ashes.
Rhodomyrtus macrocarpa	Finger cherry	Qld	Fleshy fruit (like a lengthened lillypilly) causes blindness if eaten. Aborigines knew the right time to harvest the plant.
Rhyncharrhena linearis		Central desert	Leaves and bean an important food: leaves eaten if found while hunting. FOOD VALUE: High water; some carbohydrates, energy, protein and fat.
Rubus parviflorus	Native raspberry	Vic, NSW	Small red fruits eaten raw.
Santalum acuminatum	Quandong, native peach	Central desert, Vic, NSW	Globular fruit 2–3 cm long. Stones cracked to extract kernel, eaten raw, and oil extracted for cosmetic purposes. Dehydrated fruit gathered and pounded into paste. FOOD VALUE: Kernel very high in energy, protein and fat. Fruit high in water and carbohydrates.
Santalum lanceolatum	Wild plum	Central desert	Berry eaten – considered good food. FOOD VALUE: High water content; some protein, fat and energy.
Solanum centrale	Bush raisin	Central desert	Fruits can be left to dry on bush and collected months later, mixed with water and crushed, moulded into balls and eaten fresh or dried in sun. FOOD VALUE: Very high energy, carbohydrates, protein, some fat, nectar.
Solanum chippendalei	Bush tomato	Central desert	Very prolific fruit; many kilograms can be collected in a morning. FOOD VALUE: High water and carbohydrates; some energy, protein, fat. Consistent source of vitamin C, thiamine, (vitamin B_1).
Solanum cleistogamum		Central desert	Yellow berries eaten.
Solanum ellipticum	Desert raisin	Central desert	Small perennial plant. Fruit abundant in June and July and can bear all year provided conditions not too dry. FOOD VALUE: High water content; some carbohydrates and protein; a little fat.
Solanum esuriale *S. melanospermum* *S. orbiculatum* *S. phlomoides*		Central desert, Vic	Fruit eaten raw; some types dried and soaked.
Solanum laciniatum *S. linearifolium*	Kangaroo apple	Tas, Vic, NSW	Large fruit eaten raw or roasted.

BOTANICAL NAME	COMMON NAME	REGION	USE
Solanum petrophilum		Central desert	Fruit eaten. Confined to rocky sites.
Sorghum leiocladum	Wild sorghum grass	Vic, NSW	Seeds (abundant in summer) ground and baked.
Sterculia quadrifida	Peanut tree	Arnhem Land	Seeds enclosed in a thick leathery pod which is red when ripe. Large oval seeds in black shiny skin eaten raw. Also used as a flavouring; leaves placed around fish or meat in oven.
Syzygium forte *S.suborbiculare*	Red love apple, lady apple, wild apple	Cape York, Arnhem Land	Sweet scarlet-skinned, white fleshed fruit eaten. Very large stone. A popular and important food. FOOD VALUE: High in water; some carbohydrate, protein, fat and trace elements.
Tacca leontopetaloides	Arrowroot	Northern Australia	Each plant has a pair of globular tubers, usually dug after the stem and leaves have withered. Tubers are peeled, grated, leached. The starch is dried and roasted.
Tamarindus indica	Tamarind	Arnhem Land	Tree introduced before European settlement. When fruit is ripe, shell of pod becomes thin and papery — this is discarded and pulp around large seeds eaten; seeds spat out. Rather sour pulp resembles dried apricot in appearance. Popular and important food.
Terminalia carpentariae	Wild peach	Arnhem Land	Bark chipped and clear gum eaten — a very popular food. Green, peach-like fruit eaten raw.
Terminalia ferdinandiana	Green plum	NT, western Arnhem Land	Tall slender tree with large green to yellow leaves. Fruit grows along branches and matures from March to August; looks and tastes like an English gooseberry. Not a staple; eaten especially by children. FOOD VALUE: Ascorbic acid extremely high; richest natural source of vitamin C in the world.
Terminalia grandiflora	Native almond	WA	Small tree produces edible nuts; shells cracked to eat kernel — Kimberleys.
Terminalia melanocarpa	Black fruit	Cape York	Black fruit, around 2 cm long, eaten in times of scarcity.
Themeda australis	Kangaroo grass	Vic, NSW	Seeds ground and baked. Common and prolific seeder, ripe from December to March.
Thysanotus tuberosus	Fringed lily	Vic, NSW	Roots and base of stem eaten. Edible root is in hard shell, which splits open when the tuber is cooked in hot ashes. Also eaten in Kimberleys.
Triglochin procera	Creek lily, water ribbon	Arnhem Land, Vic	Grows in billabongs — small tubers form on roots. Dug seasonally; can be eaten raw but frequently cooked.
Typha orientalis *T. domingensis*	Bulrush	All states	During spring and summer, young shoots pulled up and eaten raw. Glutinous rhizomes also roasted.
Typhonium brownii	Lily	NT, Qld	Rootstock gathered in large quantities. Roasted, hammered, then cooked again. Colour, appearance and texture of crepe rubber. Causes headache if too much is eaten.
Typhonium liliifolium		WA	Red flowered lily of flood pain. Bulb causes bad burns to the mouth without careful preparation: pounded, cooked, pounded again, cooked again, finally shaped into a sausage-like form that has good keeping qualities — Kimberleys.
Uvaria sp.	Custard finger	Arnhem Land	Sausage-shaped fruit eaten raw; Popular food. FOOD VALUE: Moderate energy; high water and carbohydrates; some protein and fat, trace elements.
Vigna lanceolata	Pencil yam	Central desert, northern Australia	Ground creeper, sometimes found growing at base of boab trees. Roots eaten raw, or cooked in hot ashes (in Kimberleys). FOOD VALUE: High water, carbohydrate; some protein and fat; moderate energy.
Vigna vexillata		Cape York,	Flattened cake made by roasting roots in fire, removing epidermis then hammering. FOOD VALUE: Very high fibre.
Vitex glabrata	Black fruit	Northern Australia	Fruit available from December to March. Important in Kimberleys.
Xanthorrhoea australis	Grass tree	All states	Flowering spike soaked in water to collect sweet nectar. Soft white leaf bases and growing point at top of stem eaten.

Appendix

TABLE OF HERBAL MEDICINES

This listing of herbal medicines includes those used historically, as well as plants used in current healing practices. Aborigines consider health and healing as a total process and use plants as a component of treatment for ailments caused by both natural and unnatural phenomena. Unfortunately the active chemical compounds of many of these potentially valuable medicines have not yet been established.

Darwin wattle (*Acacia* species) in
flower. Decoctions from both bark
and gum may be used to treat wounds.
PHOTO: JENNIFER ISAACS

230

BOTANICAL NAME	COMMON NAME	REGION	USE
Acacia spp.	Wattle	Vic	Bark used for a decoction for skin conditions such as boils and for venereal disease. Taken orally for diarrhoea during the day; pills made from bark, gum used night and morning. Gum mixed with wattle ash or bark used to treat wounds and sores.
Acacia ancistrocarpa		NT, WA	Leaves chewed with water and mixture spat on sores to stop infection. Leaves mashed in water and used to bathe sore head.
Acacia cuthbertsonii	Wattle	Central desert	Stringy bark peels readily in long tough ribbons — uncommon tree, so highly prized. Bark ribbons wrapped tightly around forehead for headaches; also used as bandages.
Acacia estrophiolata	Wattle	Central desert	Root bark heated and red liquid used to bathe sores and wounds. Effect probably explained in terms of tannin content. Gum scraped off tree and soaked until soft, then used as ointment for scabies.
Acacia farnesiana	Mimosa bush	Central desert	Thorns used to pick out splinters.
Acacia holosericea		Qld, NT, WA	Spreading shrub three to four metres high, with 'soapy pods'. Infusion of roots drunk for laryngitis.
Acacia kempeana	Witchetty bush	NT	Leaves chewed to relieve congestion or a wash made by soaking leaves in hot water.
Acacia leptocarpa	Wattle	WA	Yellow-flowered small tree; leaves hammered and soaked, then liquid applied externally. Good for sore eyes — Kimberleys.
Acacia ligulata	Wattle	Central desert	Bark boiled or soaked and drunk as cough medicine. Also good for dizziness, nerves and fits. "When man very sick, dig a hole, place embers and coals in bottom and cover with a thick layer of branches and leaves so there will be plenty of smoke. Lay sick man on branches and cover him with more leaves. Smoke heat cause sweating, sickness comes out in sweat."
Acacia lysiphloia		Central desert	Used like *A. ligulata* for 'smoking' ill people.
Acacia melanoxylon	Blackwood tree	Vic	A hot infusion of the roasted bark was used for bathing rheumatic joints.
Acacia pellita	Soap brush	NT	Body wash used to soothe aching muscles made by soaking leaves in hot water.
Acacia pruinocarpa	Wattle	Central desert	"When a woman is about to have a baby she goes to women's camp to give birth — women dig hole of crushed anthills heated to keep the mother warm. They get mulga witchetty and mantarla to make a lot of smoke. Mother first laid on top of leaves, then the baby — to smoke out the blood."
Acacia salicina	Cooba	Qld	Leaves burnt and ash smoked to produce drunkenness, drowsiness or dopiness and finally deep and lengthy sleep combined with *Duboisia hopwoodii*.
Acacia tetragonophylla	Dead finish	Qld, NSW, SA, WA, NT	Inner bark soaked or boiled and liquid drunk as a cough medicine.
Ajuga australis	Bugle	NSW, Qld, SA, Tas	Decoction of fresh leaves used to bathe sores and boils
Alocasia macrorrhiza	Cunjevoi	Qld, NSW, Vic	Antidote to sting of giant nettle tree (*Laportea gigas* and other species): milky juice rubbed on affected part. Pounded roots used to treat sting of rays and snakes, and insect bites. Warmed leaf said to relieve rheumatism, burns, boils and ulcerated sores.
Alphitonia excelsa	Red Ash	NSW, Qld, NT	Young leaf tips chewed for upset stomach and decoction of bark and wood used as liniment for muscular pains or gargled to relieve toothache.
Alphitonia petriei	White-leaf	NT	Tree burned and ashes mixed with water to form a paste for sores, boils or ringworm.
Alstonia actinophylla	Milkwood	NT	Sap collected and applied to sores. Latex painted on breast of nursing mother to improve milk supply.
Alstonia constricta	Quinine bush	Qld, NSW	A deadly poison. Latex used to cure infectious sores, though very severe on the skin.
Annona sp.	Custard apple		Inner bark of introduced custard apple tree applied to aching tooth to relieve pain.

231

BOTANICAL NAME	COMMON NAME	REGION	USE
	Ant bed	NT	Ant bed used throughout the Northern Territory for treating diarrhoea. Top surface of ant hill is removed, mixed with water and drunk. Analysis shows the mixture has a high salt content, which would give relief. Sometimes mixed with honey.
Asparagus racemosus	Wild asparagus	NT	Roots pounded with rocks and rubbed on the stomach to ease the pains of diarrhoea.
Avicennia marina	Mangrove	NT	Leaves and twigs used to ease stings from certain sea creatures. Ash obtained from burnt sticks mixed with water and rubbed on the skin for scabies.
Banksia dentata	Swamp banksia	NT	Cones burned in a hole in the ground: the patient squats in the smoke, allowing it to come up around the anal region. A cure for diarrhoea.
Barringtonia acutangula	Fresh water mangrove	Qld, WA, NT	Bark pounded between rocks and thrown into rock pools, where it produces a dark stain that fish try to avoid. They are therefore driven to one end of the pool. Sapomins also asphyxiate fish.
Boronia lanuginosa	Star boronia	·NT	Leaves crumbled into hot water and left to steep: liquid used to bathe body to soothe aches and pains such as headaches. Aromatic leaves could be crumbled in hands and scent inhaled.
Brachychiton diversifolium	Kurrajong	NT	Inner bark crushed in water and the liquid used as an eyewash.
Buchanania arborescens	Wild plum	NT, Qld	Shavings of inner bark soaked in warm water and the liquid used as an eyewash. Inner bark and sapwood pounded and soaked; infusion used as mouthwash for toothache — but not swallowed.
Buchanania obovata	Wild plum	NT	Inner bark and sapwood from young plants crushed and put in water to soak. After several hours the solid material is removed and the liquid used as an eyewash. Leaves crushed and applied to sores, boils, wounds and ringworm. Inner bark and sapwood pounded and soaked and used for toothaches, but dangerous to swallow. Ashes of burnt sapwood packed around sore tooth.
Callitris columellaris	Native pine	Central desert	Leaves and small twigs boiled and liquid patted on chest for bad colds. Also put on rashes. When used as a smoking medicine, a hole is dug and filled with leafy branches that smoke profusely when lit. The sick person stands over the hole in the smoke and sickness 'comes out' with the sweat.
Canarium australianum	Styptic tree	NT	Inner bark scraped off, pounded and applied to minor sores.
Canavalia obtusifolia		NT	Infusion of roots used for colds; also rubbed on for rheumatism, aches and pains and for leprosy.
Capparis spp.		NT	Forehead cut, then bound with bark or rag soaked in decoction of root bark to relieve headache.
Capparis lasiantha		NT	Honey from flowers used as a remedy for coughs. Plant, including roots, macerated and soaked, and water applied to swellings, snake bites, insect bites and stings.
Capparis umbonata	Wild orange	NT	Bark boiled in water until liquid turns red. The patient is washed in the fluid to relieve body aches. Infusion drunk as a treatment for sore throat and stomach pains, including diarrhoea.
Carissa lanceolata	Conkerberry	NT	Bark removed from root and root boiled; liquid used as an all-purpose rubbing, washing and drinking medicine. Also used for toothache. Pieces of root from young shrub soaked in water, liquid used as a wash for scabies. Whole plant (including roots) chipped into small pieces to collect oily sap used as a rub for rheumatism.
Cassia barclayana	Pepper-leaf senna	NT, Qld, NSW	Plant soaked in hot water and steam inhaled to relieve congestion.
Castanospermum australe	Native chestnut	Qld, NSW	Inner white bark boiled in water to make a poisonous solution allegedly placed in victim's food or drink.
Casuarina equisetifolia	Whistling tree	NT	Inner bark and sapwood shavings soaked in water and liquid gargled for toothaches.
Centaurium erythraea	Introduced centaury	Vic	Whole plant covered with boiling water; resulting bitter decoction drunk to relieve 'bilious' headaches.
Centaurium spicatum	Spike centaury	NSW	Decoction applied for piles and inflammation of genitals.

Banduk gathers branches from the scabies treatment tree, *Avicennia marina*.

PHOTO: JENNIFER ISAACS

Blossoms of the northern kurrajong (*Brachychiton diversifolium*).

PHOTO: JENNIFER ISAACS

Buchanania aborescens or *munjudj*. Bark from a young sapling is used for eye medicine.

PHOTO: JENNIFER ISAACS

Flowers of a northern *Capparis* species.

PHOTO: VIC CHERIKOFF

BOTANICAL NAME	COMMON NAME	REGION	USE
Centipeda cunninghamii	Sneezeweed	Vic	Plant boiled; resulting black liquid drunk for tuberculosis and used as a lotion for skin infections.
Centipeda thespidioides		NSW	Decoction drunk for colds, sore throats and sore eyes; very strong and causes sneezing. Poultice applied to sprained and jarred limbs.
Ceriops tagal	Mangrove	NT	Leaves used for treating sores.
Chenopodium cristatum	Crested goosefoot	NSW	Poultice applied for septic inflammation and breast abscesses.
Cissus adnata		NT	Fruit mashed and applied to stingray injuries or cuts from handling shellfish.
Citrullus colocynthis	Paddymelon	NT	Fruit warmed; juice squeezed out and dabbed on scabies or ringworm.
Clematis glycinoides	Headache vine	NT, Qld, NSW, Vic	The odour of the leaves of this plant is apparently so strong the patient supposedly forgets the headache after just one whiff.
Cleome viscosa	Tickweed	Central desert	Decoction of entire plant used for colds, sickness and sores. Head and body wash; infusion applied externally to swellings and for rheumatism.
Clerodendrum cunninghamii		NT	Leaves soaked in water and liquid drunk for general aches and pains. Leaves also soaked in water and placed on patient's stomach; liquid used for diarrhoea and vomiting.
Clerodendrum floribundum	Thurkoo	NT	Leaves and inner bark placed in a container of water and left to soak — liquid drunk or rubbed on the body to relieve colds, aches and pains.
Clerodendrum ovalifolium		WA	Used as a tobacco; leaves chewed with ashes — Kimberleys.
Convolvulus erubescens	Blushing bindweed	NSW	Decoction drunk for diarrhoea, indigestion, stomach pain.
Crinum asiaticum *C. uniflorum*	Bush lily	NT, Qld	Bulb pounded and soaked in water. The crushed bulb and liquid rubbed on sores, used to wash wounds. Thin sheets of plant material sometimes peeled off the roots and laid on the wound as a dressing.
Crotalaria cunninghamii	Rattle pod	NT	Decoction of bark used to bathe swellings on body or legs. Decoction of leaves used as an eyewash.
Cycas media *C. armstrongii*	Cycad	NT	Used specifically for spear wounds. Soft insides of the male flower stalk are combined with human urine in a paperbark container. Hot stones dropped into the container to heat liquid which is then used as an antiseptic.
Cymbidium madidum	Orchid	Qld	Seeds said to confer sterility. Bulb chewed for dysentery.
Cymbopogon spp.		NT	Decoction of root poured in ear to relieve earache. Aromatic leaves rubbed into ball and inhaled through nose to relieve colds. Infusion of leaves used as liniment or drunk for influenzas, fevers, general aches and pains.
Cymbopogon ambiguus	Lemon grass	Central desert	Whole plant dried, crushed placed in boiling water. Used as a liniment for scabies, sores, cramp and sore heads. Up to 5 ml drunk if feeling sick. Fresh grass crushed between hands and scent inhaled to relieve congestion. A very important medicine, known and used wherever it grows.
Dendrobium dicuphum	Tree orchid	NT	Bulb crushed in the mouth and spit dabbed on spear wounds. Ends of pseudo-bulbs chewed, and mucilage dabbed on burns, where skin not destroyed.
Denhamia obscura	Yellow-fruited tree	NT	Inner bark moulded into plugs for holes in the teeth. Inner bark burned and woman who wanted no more children would stand over the smoke. This treatment was believed to stop the flow of breast milk and cause sterility.
Dodonaea lanceolata	Hop bush	NT	Decoction diluted and drunk and leaves tied under belt. Also used for bathing painful areas and for snakebite.
Dodonaea polyandra	Hop bush	Qld	Decoction of root applied daily to cuts and open wounds until they heal. For stonefish and stingray stings, chewed leaf juice applied to wound and bound up for four to five days.
Dodonaea viscosa	Hop bush	NT, Qld	Used for burning to 'smoke' newborn babies. Boiled root or juice of root applied for toothache.

BOTANICAL NAME	COMMON NAME	REGION	USE
Duboisia hopwoodii	Pituri	Central desert	Contains d-nor-nicotine, an alkaloid four times more potent than nicotine. An article of barter along trade routes. Emu poison: infusion of crushed leaves is placed in animals' drinking water; will also kill humans. Leaves ground up and rolled into balls with ashes; prepared balls are also strewn near water holes to catch game, especially emus. Also used as an intoxicant; chewed and mixed into ball with ashes of *Acacia salicina* and *Geijera parriflora*, *Acacia ligulata* or eucalyptus bark. Smoke of leaves used as an anaesthetic in surgical operations.
Duboisia myoporoides	Cork tree	NSW, Qld, New Caledonia	Alkaloid-rich sap drunk to produce stupor; also used as fish poison.
Eleocharis dulcis	Saltwater spike rush	NT	Plant soaked in seawater and liquid poured over wounds. Stems packed over the area as a medicinal dressing; thought to be highly effective treatment. Moisture from decaying plant squeezed on burns and rotten pulp bound on the wound.
Eremophila alternifolia	Native fuschia	NT	One of only a few plant medicines stored for later use rather than used fresh. Branches and leaves dried in the sun for a few days, then crumbled into water and heated. Steam can be inhaled or liquid used as a wash or in small amounts as a drink for general illnesses.
Eremophila gilesii	Desert fuschia	NT	Plant heated or boiled and liquid used as a wash for scabies.
Eremophila latrobei	Emu bush, native fuschia	NT	Leafy branches picked, covered with water and boiled. Mixture can be drunk or rubbed on body to treat colds.
Eremophila longifolia		NT, NSW	Fresh plants broken up and soaked in water. The liquid is used as a medicinal bath for general sickness (and colds, by Bogan tribe in NSW). Decoction applied to sores.
Erythrina vespertilio	Coral tree	WA	Inner bark used for treatment of headaches and sore eyes. Bark and inner bark soaked in water and applied externally — Kimberleys.
Erythrophleum chlorostachyum	Ironwood, Cooktown poison tree	NT	Leaves boiled in water and liquid used to bathe sores and cuts. Infusion from bark and roots used for this purpose, also to ease stomach pains. Bark burned and women who do not want any more children stand in smoke, believed to stop flow of breast milk and cause sterility. Wood, leaves and bark used to 'smoke' person suffering from constipation. Pulverised leaves placed in nostrils to relieve diarrhoea.
Eucalyptus spp.	Gum tree	Vic	Gum mixed with water and taken internally for diarrhoea. Dental cavities filled with gum to relieve pain. John White, Sydney's first surgeon, in 1788 considered resin of red gum good astringent, effective for dysentery. Leaves of peppermint gum used to distil essential oil very good for colic.
Eucalyptus camaldulensis	River red gum	NT	Sap collected and boiled in water until it dissolves. The solution is rubbed on sores and cuts and is said to be a strong disinfectant. For diarrhoea in children the heartwood is boiled in water, and water drunk.
Eucalyptus citriodora	Lemon-scented gum	Nth Qld	When mosquitoes are troublesome, piles of branches are stacked at some distance from camp to attract insects away.
Eucalyptus dichromophloia	Bloodwood	NT	Kino or gum boiled with water, sugar added and liquid drunk to treat pulmonary complaints. Nectar used as remedy for coughs and colds. Gum also mixed with water and drunk as a general tonic and rinsed in the mouth for toothache. Gum plugged in hole of aching tooth to relieve pain.
Eucalyptus dives	Broad leaved peppermint	NSW, Vic	Used for fevers: leaves burnt and the sick person 'smoked' in the smoke of the fire.
Eucalyptus globulus	Tasmanian bluegum	Tas, Vic, NSW	Poultices made of bruised and heated gum leaves. Also, shallow pit dug, bottom covered with hot ashes, then filled with leaves. Patient lies with his back over steaming mass for backache and rheumatism. Headaches treated by inhaling steam of heated leaves; infusion of leaves drunk for colds.
Eucalyptus gummifera	Bloodwood	Qld, NSW, Vic	Exudation or gum taken internally or dusted on locally in powder form, for venereal sores. Also used with leaves and mud on wounds to stop bleeding.
Eucalyptus microtheca	Coolibah, dwarf box	Qld	Inner beaten and applied as poultice for snake bite and for severe headache.

BOTANICAL NAME	COMMON NAME	REGION	USE
Eucalyptus miniata	Woollybutt	NT	Inner bark soaked in water and liquid drunk to cure diarrhoea. Also used as a lotion for treatment of swellings.
Eucalyptus papuana	Ghost gum	Central desert	Sap or resin collected in crystallised or liquid form from wounded or infected trees. Boiled until dissolved, concentrated and bathed on sores, cramps, pains and cuts. Powerful disinfectant and when used on cuts, skin soon closes. Used by majority of central Australian tribes — highly regarded. Infusion of bark drunk for colds and to wash sore eyes.
Eucalyptus polycarpa	Bloodwood	NT	Gum is collected, dissolved in water and the liquid used as a wash for sores, cuts or burns, ulcers and yaws. Treatment repeated daily.
Eucalyptus terminalis	Bloodwood	NT	Sap collected and dissolved in boiling water. Solution rubbed on sores and cuts is said to be a strong disinfectant: mixture of sticky gum and water is dabbed on the face in the area where pain from toothache can be felt.
Eucalyptus tetrodonta	Stringybark	NT	Young shoots chewed for colds, or crushed and placed on sores and cuts. Infusion of leaves and bark drunk for aches and pains, coughs and diarrhoea. Gum boiled after dissolving in water to produce a concentrated solution that is applied to sores. An effective antiseptic. Infusion of inner bark made in hot water and drunk to stop pain and bleeding after childbirth and to 'bring on milk'.
Eucalyptus viminalis	Manna gum	Qld	Leaves applied to eyes for opthalmia and eaten for diarrhoea. Leaves contain eucalyptol and tannin.
Euphorbia drummondii	Caustic weed	Vic, NSW, WA, SA, Qld	Prostrate annual herb with milky sap and bright green leaves. Whole plant boiled and liquid applied for scabies or rubbed vigorously for pains in the chest. Bogan tribe of NSW applies latex to treat sore eyes; milky juice applied for venereal infection and genital sores. NOT TO BE DRUNK.
Exocarpus aphyllus	Leafless ballart	NSW	Decoction used for sores and colds. Also applied as poultice on chest for 'wasting diseases'.
Ficus opposita	Sandpaper fig	NT, Qld	Eyewash made by soaking inner bark in water. Leaves warmed by laying over heated stones, then placed over swollen areas of the body. Infusion drunk to treat diarrhoea. Pulverised roots also used in lagoons to stupefy fish.
Ficus racemosa	Cluster fig	NT	Inner wood scraped into a container of water and left to soak for several hours; patient later bathed in the liquid as a cure for diarrhoea.
Flagellaria indica	Supplejack	Arnhem Land	Plant bound around upper arm of children with diarrhoea or stomach pain; used in adults as a preparation for menstruation or circumcision. When chewed, firm green stem gives relief from toothache, making lips and tongue numb. Young tips cut and juice squeezed into eye. Inner part of plant stem soaked in water and used as an eyewash. Leaves soaked in water and liquid used to massage sore muscles.
Gardenia spp.		NT	Leaves and bark crumbled into hot water and left to soak until the water turns brown: liquid used as a bath for general ailments.
Gardenia megasperma		NT	Fruit used to treat toothache.
Grevillea heliosperma		NT	Fruit used to treat toothache
Grevillea pyramidalis		NT	Greenish inner bark mashed, stirred into paste with a little water and rubbed on breasts to induce lactation.
Grevillea striata	Beefwood	NT	Dried sap scraped off damaged trees and grated into a powder that is sprinkled on sores, burns and cuts. It is said to dry them and cause them to heal rapidly.
Grewia latifolia		NT	Decoction made from roots used to treat diarrhoea.
Grewia polygama		WA	Fruit said to cure diarrhoea and dysentery.
Grewia retusifolia	Paper berry, emu berry	NT	Root cooked in hot ashes, pounded, soaked in water and liquid drunk to treat diarrhoea. Leaves pounded, placed on wounds and cuts. Liquid also used for sore eyes: one person takes some of the liquid into his mouth and spits it into the eyes of the suffering patient. Inner bark of roots is pounded, immersed in water and applied to boils to soften them so that pus may be removed.

BOTANICAL NAME	COMMON NAME	REGION	USE
Gyrocarpus americanus		NT, Qld	Roots and young shoots mashed, soaked in water and liquid rubbed on for rheumatism. Infusion of roots and young shoots applied to cuts (but not fresh cuts). Wood also burnt and powdered charcoal used to heal fresh cuts and open sores.
Hakea arborescens	Yellow hakea	NT	Leaves and seed pods left in boiling water until it turns brown: liquid used as a wash for scabies.
Hakea macrocarpa	Corkwood	NT	Bark burned and the ashes sprinkled on itchy areas. Wood burnt and powdered charcoal applied to open sores and cuts. Also, the tip of a single needle is used to remove warts.
Hibiscus tiliaceus	Yellow hibiscus, cottonwood	NT	Pieces of inner bark and sapwood soaked in (salt or fresh) water, then heated with hot stones or over a fire. Liquid used to wash wounds: bark removed in strips and wrapped around wounds to cover and close them.
Imperata cylindrica	Blady grass	All states	Sharp unfolded grass leaves used to tickle the nose to cause sneezing.
Indigofera spp.		All states	Roots hammered and placed in fresh or salt water as a fish poison.
Ipomoea brasiliensis	Purple-flowered beach convolvulus, coast morning glory	NT, NSW, Qld	Leaves made into infusion for treating both marine stings and for relieving the itch of scabies. Whole plant boiled and decoction drunk to cure venereal disease. Leaves heated and applied to 'blind' boils to make them discharge.
Jacksonia dilatata	Broom pea	NT	Infusion of inner wood drunk to relieve internal pain and stomach upset.
Leptomeria acida	Native currant	NSW	Berries (which contain as much vitamin C as tomatoes) were valued as an antiscorbutic: used by Europeans in Sydney from 1788.
Litsea spp.	Native bay tree	Arnhem Land	Aromatic leaves pounded and soaked in water: liquid used as a medicinal bath.
Litsea glutinosa		Qld	Decoction of leaves and bark applied for aches and pains; a 'rubbing medicine'. On Palm Island, Qld, chewed leaves applied directly to skin infections, sores and cuts and infusion of leaves drunk to cure vomiting.
Lysiphyllum carronii	Bauhinia	NSW, Qld	Infusion of bark applied to sores.
Melaleuca spp.	Paperbark	All states	Leaves contain pleasant-smelling oils used in treatment of colds. Flexible and absorbent bark of all species used as bandages.
Melaleuca cajuputi	Small-leaved paperbark	NT	Leaves containing eucalyptol crumbled into hot water and left to steep: liquid used as body wash for general aches and pains, including constipation, and as a decongestant.
Melaleuca leucadendron	White paperbark	NT, Qld	Leaves used as decongestant and inhalant; as a liniment and an effective cough medicine. Inner bark pounded and soaked in warm water: used as beverage or wash, for coughs and applied to head, neck and ears to treat headache.
Melaleuca symphyocarpa	Liniment tree		Leaves crumpled in the hands and rubbed on the chest to treat general illnesses. Leaves crushed and aroma inhaled for a running nose or rubbed on chest for congestion.
Morinda citrifolia	Great morinda or cheese fruit	NT, Qld	Fruit eaten to cure diarrhoea or a beverage made for the same purpose by soaking leaves in water. Unripe fruit collected, pounded and applied to sores. Fruit eaten to relieve colds.
Mukia maderaspatana		NT	Berries rubbed on burns and wounds. Creeper wrapped around the wound and antbed mud packed on top to make a medicinal bandage.
Myoporum montanum	Water bush	NT, Qld, SA, Vic, NSW	Plant left in hot or boiling water for several minutes: liquid used to scrub the head to treat general ailments.
Nauclea orientalis	Leichhardt tree	NT	Fruit eaten or seed crushed in water and liquid drunk to cure general illness.
Nicotiana gossei N. ingulba N. benthamiana N. cavicola	Native tobacco	Central desert	Dried leaves ground up, mixed with ashes of mulga or other acacia, and chewed. A rather rare plant, highly prized.

BOTANICAL NAME	COMMON NAME	REGION	USE
Oecophylla smaragdina	Green ant	Arnhem Land, Elcho Island	Green ants and white pupae collected and crushed in the hands. Nursing mothers rub their breasts with the paste: when a baby with a cough or cold smelled the rubbing medicine, it 'made the baby better'. For adults it 'took away coughs from the chest and cleared the head of cold'. Pupae are a good food, rubbed into a ball and eaten.
Owenia acidula		NT, Qld, SA, NSW	Decoction of wood applied to sore eyes.
Owenia vernicosa	Marble tree	NT, Qld	Shavings of sapwood and innerbark soaked in water and used as a wash for sore eyes. Liquid also drunk to cure coughs.
Pandanus spiralis	Screw palm	NT	Inner core of young tree eaten to cure diarrhoea. It has a bitter taste but said to be quite effective at easing stomach pains. Eating the upper inner core of the tree is a treatment for colds. Inner wood pounded until a white substance exuded, mixed with water and drunk as a cure for mouth sores and toothaches, or dabbed on wounds.
Pemphis acidula	Digging-stick tree	NT	Sharpened twigs heated and inserted in a hole in a tooth; left in until toothache is eased.
Persoonia falcata	Geebung	NT, Qld, WA	Inner wood and bark shavings soaked in breast milk and used as an eyewash.
Petalostigma pubescens	Quinine bush	NT, Qld, NSW	Fruit peeled and peelings soaked in water: women drink the liquid, have stomach pains and some abdominal swelling for a while but will never conceive again. Decoction of fruit applied to aching tooth and to 'make skin shiny'.
Petalostigma quadriloculare	Quinine tree	WA	Fruit held in the mouth for toothache. Bark put in water and sore eyes bathed with it or a berry in a mug of water is used as an antiseptic wash — Kimberleys.
Phellinus sp.	Plate fungus	NT	Fungus chopped from tree, placed on fire and patient inhales the smoke. Lightly charred fungus scraped into water and patient drinks infusion as treatment for coughs, 'bad chest' or fevers.
Pittosporum phillyreoides	Wild apricot	Central desert	Seed ground to make an oily paste, which is then rubbed on sore areas of the body. A compress of warmed leaves is placed on the breasts of new mothers to induce milk flow. Red seeds are poisonous and to be avoided.
Planchonia careya	Cocky apple, bush mango	NT, Qld WA	Inner bark pounded and soaked in water until water turns red; liquid used as a wash for open boils and burns. Leaves warmed in hot water and laid on forehead for headaches. Sheets of bark heated and laid over spear wounds. Small, fine roots mashed, soaked in water and applied to relieve itching of prickly heat, rashes or chicken pox. Also a fish poison: roots and bark mashed and placed in salt water.
Prostanthera striatiflora	Streaked mint bush	Central desert	Leaves dried and crushed; powder scattered over surface of waterholes. Fifteen minutes later, water is sufficiently poisoned to drug birds up to the size of an emu. Too powerful to be used widely, and branches always placed beside the waterhole to show it is poisoned. Leaves may be steeped and liquid used as a medicinal wash.
Pterigon odorus	'Stinking Roger'	Central desert, northern Australia	Aromatic herbaceous plant, used as decongestant; rubbed on chest. Caustic latex or sap applied to sores and scabies. Volatile aromatic oils known to repel insects. Leaves rubbed directly on scabies to ease itching.
Pterocaulon serrulatum	Apple bush	NT	Aromatic leaves crumbled and vapours inhaled to relieve congestion. Used for colds, flu and sore throats. Decoction of leaves drunk and crushed leaves stuffed up nose.
Pterocaulon sphacelatum	Daisy	Central desert	Sniffing and rubbing medicine for colds and sores. Leaves crumbled and aroma inhaled, or rubbed on chest.
Rhizophora stylosa	Spider mangrove	NT	Inner bark scraped and soaked in water: liquid drunk to relieve the pain of ulcers, or used to treat ulcers and yaws.
Rubus spp.	Native raspberry	NSW	Decoction of young leaves drunk for 'bad belly'.

BOTANICAL NAME	COMMON NAME	REGION	USE
Santalum lanceolatum	Quandong	NT	The shell of the seed is discarded and the contents pounded into a paste by adding water or saliva. The paste is rubbed on sore areas. Bark shavings are soaked, and liquid rubbed on itchy areas. Decoction of leaves and bark drunk as a purgative. Decoction of outerwood drunk for 'sickness of the chest'. Infusion of roots used for rheumatism and applied to the body for refreshment when hot and tired. Leaves are burnt to drive away mosquitoes, and people 'smoke' themselves and their babies to gain strength for long trips.
Santalum obtusifolium	Sandalwood	NT	Decoction of wood drunk for constipation and for general aches and pains.
Sarcostemma australe	Snake vine, caustic vine	NT, Qld, NSW, WA, SA	Used on scabies and irritating sores by breaking stem and dabbing on white sap. Whole vine and sap warmed and rubbed on women's breasts to induce lactation.
Scaevola spinescens	Spiny fan flower	Qld, NSW, SA, WA	Infusion of roots drunk to control pains in alimentary tract. Decoction of broken up stems reputed to cure boils, sores and rashes. Fumes of burning plant inhaled for colds.
Scaevola taccada	Lettuce tree, native cabbage	NT, Qld	Ripe fruit heated in hot sand and juice squeezed into sore eyes. Ripe fruit also squashed between palms and juices applied daily to sores.
Smilax australis	Creeper	NT, Qld, NSW	Extract used to treat sore eyes.
Smilax glyciphylla	Native sarsaparilla	NSW	Infusion of leaves esteemed as a pleasant tea. Reputation as tonic and general remedy. Berries contain as much vitamin C as tomatoes — a cupful a day needed to prevent scurvy. Decoction of leaves also drunk for coughs and chest troubles.
Solanum lasiophyllum	Flannel bush	NT, WA	Decoction of roots applied as a poultice to swellings in legs.
Sonchus oleraceus	Milk thistle	All states	Eaten raw in western Victoria to ease pain and induce sleep.
Spartothamnella juncea	Bead bush	NSW, Qld	Lung complaints and cough treated with a decoction. Also drunk for post-partum fever
Spinifex longifolius	Spinifex	NT	Juice squeezed from new shoots or growing tips and dropped into the eyes. During dry seasons the shoots and tips are pounded and soaked in warm water to make an eyewash. Young shoots or the tips of runners are pounded between two stones, then left to soak in water for two to three hours. The liquid is applied to infected sores or burns and is said to be an effective cure.
Stemodia grossa		NT, WA	Decoction of leaves, with sugar, drunk for colds and rheumatism.
Stemodia lythrifolia		NT, WA	Small, strongly scented blue flowered plant used for smelling and infused in water until water has acquired flavour. Applied over the head as a treatment for headaches.
Stemodia viscosa		NT, Qld	Aromatic herb growing to 60 cm with blue-violet flowers; used fresh as a decongestant or boiled as a disinfectant for sores and eyes. Also a sniffing and rubbing medicine. A fresh twig of this herb is pushed through the nasal septum and functions as a decongestant.
Sterculia quadrifida	Peanut tree	NT, Qld	Inner wood soaked in water or breast milk and liquid used as an eyewash. Leaves heated and placed on stonefish or stingray stings; crushed leaves put on wounds.
Suriana maritima	Vine-leaved beach shrub	NT	Sharp leaves used to tickle nose and cause sneezing.
Syzygium suborbiculare	Red wild apple	NT, Qld	Leaves soaked in water and the liquid drunk to cure diarrhoea and to bathe sores. Fruit cooked in hot ashes, juice squeezed out and consumed to clear chest congestion. Pulp of cooked fruit put in sore ears.
Tamarindus indica	Tamarind	northern Australia	Seeds removed from pod and left to soak in water overnight. In the morning the pulp is removed from the seeds and the seeds discarded. The pulp is left to soak in the liquid and later the whole mixture is drunk as a cure for diarrhoea and for coughs and colds. Fruit eaten, usually before it is ripe and acts as a laxative. Pulp of fruit used to massage head and relieve headaches, tired limbs or sore parts of the body.

BOTANICAL NAME	COMMON NAME	REGION	USE
Tamarix aphylla	Athol pine	NT	Twigs boiled in water until it turns a bluish colour: liquid rubbed on the body for itchy skin and rashes.
Tephrosia phaeosperma		Qld, WA	A fish poison: roots hammered to release poison and wrapped in paper-bark. When tide is out, they are placed under rocks where fish hide.
Terminalia carpentariae	Wild Peach, red cement tree	NT	Red sap in inner bark used for rubbing tired, swollen feet.
Terminalia ferdinandiana	Green plum	NT	Pieces of red, sticky inner bark are crushed and added to water. The patient soaks his/her sores in the sticky mixture. Leprosy sores also washed, also used for backache and sore feet.
Tinospora smilacina	Snake vine	NT, WA	Stem pounded and tied around head to relieve headaches, also used as a bandage for painful areas; prepared by beating in water until stem is soft and soaking. Sap applied to painful sores; root applied to marine stings. Widespread medicinal use: leaves chewed for a bad cold; stem wound around abdomen for stomach ache; leaves heated and combined with cockroach pieces and applied to stingray injuries.
Trachymene hemicarpa		NT, WA	Muscle cramps and tiredness relieved by rubbing preparations of leaves on affected part.
Tricoryne platyptera		Qld	Crushed leaves applied and bound over wounds, cuts and sores. Fresh leaves applied daily for two to three days.
Urtica incisa	Stinging nettle	NSW	For rheumatism, affected parts beaten with a bunch of leaves to cause a nettle rash. For sprains, infusion of leaves used to bathe affected part; boiled leaves also used as a poultice.
Ventilago viminalis	Supplejack, vine tree	Central desert	Ashes combined with native tobacco plant (Nicotiana sp.) to make a stronger chewing tobacco. Roots and bark mashed and soaked in water; good for rheumatism, swellings, cuts and sores. For toothache, roots and bark mashed and soaked in water. Infusion of roots and bark said to restore hair in bald men.
Vigna vexillata	Medicine bean, native cowpea	NT	Roots chewed and eaten for constipation or diarrhoea. Root pounded with grass and inserted into abdominal cavity when intestines replaced-after a severe abdominal wound.
Xanthorrhoea resinosa	Grass tree	NSW	Gum considered to be of great value in chest complaints by John White, first surgeon of Sydney in 1788.
Xylocarpus australasicum	Cedar mangrove	NT	Inner bark pounded and soaked in water: liquid drunk as an all-purpose medicine.
Zehmeria micrantha	Bush cucumber	Central desert	Good for headaches; fruit broken open and dabbed on the forehead has a cooling effect on hot days. Also good for earache.

A stand of grass trees (Xanthorrhoea species) survives bushfires in northwestern New South Wales.

PHOTO: MICHAEL COURTNEY

ENDNOTES

1   NATURALISTS, HUNTERS AND GATHERERS

1 These signs are known to people of Weipa and Aurukun, Cape York, Queensland.

2 For an interesting and full discussion of women's role as
gatherers see Hiatt, B., 'Woman the gatherer' in Gale F.
ed, *Women's Role in Aboriginal Society.* Canberra,
Australian Institute of Aboriginal Studies, 1974.

3 Similar percentages have been reported by Hiatt, *ibid,*
and Gould, R., *Yiwara: Foragers of the Australian
Desert.* Sydney, Collins, 1969. The opposite situation
has been reported in western Arnhem Land by Jon
Altman, who argues that men provide 80 per cent of the
diet by hunting animals with guns.

4 Golson, J., 'Australian Aboriginal food plants: some
ecological and culture-historical implications' in
Mulvaney, D. J. and Golson, J. eds, *Aboriginal Man and
Environment in Australia.* Canberra, ANU Press, 1971,
lists 227 species from Arnhem Land, Cape York and
central Australia. Lawrence, R., 'Aboriginal habitat and
economy', *Occasional Papers*, 6. Canberra, Department
of Geography, ANU School of General Studies, 1968,
lists over 200 for central Australia. Peter Latz of the
Arid Zone Research Institute, Alice Springs, has compiled numerous food sources for the Alyawara, Aranda
and other desert people. (O'Connell, Latz and Barnett,
1983).

5 For results of analysis of bush food nutrients see: Brand,
J. C., 'An outstanding food source of vitamin C', *Lancet,*
16 October 1982; Brand, J. C., Cherikoff, V., Lee, A.
and McDonnell, J., 'Nutrients in important bush foods',
Proceedings of the Nutrition Society of Australia, 1982, 7,
50–54; Brand, J. C. and Cherikoff, V., 'The nutritional
composition of Australian Aboriginal foods plants of
the desert regions' in Wickers, G. E., Goodwin, J. R.
and Fields, D. V. eds, *Plants for Arid Lands.* London,
Allen and Unwin, 1985; Brand, J. C., Cherikoff, V. and
Truswell, A. S., 'The nutritional composition of
Australian Aboriginal bush foods', *Food Technology in
Australia*, 35, 6, June 1983, 293–298; 'Animal foods',
Food Technology in Australia, 37, 5, 208–211; 'Seeds
and nuts', *Food Technology in Australia*, 37, 6, 275–279.

2   SEASONS AND THE AUSTRALIAN ENVIRONMENT

1 Gould, R. A., 'Progress to oblivion', *Ecologist, 2, 9,*
September 1972, 18.

2 Harris, D. R., 'Land of plenty on Cape York Peninsula',
Geographical Magazine, 48, 11, August 1976.

3 Thomson, D. G., 'The seasonal factor in human culture', *Prehistoric Society Proceedings*, 5, 1939, 209–221.

4 Davis, S., *The Hunter for All Seasons: an Aboriginal
Perspective of the Natural Environ.* Northern Territory,
Milingimbi School Literature Production Centre,
1984.

3 PEOPLE, PLANTS AND ANIMALS

1 Jones, R., 'The Neolithic, Palaeolithic and the hunting gardeners: man and land in the Antipodes' in Suggate, R. P. and Cresswell, M. M. eds, *Selected Papers from the IX International Congress INQUA 2–10 December 1973*, Royal Society of New Zealand, Bulletin 13, Wellington, 1975.

2 *ibid.*

3 Isaacs, J., *Australian Dreaming.* Sydney, Lansdowne, 1980, 202.

4 Batey, I., Unpublished manuscript, (undated) Royal Historical Society of Victoria, quoted in Frankel, D., 'An account of Aboriginal use of the yam daisy', *Artefact*, 7, 1982, 1–2.

5 Jones, R., *op cit.*

6 Kimber, D., 'Beginnings of farming? Some man–plant–animal relationships in central Australia', *Mankind*, 10, 3, June 1976.

7 Isaacs, J., *op cit*, 204–205.

8 Thomson, D. F. 'The hero cult, initiation and totemism on Cape York', *Journal of the Royal Anthropological Institute*, LXII, 1933.

9 Isaacs, J., *op cit*, 203.

4 COOKING TECHNIQUES

This chapter is based on personal observations with additional advice from Banduk and Thancoupie.

1 Beveridge, P., *Aborigines of Victoria.* Melbourne, M. C. Hutchinson, 1889.

5 FRUITS

Information on fruits has been compiled from numerous published sources listed in the bibliography. First-hand experience has added to the published material.

The information on solanums is largely based on Gould, R. A., 'Subsistence behaviour among the western desert Aborigines of Australia', *Oceania*, XXXIX, 4, June 1969, 253–267, with additional information from the Yuendemu Literacy Centre and O'Connell, J. F., Latz, P. K. and Barnet, P., 'Traditional and modern plant use among the Alyawara of central Australia', *Economic Botany*, 37, 1, 1983, 80–109.

1 Brand, J., 'An outstanding food source of vitamin C', *Lancet*, 16 October 1982.

6 NUTS

1 Information from a thesis by Harris, D., 'Traditional patterns of plant food in Cape York, 1974'. Department of Geography, University College, London, 1975.

2 Information on pandanus is largely based on Gaffey, P., 'A fruitful search: pandanus use in Australia and New Guinea'. B A Hons thesis, Australian National University, 1978, chapter 3, 54–64, as well as first-hand accounts of Banduk and Thancoupie.

3 Petrie, C. C., *Tom Petrie's Reminiscences of Early Queensland.* Sydney, Angus & Robertson, 1983.

4 Tindale, N. B., 'A list of plants collected in the Musgrave and Mann ranges, South Australia, 1933', *South Australian Naturalist*, 31 May 1941, 11.

7 ROOTS, TUBERS, CORMS AND BULBS

1 Lami Lami, L., *Lamilami Speaks.* Sydney, Ure Smith, 1974, 34.

2 McArthur, M., 'Food consumption and dietary levels of groups of Aborigines living on naturally occurring foods' in *Records of the American–Australian Scientific Expedition to Arnhem Land', 2: Anthropology and Nutrition.* Melbourne, Melbourne University Press, 1960, 90–145.

3 For information on *murrnong* see: Brough Smyth, R., *The Aborigines of Victoria.* 1, Melbourne, Government Printer, 1878; Oates, A. and Seeman, A., *Victorian Aborigines: Plant Foods.* Melbourne, National Museum of Victoria, 1979.

4 Leichhardt, L, *Journal of an Overland Expedition in Australia . . .* London, Boone, 1847.

5 Information supplied by Geoff Wharton at Weipa, and Thancoupie.

8 SEEDS AND DAMPER

1 Arndt, W., 'Indigenous sorghum as a food and in myth, the Tagamon tribe', *Oceania*, XXII, 2, December 1961, 109–112.

2 Silberbauer, G. B., 'Ecology of the Ernabella Aboriginal community', *Anthropological Forum*, III, 1, November 1971, 21–37.

3 Tindale, N. B., *Aboriginal Tribes of Australia.* Canberra, Australian National University Press, 1974, 99.

4 For full discussion of desert seeds see O'Connell, J. F., Latz, P. K. and Barnett, P., 'Traditional and modern plant use among the Alyawara of central Australia', *Economic Botany*, 37, 1, 1983, 80–109.

5 Scott, M. P., 'Some Aboriginal food plants of the Ashburton district, W.A.', *Western Australian Naturalist*, 12, 4, 17 August 1972.

6 *Junga Yimi*, 2, 4, 26. Yuendumu, NT, Warlpiri Literature Production, 1980.

7 Hilliard, W. M., *The People in Between: the Pitjantjatjara People of Ernabella.* London, Hodder and Stoughton, 1968.

9 GREEN VEGETABLES

1 Woolston, F., 'Ethnobotanical items from the Wellesley Islands, Gulf of Carpentaria', *Occasional Papers*, 1. Anthropology Museum, University of Queensland, 1973.

10   HONEY, GUM AND NECTAR

1 Mundine, J., *Australians in Perspecta,* 1983. Catalogue of the Art Gallery of New South Wales, 1983, 47.

2 Rudder, J., *Introduction to Yolngu Science.* Northern Territory, Galiwinku Adult Education Centre, 1977.

3 Roughsey, D., *Moon and Rainbow: the Autobiography of an Aboriginal.* Sydney, Reed, 1971.

4 Akerman, K., 'Honey in the life of the Aboriginals of the Kimberleys', *Oceania,* XLIX, 3, March 1979, 169–178.

5 Love, J. R. B., *Stone Age Bushmen of Today.* London, Blackie, 1936, 7.

6 Crawford, I. M., *The Art of the Wandjina.* Melbourne, Oxford University Press, 1968, 118.

7 Akerman, K., *op cit.*

8 MacPherson, J., 'Ethno botany: the eucalyptus in the daily life and medical practice of the Australian Aboriginals', *Mankind,* 2, 6, 1939, 175–180.

9 Mountford, C. P., *Nomads of the Australian Desert.* Adelaide, Rigby, 1976.

10 Carr, D. J. and Carr, S. G. M., 'The botany of the first Australians' in Carr, D. J. and Carr, S. G. M. *ed, People and Plants in Australia.* Sydney, Academic Press, 1981.

11 Basedow, H., *Narrative of an Expedition of Exploration in North-Western Australia, Proc. Royal Geographical Society,* Vol XVIII, 1918.

11   LAND ANIMALS

1 Altman, J. C., *The Dietary Utilization of Flora and Fauna by Contemporary Hunter Gatherers in North–Central Arnhemland.* Canberra, Department of Political and Social Change, Research School of Pacific Studies, ANU, 1982. This information was based on Altman's fieldwork at Momega outstation in the Mann–Liverpool rivers region, western Arnhem Land.

2 Akerman, K., 'Ngala and Mei: living on bush foods in the central Kimberley', *Earth Garden,* 1978.

3 Roth, W. E., *A Report on the Aboriginals of the Pennefather River Districts and Other Coastal Tribes Occupying the Country Between the Batavia and Embley Rivers.* 1900.

4 Meggitt, M. J., *Desert People: a Study of the Walbiri Aborigines of Central Australia.* Sydney, Angus & Robertson, 1962.

12   MARINE ANIMALS AND FISH

1 Roughsey, D., *Moon and Rainbow: the Autobiography of an Aboriginal.* Sydney, Reed, 1971.

2 Mitchell, T. L., *Three Expeditions into the Interior of Eastern Australia, with Descriptions of the Recently Explored Region of Australia Felix, and the Present Colony of New South Wales.* London, Boone, 1838.

3 Petrie, C. C., *Tom Petrie's Reminiscences of Early Queensland.* Sydney, Angus & Robertson, 1983, 73.

4 Rudder, J., *Introduction of Yolngu Science.* Northern Territory, Galiwinku Adult Education Centre, 1977.

5 Roughsey, D., *op cit.*

13   SHELLFISH

1 Meehan, B., *Shell Bed to Shell Midden.* Canberra, Australian Institute of Aboriginal Studies, 1982, 86.

2 *ibid,* 155.

3 Davis, S., *The Hunter for All Seasons: an Aboriginal Perspective of the Natural Environ.* Northern Territory, Milingimbi School Literature Production Centre, 1984, 57.

14   BILLABONG AND SWAMP ANIMALS

This chapter is based on first-hand observation.

15   INSECTS AND GRUBS

1 Flood, J., *The Moth Hunters: Aboriginal Prehistory of the Australian Alps.* Canberra, Australian Institute of Aboriginal Studies, 1980.

2 Ling Roth, H., *The Aborigines of Tasmania.* Hobart, Fullers Bookshops, 1899.

3 Dawson, J., *Australian Aborigines: the Languages and Customs of Several Tribes of Aborigines in the Western District of Victoria, Australia.* Melbourne, George Robertson, 1881. Facsimile published by Australian Institute of Aboriginal Studies, Canberra, 1981.

4 Petrie, C. C., *Tom Petrie's Reminiscences of Early Queensland.* Sydney, Angus & Robertson, 1983.

5 Crawford, I. M., 'Traditional plant resources in the Kalumburu area: aspects in ethno economics', *Records of the Western Australian Museum,* Supplement 15, Perth, 1982.

16   HERBAL MEDICINE

1 Henshall, T. and Yuendumu Health Workers, *Ngurrju–Maninjukurlangu: Bush Medicine.* Yuendumu, Warlpiri Literature Production Centre, 1982.

2 Djaypila and Yalwidika, 'Medicinal plants on Elcho Island', *Aboriginal Health Worker,* 3, 1979.

3 Henshall, T. and Yuendumu Health Workers, *op cit.*

4 Scarlett, N., White, N. and Reid, J., 'Bush medicines: the pharmacopoeia of the Yolngu of Arnhem Land. Commenting on comparisons with Burkill, I. H., *A Dictionary of the Economic Products of the Malay Peninsula.* 1966' in Reid, J. *ed, Body, Land and Spirit: Health and Healing in Aboriginal Society.* St Lucia, University of Queensland Press, 1982.

5 Webb, L. J., 'Guide to the Medicinal and Poisonous Plants of Queensland.' *Bulletin 232,* Council for Scientific and Industrial Research, Melbourne, 1948.

BIBLIOGRAPHY

Akerman, K.,   'Ngala and Mei: living on bush foods in the central
                  Kimberley', *Earth Garden*, 1978, 20–24.

Akerman, K.,   'Honey in the life of the Aboriginals of the Kimberleys',
                  Oceania, XLIX, 3, March 1979, 169–178.

Altman, J. C.,   'The Dietary Utilisation of Flora and Fauna by Contempo-
                  rary Hunter-Gatherers in North–Central Arnhemland',
                  Canberra, Department of Political and Social Change,
                  Research School of Pacific Studies ANU, 1982.
                  Typescript.

Arndt, W.,   'Indigenous sorghum as food and in myth',
                  Oceania, XXXII, 2, December 1961, 109–112.

Barrett, M. J.,   'Walbiri customs and beliefs concerning teeth', *Mankind*,
                  6, 3, May 1964, 95–104.

Basedow, H.,   'Narrative of an Expedition of Exploration in North-West
                  Australia', *Proc. Royal Geographical Society*, XVIII, 1918.

Beck, W.,   'Aspects of plant taxonomy in Australian archaeology'.
                  MA Thesis, La Trobe University, 1980. Typescript.

Bennett, G.,   *Gatherings of a Naturalist in Australia 1860* (Facsimile
                  edition), Currawong, 1982.

Blainey, G.,   *Triumph of the Nomads: a History of Ancient Australia*.
                  Melbourne, Macmillan, 1975.

Blainey, G.,   'The early Australian pharmacists', *Australian Journal of
                  Pharmacy*, July 1977, 416–417.

Blombery, A. M., *What Wildflower is That?*. Sydney, Lansdowne, 1972.

Bowdler, S.,   'Hook, line and dilly bag: an interpretation of an Australian
                  coastal shell midden', *Mankind*, 10, 4, 1976, 248–256.

Bowdler, S.,   'Rainforest: colonised or coloniser', *Australian Archaeology*,
                  17, December 1983, 59–66.

Brand, J. C.,   'An outstanding food source of vitamin C', *Lancet*,
                  16 October 1982.

Brand, J. C. and Cherikoff, V., 'The nutritional composition of Australian Aboriginal foods, plants of the desert regions' in Wickers, G. E., Goodwin, J. R. and Fields, D. V. *eds, Plants for Arid Lands,* London, Allen and Unwin, 1985.

Brand, J. C., Cherikoff, V., and Truswell, A.S., 'The nutritional composition of Australian Aboriginal bush foods', *Food Technology in Australia,* 35, 6, June 1983, 293–298.

Brand, J. C., Cherikoff, V., and Truswell, A. S., 'The nutritional composition of Australian Aboriginal bush foods, 3, Seeds and nuts', *Food Technology in Australia,* 37, 6, 1985, 275–279.

Brand, J. C., Cherikoff, V., Lee, A. and McDonnell, J., 'Nutrients in important bush foods', *Proceedings of the* Society of Australia, 1982, 7, 50–54.

Brough Smyth, R., *Aborigines of Victoria,* I, Melbourne, Government Printer, 1878.

Calder, W. B., 'A history of the Mornington Peninsula as it relates to vegetation', *Victorian Historical Magazine,* 45, 1, February 1974, 5–30.

Campbell, A., 'Pharmacy of Victorian Aborigines', *Australian Journal of Pharmacy,* December–January 1973–4, 894–900.

Campbell, V., 'Ethnohistorical evidence on the diet and economy of the Aborigines of the Macleay River valley' in McBryde, I. *ed, Records of Times Past: Ethnohistorical Essays on the Culture and Ecology of the New England Tribes.* Canberra, Australian Institute of Aboriginal Studies, 1978.

Cane, S., Stockton, J. and Vallance, A., 'A note on the diet of the Tasmanian Aborigines', *Australian Archaeology,* 9, 1979, 77–79.

Carr, D. J. and Carr, S. G. M., 'The botany of the first Australians' in Carr, D. J. and Carr, S. G. M. *eds, People and Plants in Australia.* Sydney, Academic Press, 1981.

Cherikoff, V., Brand, J.C., and Truswell, A. S., 'The nutritional composition of Australian Aboriginal bush foods 2, Animal foods', *Food Technology in Australia,* 37, 5, 208–211, 1983.

Chase, A. and Sturmer, J. Von, 'Anthropology and botany; turning over a new leaf'. Canberra, Australian Institute of Aboriginal Studies, Ethnobotany Workshop, 15–16 May 1976, Typescript.

Cleland, J. B., 'Plants, including fungi, poisonous or otherwise injurious to man in Australia', *Medical Journal of Australia,* 19 December, 1931, 775–778.

Cleland, J. B., 'Ethno-botany in relation to the central Australian Aboriginal', *Mankind,* 2, 1, April 1936, 6-9.

Cleland, J. B. and Johnston, T. H., 'Aboriginal names and uses of plants at the granites, central Australia', *Transactions of the Royal Society of South Australia,* 63, 1939, 22–27.

Colliver, F. S., 'The Aboriginal and his medicine chest', *Anthropological Society of Queensland,* 44, April 1972.

Colliver, F. S., 'Some plant foods of the Queensland Aborigine', *Queensland Naturalist,* 21, 1–2, 1973, 22–31.

Cook, C. E., 'Medicine and the Australian Aboriginal: a century of contact in the Northern Territory', *Medical Journal of Australia,* 14, 2 April 1966, 559–564.

Crawford, I. M., *The Art of the Wandjina.* Melbourne, Oxford University Press, 1968.

Crawford, I. M., 'Traditional plant resources in the Kalumburu area: aspects in ethno-economics', *Records of the Western Australia Museum,* Supplement 15, 1982.

Cribb, A. B. and Cribb, J. W., *Wild Food in Australia.* Sydney, Collins, 1975.

Cribb, A. B. and Cribb, J. W., *Wild Medicine in Australia.* Sydney, Collins, 1981.

Cribb, J. W., 'Australia's medicinal plants', *Medical Journal of Australia,* 143, 9–23 December 1985, 574–577.

Dargin, P., *The Aboriginal Fisheries of the Darling and Barwon Rivers.* Brewarrina, Brewarrina Historical Society, 1976.

Davis, S., *The Hunter for all Seasons: an Aboriginal Perspective of the Natural Environ.* Northern Territory, Milingimbi School Literature Production Centre, 1984.

Dawson, J., *Australian Aborigines: the Languages and Customs of Several Tribes of Aborigines in the Western District of Victoria, Australia.* Melbourne, George Robertson, 1881, Facsimile published by Australian Institute of Aboriginal Studies, Canberra, 1981.

Djaypila and Yalwidika, 'Medicinal plants on Elcho Island', *Aboriginal Health Worker,* 3, 2, June 1979, 50–56.

Duyker, E., 'Land use and ecological change in central New South Wales', *Journal of the Royal Australian Historical Society,* September 1983, 120–132.

Dyall, L. K., 'Aboriginal occupation of the Newcastle Coastline', *Hunter Natural History,* 3, 3, August 1971, 154f.

Elkin, A. P., *The Australian Aborigines.* Sydney, Angus & Robertson, 1974.

Flood, J., *The Moth Hunters: Aboriginal Prehistory of the Australian Alps.* Canberra, Australian Institute of Aboriginal Studies, 1980.

Ford, E., 'Medical practice in early Sydney', *Medical Journal of Australia,* 11, 9 July 1955, 41–54.

Frankel, D., 'An account of Aboriginal use of the yam-daisy', *Artefact,* 7, 1–2, 1982, 43–45.

Gaffey, P., 'A fruitful search: pandanus use in Australia and New Guinea'. BA Hons Thesis, ANU, 1978. Typescript.

Golson, J., 'Australian Aboriginal food plants: some ecological and culture-historical implications' in Mulvaney, D. J. and Golson, J. eds, *Aboriginal Man and Environment in Australia.* Canberra, ANU Press, 1971.

Gould, R. A., *Yiwara: Foragers of the Australian Desert.* Sydney, Collins, 1969.

Gould, R. A., 'Subsistence behaviour among the western desert Aborigines of Australia', *Oceania,* XXXIX, 4, June 1969, 253–267.

Gould, R. A., 'Progress to oblivion', *Ecologist,* 2, 9, September 1972, 17–23.

Hamilton, A., 'Blacks and whites: the relationships of change', *Arena,* 30, 1972, 34–48.

Hamlyn-Harris, R. and Smith, F., 'On fish poisoning and poisons employed among the Aborigines of Queensland', *Memoirs of the Queensland Museum*, 5, 1916, 1–22.

Hardley, R. G., 'Some of the factors that influenced the coastal riverine and insular habitats of the Aborigines of south east Queensland and of northern New South Wales'. BA Hons Thesis, University of Queensland, 1968. Typescript.

Harney, W. E., *Tales from the Aborigines*. Adelaide, Rigby 1976.

Harris, A., 'Goannas for tea', *Your Museum*, August 1982.

Harris, D. R., 'Traditional patterns of plant-food procurement in the Cape York Peninsula and Torres Strait Islands'. Report on field work carried out August–November 1974. Department of Geography, University College London, 1975. Typescript.

Harris, D. R., 'Aboriginal use of plant foods in the Cape York Peninsula and Torres Strait Islands', *Australian Institute of Aboriginal Studies Newsletter*, 6, 3–10, June 1976, 21–22.

Harris, D. R., 'Land of plenty on Cape York Peninsula', *Geographical Magazine*, 48, 11, August 1976, 657–661.

Hart, G. W. M. and Pilling, A. R., *The Tiwi of North Australia*. NY, Holt, Rinehart and Winston, 1960.

Henshall, T. and Yuendumu Health Workers, *Ngurrju-Maninjakurlangu Nyurnukurlangu, Bush Medicine*. Yuendumu, Warlpiri Literature Production Centre, 1980.

Hiatt, B., 'Woman the gatherer' in Gale, F. ed., *Women's Role in Aboriginal Society*. Australian Aboriginal Studies 36; Social Anthropology Series 6, Canberra, Australian Institute of Aboriginal Studies, 1970.

Hiddins, L. J., *Survive to Live*. James Cook University of Northern Queensland, 1981.

Hilliard, W. M., *The People in between: the Pitjantjatjara People of Ernabella*. London, Hodder and Stoughton, 1968.

Holly, A., 'Traditional herbal medicines of the Northern Territory'. Paper submitted to Dr E. Florence, Lewis and Clark College Portland, Oregon, USA, Canberra, 1982. Typescript.

Horwood, J. M., 'Aboriginal people in north east Australia' in Wood, B. ed, *Tucker in Australia*. Melbourne, Hill of Content, 1977.

Horwood, J. M., Wallace, F. J. and Campbell C., 'A model of food values for two Australian cultures', *Proceedings of the Nutrition Society of Australia*, 8, 1983, 157–160.

Hyam, G. N., 'Living off the land in Victoria', *Victorian Naturalist*, LIX, February 1943.

Hynes, R. A. and Chase, A. K., 'Plants, sites, and domiculture: Aboriginal influence upon plant communities in Cape York Peninsula', *Archaeology in Oceania*, 17, 1, April 1982, 38–51.

Irvine, F. R., 'Wild and emergency foods of Australian and Tasmanian Aborigines', *Oceania*, 88, 1957–1958, 113–142.

Irvine, F. R., 'Evidence of change in the vegetable diet of Australian Aborigines' in Pilling, A. R. and Waterman, R. A. eds, *Diprotodon to Detribalisation: Studies of Change among Australian Aborigines*. Michigan State University Press, 1970.

Isaacs, J.,   *Australian Dreaming: 40,000 Years of Aboriginal History.* Sydney, Lansdowne, 1980.

Jones, R.,   'The Neolithic, Palaeolithic and the hunting gardeners: man and land in the Antipodes' in Suggate, R. P. and Creswell, M. M. *eds, Selected Papers from the IX International Congress INQUA, 2–10 December, 1973,* Royal Society of New Zealand, Bulletin 13, Wellington, 1975.

Kimber, R. G.,   'Beginnings of farming? Some man–plant–animal relationships in central Australia', *Mankind,* 10, 3, June 1976, 142–150.

Kirk, R. L.,   *Aboriginal Man Adapting.* Melbourne, Oxford University Press, 1983.

Knuckey, M.,   'The disappearing bush', *Aboriginal News,* 3, 5, 1978, 3–5.

Jenkin, G.,   *Conquest of the Ngarrindjri.* Adelaide, Rigby 1979.

Lamilami, Rev L.,   *Lamilami Speaks.* Sydney, Ure Smith, 1974.

Lassak, E. V. and McCarthy   *Australian Medicinal Plants.* Methuen, 1983.

Latz , P. K. and Griffin, G. F.,   'Changes in Aboriginal land management in relation to fire and to food plants in central Australia' in Hetzol, B. S. and Frith, H. J. *eds, The Nutrition of Aborigines in Relation to the Ecosystem of Central Australia.* Canberra, CSIRO, 1976.

Lawler, L. J. and Slaytor, M.,   'Uses of Australian orchids by Aborigines and early settlers', *Medical Journal of Australia,* 26 December 1970, 1259–1261.

Lawrence, R.,   *Aboriginal Habitat and Economy.* Occasional Papers No. 6. Canberra, Department of Geography, ANU School of General Studies, 1968.

Lawrence, R.,   'Habitat and economy: a historical perspective' in Mulvaney, J. and Golson, J. *eds, Aboriginal Man and Environment.* Canberra, ANU Press, 1971.

Leichhardt, L.,   *Journal of an Overland Expedition in Australia from Moreton Bay to Port Essington, a Distance of 3000 Miles, during the Years 1844–1845.* London, Boone, 1847.

Levitt, D.,   *Plants and People: Aboriginal Uses of Plants on Groote Eylandt.* Canberra, Australian Institute of Aboriginal Studies, 1981.

Ling Roth, H.,   *The Aborigines of Tasmania.* Hobart, Fuller's Bookshop, 1899.

Longmore, R. B.,   'Aboriginal medicinal plants', *Scientific Australian,* December 1978, 25.

Love, J. R. B.,   *Stone Age Bushmen of Today.* London, Blackie, 1936.

Lucich, P.,   *Children's Stories from the Worora.* Australian Aboriginal Studies, 18. Canberra, Australian Institute of Aboriginal Studies, 1969.

McArthur, M.,   'Food consumption and dietary levels of groups of Aborigines living on naturally occurring foods' in Mountford, C. P. *ed, Records of the American–Australian Scientific Expedition to Arnhem Land, 2, Anthropology and Nutrition.* Melbourne, Melbourne University Press, 1960.

McBryde, I. *ed,*   *Records of Times Past: Ethnohistorical Essays on the Culture and Ecology of New England Tribes.* Canberra, Australian Institute of Aboriginal Studies, 1978.

McDonald, D. I.,   'The Bogong moth: an Aboriginal Feast', *Newsletter of the Royal Australian Historical Society*, January–February 1979, 6.

Macpherson, J.,   'The toxicology of the arum lily and cunjevoi lily', *Medical Journal of Australia*, 9 November 1929, 671–673.

Macpherson, J.,   'Australia: ethno-botany, the eucalyptus in the daily life and medical practice of the Australian Aborigines', *Mankind*, 2, 6, May 1939, 175–180.

Meehan, B.,   *Shell Bed to Shell Midden*. Canberra, Australian Institute of Aboriginal Studies, 1982.

Meggitt, M. J.,   *Desert People: a Study of the Walbiri Aborigines of Central Australia*. Sydney, Angus & Robertson, 1962.

Mirritji, J.,   *My People's Life: an Aboriginal's Own Story*. Northern Territory, Milingimbi Literature Centre, 1978.

Mitchell, T. L.,   *Three Expeditions into the Interior of Eastern Australia, with Descriptions of the Recently Explored Region of Australia Felix, and the Present Colony of New South Wales*. London, Boone, 1838.

Morris, P. F.,   'Some vegetable foods of the Wimmera and Mallee', *Victorian Naturalist*, LIX, February 1943, 167–171.

Mountford, C. P.,   'Aboriginal methods of fishing and cooking as used on the southern coast of Eyre's Peninsula, S.A.', *Mankind*, 2, 7, 1939, 196–200.

Mountford, C. P.,   *Ayers Rock: Its People, Their Beliefs and Their Art*. Sydney, Angus & Robertson, 1965.

Mountford, C. P.,   *Nomads of the Australian Desert*. Adelaide, Rigby, 1976.

Mulvaney, D. J.,   *The Prehistory of Australia*. Ringwood, Vic, Penguin, 1975.

Mundine, J.,   'Guku (honey)' in *Australians in Perspecta Catalogue*. Sydney, Art Gallery of New South Wales, 1983.

Nabarula, A. D.,   'Bush Medicines used at Warrabri', *Aboriginal Health Worker*, 2, 4, December 1978.

Napaljarrirli Manu S. and Nakamarrarlu C.,   *Junga Yimi*, 2, 1, 1979, 27.

Nungarrayirlid J. and Davis, A.,   *Yakajirri Kapurdu-Kurlu*. Northern Territory, Warlpiri Literature Production Centre, 1981.

Nungarrayirli J. and Davis, A.,   *Wataki-Kurli, Pirdijirri-Kurli*. Northern Territory, Warlpiri Literature Production Centre, 1981.

Oates, A., and Seeman, A.,   *Victorian Aborigines: Plant Foods*. Melbourne, National Museum of Victoria, 1979.

O'Connell, J. F., Latz, P. K. and Barnett, P.,   'Traditional and modern plant use among the Alyawara of central Australia', *Economic Botany*, 27, 1, 1983, 80–109.

Parker, A. Z.,   'An ethnobotanical study of Leonora, W. A.'. Australian Institute of Aboriginal Studies. Manuscript.

Peile, A. R.,   'Preliminary notes on the ethno-botany of the Gugadja Aborigines at Balgo, W.A.', *Western Australian Herbarium Research Notes*, 3, 1980, 59–64.

Petrie, C. C.,   *Tom Petrie's Reminiscences of Early Queensland*. Sydney, Angus & Robertson, 1983.

Pierce, R.,   'The evidence of J. Ainsworth on the diet and economy of the Ballina horde' in McBryde, I. ed, *Records of Times Past*. Canberra, Australian Institute of Aboriginal Studies, 1978.

Pilling, A. R. and Waterman R. A. *eds,*   *Diprotodon to Detribalisation: Studies of Change among Australian Aborigines.* Michigan State University Press, 1970.

Pink, O. M.,   'Notes on Aranda uses of flora', *Australia and New Zealand Association for Advancement of Science Report,* 21, 1932, 177.

Reid, E. J. and Betts, T. J.,   'Records of Western Australian plants used by Aboriginals as medicinal agents', *Planta Medica,* 36, 1979, 164–173.

Reid, J. and Williams, N.,   'Voodoo death in Arnhem Land: whose reality?' *American Anthropologist,* 86, 1, 1984, 121–133.

Robin, D.,   'Trial shows Aboriginal food values', *Aboriginal News,* 3, 9, 1980, 21–23.

Roth, W. E.,   'String and other forms of strand', *North Queensland Ethnography Bulletin,* 1, January 1901.

Rotherham, E. R., Blaxell, D. F., Briggs, B. G. and Carolin, R. C. *eds,*   *Flowers and Plants of New South Wales and Southern Queensland.* Sydney, Reed, 1975.

Roughsey, D.,   *Moon and Rainbow: the Autobiography of an Aboriginal.* Sydney, Reed, 1971.

Rudder, J.,   *Introduction to Yolngu Science.* Northern Territory, Galiwinku Adult Education Centre, 1977.

Ryan, J. S. *ed,*   *The Land of Ulitarra.* Armidale, University of New England, 1964.

Scarlett, N., White, N. and Reid, J.,   'Bush medicines: the pharmacopoeia of the Yolngu of Arnhemland' in Reid, J. *ed, Body, Land and Spirit.* St Lucia, University of Queensland Press, 1982.

Scott, M. P.,   'Some Aboriginal food plants of the Ashburton district, W.A.', *Western Australian Naturalist,* 12, 4, 17 August 1972, 94–96.

Silberbauer, G. B.,   'Ecology of the Ernabella Aboriginal community', *Anthropological Forum,* III, I, November 1971, 21–37.

Stefanska, A. and Barr, A.,   'Cures from the bush', *Hemisphere,* 25, 6, 1981, 368–373.

Strehlow, T. G. H.,   *Aranda Traditions.* Melbourne, Melbourne University Press, 1947.

Sullivan, S.,   'Aboriginal diet and food gathering methods in the Richmond and Tweed River valleys as seen in early settler records' in McBryde, I. *ed, Records of Times Past.* Canberra, Australian Institute of Aboriginal Studies, 1978.

Sweeney, G.,   'Food supplies of a desert tribe', *Oceania,* XVII, 4, 1947, 289–299.

Thomson, D. F.,   'The seasonal factor in human culture', *Prehistoric Society Proceedings,* 5, 1939.

Thomson, D. F.,   'The seasonal factor in human culture illustrated from the life of a contemporary nomadic group', *Prehistoric Society Proceedings,* 5, 10, 1939, 209–221.

Thorpe, W. W.,   'Aboriginal therapeutics', *Mankind,* 1, 4, March 1932, 94–95.

Tindale, N. B.,   'A list of plants collected in the Musgrave and Man-ranges, South Australia, 1933', *South Australian Naturalist,* 31 May, 1941, 8–12.

Waddy, J.,   'Amardi-Langwa Ekirra: dictionary—Plants' anuscript.

Warner, W. L.,   *A Black Civilization*. New York, Harper and Row, 1964.

Webb, L. J.,   'Guide to the medicinal and poisonous plants of Queensland', *Council for Scientific and Industrial Research, Bulletin 232, 1948*.

Webb, L. J.,   'The use of plant medicine and poisons by the Australian Aborigines', *Mankind*, 6, 2, 1959, 137–146.

Webb, L. J.,   ' "Eat, die and learn": the botany of the Australian Aborigines', *Australian Natural History*, 9, March 1973, 290–296.

Webb, T. T.,   'Aboriginal medical practice in east Arnhem Land', *Oceania*, IV, 1, September 1933, 91–99.

Webb, T. T.,   'Aboriginal medical practice in east Arnhem Land', *Oceania*, IV, 1, September 1933, 91–99.

Winkel, V.,   'Native fruits of North Queensland', *North Queensland Naturalist*, April 1982, 6–7.

Woolston, F. P.,   'Ethnobotanical items from the Wellesley Islands, Gulf of Carpentaria', *Anthropology Museum, University of Queensland, Occasional Papers 1, 1973*.

Wrigley, J. W.,   *Australian Native Plants*. Sydney, Collins, 1979.

ACKNOWLEDGMENTS

In compiling this publication particular thanks must be given to Diana Conroy, my research assistant, whose enthusiasm and love for the subject helped enormously. My mother, Carmel Pepperell, typed the manuscript, worked very hard and offered great support.

This book could not have been written without the enthusiastic help and advice of two very good friends, Banduk Marika and Thancoupie. Banduk, with her family, showed me many foods around the environment of Yirrkala and helped greatly in Sydney by identifying photographs and offering personal advice and insight. Thancoupie and her sister, Joyce Hall, took me to Hay Point, Weipa, with thirty others to a moving ceremony in remembrance of their mother, Ida Paul. Here we enjoyed the food of swamp and waterhole, as well as the skills of children and women who fished and collected shellfish. Although an established artist, Thancoupie still supports herself largely from food which she gets from the seashore and is an inspiration to my children.

I am indebted to photographers Leo Meier, Harold Weldon and Reg Morrison for their excellent work. At different times they each travelled with me; when I was able to rest and eat the spoils, they had to photograph the food. The results are splendid.

In all communities women offered the main advice as research assistants and naturalists. In Yirrkala it was my yapa (sister) Dhuwandjika and her daughter, Mararu; in Ramingining my assistants were Elsie Ganbada and family; in Mt Liebig Maude Peterson was energetic, enthusiastic and efficient and in Amata, Nellie Patterson made hard work fun.

The resources of the Australian Institute of Aboriginal Studies are extensive and I wish to thank the librarians for their patience in locating a very large bibliography of works by previous researchers and Aboriginal people themselves on bush food and medicine throughout Australia.

All comments on food values have been made on the basis of research by Dr Jennifer Brand and Vic Cherikoff at the Human Nutrition Unit, University of Sydney. Vic Cherikoff gave particular help and assistance in checking the finished manuscript, offering his own observations and providing photographs.

The staff of the National Herbarium of New South Wales at the Royal Botanic Gardens of Sydney identified the specimens I brought from the bush and Dr Peter Hind assisted by checking the appendices and correcting errors in scientific terminology. Phil Colman of the Department of Shells at the Australian Museum helped by identifying the remains of many shellfish meals which I carried in my bag back to Sydney, so that the Aboriginal names would have some meaning to enthusiasts in search of the foods discussed.

Other friends helped with accommodation, advice or support throughout Australia. In particular I would like to mention Geoff Wharton and Tony Tiplady in Weipa, John Mundine in Ramingining, Diane Moon in Maningrida, Barbara James in Darwin, and Daphne Williams, Jane and Mark Savage in Alice Springs. My thanks are also extended to the council of the Yipirinya school, Alice Springs, for permitting me to observe a school 'bush food' expedition.

My brother, Dr Julian Pepperell, a senior biologist with the Fisheries Research Institute, New South Wales Department of Agriculture, made sense of colloquial Aboriginal names of many northern waters fish and acted as consultant on the fish and marine animal chapters.

David, Joey, Sam, and Willie Isaacs all enjoyed participating in this book. They enthusiastically travelled with me, David taking some of the photographs when I was otherwise occupied with eight-month-old Willie. Joey and Sam unhesitatingly tried all new foods put before them and their own descriptions of the taste are incorporated into the text.

INDEX